Investing in Miracles

Southeast Asia

POLITICS, MEANING, AND MEMORY

Rita Smith Kipp and David Chandler

SERIES EDITORS

OTHER VOLUMES IN THE SERIES

HARD BARGAINING IN SUMATRA:
*Western Travelers and Toba Bataks in the Marketplace
of Souvenirs*
Andrew Causey

PRINT AND POWER:
*Confucianism, Communism, and Buddhism in the
Making of Modern Vietnam*
Shawn Frederick McHale

TOMS AND DEES
*Transgender Identity and Female Same-Sex Relationships
in Thailand*
Megan J. Sinnott

Investing in Miracles

El Shaddai and the Transformation

of Popular Catholicism in the

Philippines

KATHARINE L. WIEGELE

UNIVERSITY OF HAWAI'I PRESS   *Honolulu*

Library of Congress Cataloging-in-Publication Data
Wiegele, Katharine L., 1966–
    Investing in miracles : El Shaddai and the transformation of popular Catholicism in the Philippines / Katharine L. Wiegele.
        p. cm. — (Southeast Asia: politics, meaning, memory)
    Includes bibliographical references.
    ISBN 0-8248-2795-3 (hardcover : alk. paper) —
    ISBN 0-8248-2861-5 (pbk. : alk. paper)
    1. El Shaddai DWXI Prayer Partners Foundation International. 2. Pentecostalism—Catholic Church. 3. Pentecostalism—Philippines. I. Title. II. Series.
    BX809.E53W54 2004
    267'.182599—dc22

                                              2004004203

Designed by UH Press Production Department, after design by Rich Hendel
Printed by The Maple-Vail Book Manufacturing Group

For Mom and Dad

For Giovanni

and

For those who call themselves

the children of El Shaddai

CONTENTS

ACKNOWLEDGMENTS

This book was written with the support of many people and institutions. The field research was generously funded by grants from Fulbright-Hayes and the Wenner Gren Foundation for Anthropological Research as well as a Nell Signor fellowship from the Program for International Studies at the University of Illinois at Urbana-Champaign. I was sustained during the writing with financial support from the Graduate College and the Department of Anthropology at the University of Illinois at Urbana-Champaign.

My gratitude goes first to the people of Manila who opened their homes and their hearts to me. The people of the community I have fictionally called Bandong-Sinag were patient and hospitable despite my intrusions into their personal and spiritual lives. To these generous people, too numerous to name, I hope I have rendered your stories and sentiments accurately and faithfully. In particular, I am indebted to three people: Josephine for courageously approaching me at my first El Shaddai prayer meeting and for many significant introductions in the community; the energetic El Shaddai healer I have called Eddie who had enough confidence in me and my work to invite me on his sometimes painful and always intimate housecalls; and Millie, who initially brought me to the community and introduced me to her extensive network of friends and family. Millie's creativity and insight were vital to my understanding of local religious life, as were her hours of research assistance. I owe my trusting relationships with the people of Bandong-Sinag to the strength and kindness of these three individuals.

This research would have been impossible without the cooperation of El Shaddai DWXI Prayer Partners Foundation, International, Inc. The foundation's Servant Leader, Mike Velarde, allowed me access to the group's organizational staff, to the services of the foundation's various offices, to himself for several interviews, and to the multitudes of faithful members at El Shaddai events. Cathy Cruz and her staff in the statistics office, Carmen of the publications office, and Mel Robles were patient and generous with their time and expertise. In addition, many named and unnamed Roman Catholic clergymen, including Archbishop Cardinal Jaime Sin and Bishop Ted Bacani, spoke to me with frankness and offered me the contacts and insights that came from years of work within particular parishes and organizations.

Susan Russell put me in touch with my two research assistants, Fely Pacantes and Leizle Bandonill. The energy, loyalty, and intellectual effort exerted by these two able women was unsurpassed. They kept good humor and professionalism despite the grueling schedule to which I subjected them, and they lavishly shared their curiosity and intellect as we puzzled over the things we had experienced together. Their collaboration on this project is priceless, as is their friendship. I am also grateful to Yda Arce Liongson for help with my Tagalog and with difficult translations and to Miren Sanches for her brief but invaluable research assistance, insights, and translations.

Alex Calata and the staff at the Philippine American Educational Foundation provided administrative support and encouragement throughout my fieldwork. Justice Hilario Davide Jr., Soloman and Elizabeth Racho, and the Jumpay family were generous hosts, as were the families of Fhe Dolor and Pacencia and Napoleon Conte, who provided my home and family away from home in the Philippines during parts of this fieldwork and for many years. Chino Medina, Ben Razon, Victor Besa, and Patrick de Lange, along with the numerous friends they introduced me to, kept my spirits up with their humor and wit. I especially appreciate the stimulating conversations with Ben about this research, his understanding of my ideals, and his sense of irony and compassion that shows in the photos he took for this project.

Russell Mask, then at the University of Wisconsin–Madison, and Roxie Lim of the University of the Philippines–Dilliman convinced me that this topic was worthy of detailed study. Russell Mask and Arnold Jumpay provided crucial sources from Manila for the project's initial conceptualization. Vince Rafael, Nancy Abelmann, Clark Cunningham, Alma Gottlieb, Bill Kelleher, Susan Russell, Mahir Saul, and Norman Whitten helped focus my project and make it worthy of funding. Rosa de Jorio, Maria Tapias, Sandra Hamid, Sarah Phillips, Jill Leonard, Eri Fujieda, and Gina Hunter-de Bessa at the University of Illinois and Melanie McDermott-Hughes at Berkeley have been constant friends and loyal colleagues. Shanshan Du, Richard Freeman, Mwenda Ngtarangwi, and Alma Gottlieb provided helpful readings of early drafts. Discussions and correspondence with Simon Coleman and Aiwah Ong forced me to fortify my arguments. I also benefited from conversations with the writer F. Sionil Jose, Vicky Apuan of Miram College, Fernando Zialcita of

Ateneo de Manila, Prosperino Corvar and Francisco Nemenzo of the University of the Philippines–Dilliman, and many other Filipino thinkers and observers.

Mahir Saul, Nancy Abelmann, Clark Cunningham, Martin Manalansan, and Susan Russell have taught and inspired me throughout the many stages of this study and have provided invaluable comments on the entire text. Their individual contributions are too many to mention. I thank them for their hard work and dedication. Mahir Saul instilled confidence and kept my thinking clear and my writing free of jargon. Bill Kelleher taught me about theory and knowledge production and showed me it was possible to merge my ideals and my ethnography. F. K. Lehman, without knowing it, gave me permission to pursue my own writing style when he told me "a good description explains." Susan Russell introduced me to anthropology in the first place and has helped propel me through many different phases of my career. Throughout the years she has been a supportive teacher, friend, and, more recently, colleague. Despite its many flaws, I hope my work is worthy of these fine mentors.

Mary Wiegele, my mother, and Giovanni Bennardo, my husband, have filled in the many gaps in funding and afforded me the luxuries and necessities that helped make my life enjoyable during these many months. My mother has contributed much to my understanding of the complexities and contradictions of Catholic faith and has been a graceful model of critique and compassion. Although my father, Thomas C. Wiegele, passed away before this research began, he continues to be for me a model of intellectual integrity and persistence. And it is impossible to have a more supportive partner than Giovanni. At difficult junctures, he has urged me on with many discussions and careful readings of chapter drafts. Despite the demands of his own career and our very divergent work habits, he has been an expert in balance and patience, making it possible for us both to write, teach, and enjoy many happy hours together every day with our son Lucio, and more recently, our son Matteo.

And, finally, I extend sincere appreciation to the many unnamed attendees of El Shaddai rallies who talked to me and shared space on their mats, to the members of all the El Shaddai chapters in which I did research, including those in Manila, Alaminos, Bauan, Roxas City, and Baguio City, and to many others for their graciousness, their cooperation, and their willingness to reflect upon and share with me some of their most intimate and transforming moments.

Investing
in
Miracles

I

Seeking El Shaddai

For nearly fifteen minutes we pass face after face in every direction. We walk silently, at a steady pace. Were it not for the landmarks in the distance—the city's skyline on one side, the orange sunset dusting Manila bay on the other—we might be disoriented on our journey toward the rally stage. The crowd of half a million is calm but expectant. Some listen to the radio broadcast from the grandstand or browse vending stalls. Others write down their needs, worries, and dreams on pieces of paper that will be prayed over, when the sky grows dark, by the charismatic "Brother Mike" from his glowing electric stage in the distance. And somewhere behind the stage curtains, his face caked with makeup, Brother Mike is stiff with performance jitters that only his wife and his closest aides witness. Up close, with his neon plaid suit and exaggerated stage features, he looks fantastically larger than life.

Father Bert, a Filipino Catholic priest, has accompanied me to this national El Shaddai rally in which Brother Mike Velarde, as he does every Saturday night, will preach and heal the faithful.[1] Father Bert is not a member of El Shaddai nor of the Catholic charismatic movement. In fact, he explains, he opposes what El Shaddai stands for because he feels it runs counter to liberation theology. Nonetheless he wishes to attend because he wants to "see how it is done." How does Brother Mike create moods of elation, moods in which one can feel the Holy Spirit moving, moods so powerful that people, men and women alike, come from all over the nation to experience a prayer and healing rally, lasting five or six hours, sometimes ten, until dawn, even in the rain? How does he motivate millions of impoverished Filipinos to donate 10 percent or more of their income to an organization that has not even so much as a church building? How does he inspire millions to testify, often publicly, that they have been radically transformed and attest that miracles have graced their lives? Father Bert has listened to tapes of American evangelists like Jimmy Swaggart in an attempt to spice up his own oration style, but he still has not managed to fill his church and its coffers to overflowing, nor has he heard any testimonies of miracles or lives transformed. How does Brother Mike, and the preachers and evangelists under him, do it? After the rally, as we weave through the crowds and traffic on the way home, Father Bert tells me vaguely that experiencing the rally will help in his community organizing, but how, exactly, he cannot say.

* * *

This is a book about people who have been in the public eye in the Philippines since they began gathering for miracle and healing rallies in the early 1980s. Throughout the 1980s and 1990s, the El Shaddai movement's ever-growing numbers have posed a challenge to religious institutions in the Philippines, particularly the Philippine Roman Catholic Church (PRCC). Their unorthodox ways not only threaten status quo religious boundaries of practice and belief but also present opportunities for the PRCC to stop the massive flow of Catholics to Protestant and evangelical groups in the Philippines. In the past several decades these groups have enticed followers with what many El Shaddai faithful see as more spiritually, socially, and materially relevant (and, some say, authentic) forms of religion. Observers have often found it difficult to categorize the El Shaddai movement. Its prosperity theology often prompts debates as to what constitutes Catholic or even religious activity and has even led to questions about the meaning of religion itself. Its boundary crossing has produced both uneasiness and curiosity.

The El Shaddai movement has also been fascinating to journalists and other observers. El Shaddai practices like "seed-faith" offerings, "positive confession," and "prayer requests," all part of its controversial prosperity theology, have provided fodder for debate on the compatibility of material desires and religious motivations. This obsession with El Shaddai's prosperity theology has often led to journalistic reductions of the movement that see El Shaddai rituals as designed solely to elicit favors, often material, from God. While focusing our attention on the relationship between religious and capitalistic moralities—and perhaps prompting self-reflection on the part of Filipino and Western observers—these reductions seriously underestimate the complexity and sophistication of contemporary Filipinos.

In this work I document the rise of the El Shaddai movement, its ethos and its ritual practices, and the new sociocultural forms it has spawned. In so doing, I seek to understand how and why this movement grew so rapidly to the point where it yields considerable influence in the public arenas of political, economic, and religious discourse in Filipino civil society. Ultimately the El Shaddai movement reveals the changing culture of Filipino lower and aspiring middle classes at a time when old understandings of class struggle and Catholic sacrifice no longer resonate with contemporary aspirations.

The movement's rise to popularity coincides with a period of intense social, political, and economic change in the Philippines—namely the People Power Revolution of 1986, which ended the Marcos dictatorship and restored democracy, and the rapid economic growth that took place during much of the Fidel Ramos presidency. Mike Velarde, the movement's leader, has capitalized on his strong ties with the Philippine Roman Catholic Church and successive Filipino governments. He supported the economic and political initiatives of the Ramos presidency and more recently aligned with many Protestant denominations in support of President Estrada, even as Catholic Church leaders and the Filipino public rallied against Estrada and eventually forced him from office.

THE MOVEMENT IN CONTEXT

Mike Velarde assesses the El Shaddai movement this way:

With the El Shaddai DWXI–PPFI [Prayer Partners Foundation International] Ministry, the Philippines is witnessing a real spiritual and moral revival, shaking established religious organizations and denominations. The Catholic Church, which El Shaddai DWXI–PPFI primarily aims to serve, is divided on the issue. Protestants, Pentecostals, Fundamentalists, Iglesia ni Cristo members, and members of other denominations are trooping to El Shaddai fellowships and mass and healing rallies regularly all over the land. Communities and cell groups are sprouting everywhere like mushrooms, in different cities and capital towns all over the Philippines. [Velarde 1993a:20]

While this enthusiastic assessment by Brother Mike may seem to exaggerate El Shaddai's influence and growth, in fact his description is close to the truth. The El Shaddai movement—formally called El Shaddai

DWXI Prayer Partners Foundation International, Inc. (also called El Shaddai Ministries)—began in 1981 as a nondenominational Christian radio program. One Sunday a small group of listeners gathered in thanksgiving outside the DWXI radio station. Within fifteen years the group had become a substantial movement with a followership of 9 to 11 million. (Even the most conservative estimates fall within this range.) By 1997 the group had chapters in nearly every province in the Philippines and more than thirty-five countries, with an overseas membership comprising around 20 percent of the total.[2] Velarde airs El Shaddai television programs throughout the country and broadcasts El Shaddai radio on dozens of his own stations nationwide. Tapes of his sermons circulate widely among Filipino overseas workers. Today he is also part owner of television Channel 11 in Manila, another prominent venue for El Shaddai religious programming. Up to a million followers gather each week in Manila for nighttime prayer and healing rallies led by Brother Mike. Indeed, Velarde has been called one of the fifty most powerful people in Asia (*Asiaweek*, July 5, 1996) and one of the ten people "who made a difference" in the Philippines in the decade following the People Power Revolution *(Philippine Daily Inquirer)*. He has also been instrumental in national Filipino politics during successive presidencies since the mid-1980s.

The El Shaddai movement takes its name from a booklet written by Rev. Kenneth E. Hagin, a popular American preacher of the prosperity gospel. Velarde renders the name in English for members of El Shaddai Ministries as "God Almighty" and "The God Who Is More Than Enough"—an image of God well suited to the group's prosperity orientation. The name is actually of Hebrew origin. According to the religious historian Karen Armstrong, El Shaddai was a name used by Abraham for his deity. Drawing from biblical sources, she writes: "It is highly likely that Abraham's God was El, the High God of Canaan. The deity introduces himself to Abraham as El Shaddai (El of the Mountain), which was one of El's traditional titles" (Armstrong 1993:14).

The organizational structure of El Shaddai DWXI–PPFI, which has been "inspired by the Holy Spirit," is authoritarian with Brother Mike at the top as the group's "servant-leader." Below him the Executive Secretariat is composed of sixteen "senior disciples," two of whom are closely related to Velarde (a brother and a son). These sixteen make recommendations to Velarde and lead the seven "ministries" or departments that compose the foundation.[3] Two Catholic priests appointed by Bishop Ted

Bacani serve as spiritual directors, helping in the training ("lay forma-tion") of El Shaddai's disciples, pastors, evangelists, service volunteer disciples/trainees, and prayer group coordinators.[4] The movement has several main venues: national prayer and healing rallies held on Satur-days and Tuesdays at two different public spaces in Manila; daily prayer and healing *gawain* (ritual events) at El Shaddai's main headquarters in Makati, Manila; smaller *gawain* organized weekly by local El Shaddai chapters throughout the Philippines; weekly *gawain* hosted by interna-tional El Shaddai chapters; national rallies held during special events such as chapter anniversaries, Christmas, and Pentecost; and extensive radio and television programming.

Velarde began describing his group as "Catholic charismatic" shortly after its nondenominational beginnings. Although this label is indeed fitting, it does not exhaust the movement's range of activities and impli-cations. Like other charismatic Christians worldwide, El Shaddai practice emphasizes the Holy Spirit and experience over religious doctrine. The term "charismatic Christianity" is used here in the sense in which Karla Poewe defines it: "encompass[ing] all Christianity, from its beginning in the first century, that emphasized religious or spiritual experiences and the activities of the Holy Spirit" (1994:2). Charismatic Christianity also involves the reinterpretation of and healing of one's life—a process that relies on religious language and the use of signs (Roelofs 1994; Poewe 1994:21).

Charismatic Christianity differs from Pentecostalism in several impor-tant ways. Broadly speaking, Pentecostals form their own denominations whereas the term "charismatic" usually describes Christians from main-line denominations who have adopted Pentecostal-like beliefs and prac-tices. As Russell Spittler writes in an article reviewing the use of these categories: "Pentecostals share with charismatics affirmation of spiritual gifts, speaking in tongues, healing, and prophecy. And the religious services of both are likely to be characterized by lively singing, manifest spiritual gifts, personal testimony, prayer for healing, and nonliturgical informality. But the two groups may have quite divergent theological views, eschatological expectations, worldviews, and attitudes toward social action" (1994:106). Charismatics can be found in nearly every Christian denomination, and their theological views vary accordingly. Pentecostals and fundamentalists, by contrast, share a "precritical and uncomplicated" approach to the Bible but diverge on such matters as speaking in tongues and style of worship—those aspects Pentecostals share with charismatics (p. 106).

By these definitions and by self-definition, El Shaddai is a Catholic charismatic group, although it does not emphasize speaking in tongues and other spiritual gifts for laypeople as much as some charismatic groups do. And while the group shares some doctrine with conservative Protestant charismatics (Coleman 2000), it is Catholic not only because it "aims to serve" the church but also because it is officially recognized by the Philippine Roman Catholic Church as a Catholic lay movement. In 1989 the Catholic Bishops Conference of the Philippines, after some scrutiny, declared Velarde to be a faithful Catholic, albeit a businessman and entrepreneur without formal religious training. The Philippines' highest Catholic official, Archbishop Cardinal Jaime Sin, has publicly recognized the movement as Catholic, and the church has appointed a spiritual director to advise Velarde and his pastors on theological matters. Velarde avoids blatantly preaching against official Catholic doctrine. (Nevertheless, many El Shaddai pastors and evangelists look to conservative Protestant preachers such as Jimmy Swaggart as stylistic models for their preaching.) A Catholic mass is said by a clergyman at every El Shaddai national rally, and Velarde gives a portion of the group's collections to the Catholic Church. Local El Shaddai chapters since 1995 have been required to affiliate with a Catholic parish. The pope, during his popular visit to the Philippines in 1995, inquired about the group after seeing thousands of El Shaddai banners and other insignia among the millions who gathered in his presence in this Catholic country, but he has not made an official declaration about the group.

El Shaddai can be classified as belonging to a specific wing of charismatics worldwide called the "prosperity movement" (also called variously "faith," "faith formula," "health and wealth," or "word movement"). The prosperity movement in general has also been called "neo-Pentecostal" owing to its origins in Pentecostalism, its acceptance of material prosperity, and its appeal across social classes and religious denominations (Coleman 2000). El Shaddai, like other prosperity movements, typically blends what have been called "textual" and "tactile" orientations to faith—textual because they have a fundamentalistic approach to the Bible, tactile in that they emphasize religious experience in the form of testimonies, ecstatic speech, and bodily movements (Coleman 2000:24; Cox 1995:15). The ministries of American televangelists Pat Robertson and

Oral Roberts and preacher Kenneth Hagin, key figures in the origins and development of prosperity teachings, have each to varying degrees influenced the development of El Shaddai. Because many of the beliefs and practices associated with prosperity theology are inconsistent with normative Filipino Catholicism, some controversy exists among mainstream Catholics and the Catholic clergy in the Philippines as to whether the El Shaddai movement should be considered legitimately Catholic.

The El Shaddai movement clearly exhibits the main theological features of prosperity movements globally: healing, prosperity, and "positive confession." Simon Coleman (2000:28) explains that in prosperity teachings, healing and prosperity (or health and wealth) are said to be promised to all believers based on a covenant made with Abraham in the Old Testament. Positive confession refers to the idea that not only faith and obedience but also one's specific statements can elicit God's power and intervention in the lives of the faithful: "Thus 'positive confession' is a statement that lays claim to God's provisions and promises in the present" (Coleman 2000:28; Hollinger 1991:57). Healing, prosperity, and positive confession are three prominent features of El Shaddai theology and practice.

Mike Velarde is unique among prosperity leaders in that he, and El Shaddai Ministries, remain officially part of a fixed denomination. Most leaders of prosperity movements have distanced themselves from mainline denominations (Coleman 2000:30), just as charismatic leaders in general (that is, leaders with a gift for attracting a large following) have distanced themselves from larger institutions (Weber 1946, 1968; Lindholm 1990). Moreover, El Shaddai's Catholic affiliation makes it unique among these prosperity movements because religious congregations of this kind have traditionally been made up of denominational Protestants. Although the Catholic charismatic movement has been accepted globally by the Roman Catholic hierarchy for some time, a prosperity movement whose membership is dominated by Catholics appears to be without precedent. And yet, while El Shaddai's followership is mainly Catholic and the group maintains legitimate ties to the Philippine Roman Catholic Church, Velarde, like his prosperity counterparts in other countries, still functions as a leader who is not obligated to any denomination. Velarde fits Kenneth Hagin's entrepreneurial model of "establishing an overtly independent ministry that is a vehicle for evangelistic activity far beyond the level of the local congregation" (Coleman 2000:30). Among many other similarities, El Shaddai also shares with prosperity groups in Africa and Latin America an accommodation to (or even ideological emphasis on) globalism and, as well, an organization that favors large congregations in urban settings.

Prosperity movements vary insofar as they develop within particular local contexts even though the preachers, doctrine, and organizational structures may be imported to varying degrees, especially from the United States. (Prosperity movements worldwide, including El Shaddai, now send preachers overseas, maintain radio stations or programming abroad, and evangelize in places like the United States and Hong Kong.) El Shaddai is probably the largest prosperity movement worldwide in terms of followers—significantly bigger than other movements of its kind. As mentioned, its denominational connection with the Roman Catholic Church is unique, and this gives rise to a host of particularities not only in El Shaddai practice but also in the dialectics of El Shaddai's relations with Philippine society at large. Aside from these obvious features, the cultural forms that El Shaddai has taken (and created) result from the specifics of Filipino culture and history.

CHRISTIANITY IN THE LOWLANDS

Filipinos have never been empty vessels for imported ideologies, religious or otherwise. Vicente Rafael (1988) describes the process of Tagalog conversion to Roman Catholicism under early Spanish rule as translation—as a reinvention of symbols and signs, an interpretation of events and symbols through local categories, and resistance to colonial authority through slippages of meaning in colonial power relations. Precolonial notions of reciprocity and debt combined with Roman Catholicism to form uniquely Filipino concepts and practices within—and in opposition to—Catholicism and Spanish rule. Concepts such as *utang na loob* (debt of gratitude) and *hiya* (shame)—central to reciprocity and the formation of social relationships—contributed to the nature of Tagalogs' indigenized relationships with the Christian God and Catholic religious authorities. According to Rafael, Tagalogs conceived of God as a benefactor to whom they were constantly in debt, a debt that could be repaid only at death. This perspective bound the Filipino in an obligatory relationship with God and the church.

Relationships of debt and reciprocity are still significant elements of contemporary Filipino society. El Shaddai members, however, through financial offerings to God and positive confession (which allows the believer to elicit God's intervention), become the initiators of the reciprocal relationship with God. By obligating God through these acts, El Shaddai members can be said to reverse the direction of the debt relationship with God. Moreover, El Shaddai changes the primary focus of one's relationship with God—from salvation in the afterlife to this-worldly uplift. Rather than waiting to repay one's debts to God in the afterlife, they invoke God's generosity here and now through positive confession and tithing and, in so doing, lay claims on the power of God by indebting God to them. Popular Catholic notions of suffering are also transformed through El Shaddai ideology and practice. Older modes of Catholic expression that made suffering virtuous have been replaced by the pervasive image of a God who wants humans to be healthy and prosperous, a God who dislikes suffering. Rafael also focuses attention on the unexpected ways in which early Tagalog converts understood the Catholic sacraments of communion and confession. El Shaddai healers manipulate the normative meanings connected to these sacraments, wrest from them their spiritual efficacy, and relegate them to tradition and obligation without ever discarding them.

Religion in the Philippines has always been part of the language through which power relationships and radical political and economic change have been understood, manipulated, and resisted. As Filomeno Aguilar documents, Spanish colonialism and the penetration of foreign merchant capitalism in Negros, a Visayan island, was understood by Filipinos as a "clash of spirits" between competing cosmic forces—the foreign merchant capitalists represented on one side and the Spanish friars on the other (Aguilar 1998:26). Reynaldo Ileto (1979) writes about Tagalog resistance to Spanish colonialism from 1840 to 1910 and tells how grassroots movements utilized local conceptions of the passion story of Christ *(pasyon)*. While Spanish clerics intended the *pasyon* to encourage acceptance of suffering and submission to Catholic doctrine and colonial power, the story was mobilized for revolution and resistance. Ileto shows how Filipinos combined the *pasyon* with local notions of *loob* (inner self), *utang* (debt), and other salient cultural concepts to produce relevant religious practices and ideologies. Fanella Cannell's (1999) study of contemporary Christian practice in Bicol shows how inequalities and power relationships are mediated and understood through cultural and religious idioms of persuasion, reluctance, and pity. Heather Claussen (2001) describes feminist Catholic nuns in the Philippines who, through their unique blend of faith and politics, are attempting to address contemporary inequalities and reshape Filipino culture and gender norms.[5]

From these works we learn how Filipinos have transformed Catholic practice and symbols into idioms through which they resist, cope with, bring about, and understand change. According to John Bowen, one way to study broad cultural change is "by analyzing those 'mediating' institutions and cultural forms through which people redefine who they are" (1995:1062). Religion is one of the ways through which Filipinos have reinvented themselves—both in the past and, I believe, today—in the context of recent religious innovations such as the El Shaddai movement. Through El Shaddai, Filipinos are transforming Catholicism in specific ways to cope with economic, political, and social change. New religious ideas and practices are co-opted to achieve personal transformations when Catholic traditions no longer satisfy changing spiritual needs and leftist ideologies of struggle and oppression no longer articulate the aspirations of contemporary Filipinos.

Apart from these issues connected specifically to the Filipino milieu, the El Shaddai movement offers an interesting case study of charisma, sacred power, and influence in Southeast Asia. This book also addresses questions connected to religion and power in general—namely some of those raised by Talal Asad (1993), who asks how religious "moods and motivations," religious authenticity, and spiritual authority are actually created.[6] What conditions have led to the acceptance of different religious authorities and different logics of spirituality in the Philippines? And, finally, if religion is a mediating institution for broad cultural change, what does the El Shaddai movement tell us about change in Filipino society?

MY FIELDWORK: FROM METRO MANILA TO ROME

I got my first glimpse of Brother Mike on television while the biggest typhoon in decades was thrashing the capital city. While the majority of greater Metro Manila was having a power outage, Brother Mike's green and pink checked suit glowed from the generator-powered color TV in my hotel room as his dramatic Tagalog speech competed with the wind and rain crashing against the window. It was a replay of last week's prayer and healing rally. As the camera panned the seemingly endless expanse of followers, I wondered how I would get from *here* to *there*—from behind the TV screen into the homes and the individual lives of the people whose sincere, emotion-filled faces drew me into the intense mood of the nighttime rally. Who were they, exactly, and how would I find them? Eventually I did come to know a small fraction of these people—by living with them and sharing the drama of their lives in an interior section of a semi-squatter neighborhood in Manila. Yet the *bridge* between these two worlds—that is, the anonymous, imagined world of the mega-rally on TV, broadcast nationwide and internationally for public consumption, and the everyday worlds of the followers into whose homes these programs are broadcast—came to permeate nearly every aspect of my research.

In many ways, the idea of bridging these two levels of experience not only framed the direction of my research but also characterized the difficulties in finding appropriate anthropological frameworks and methodologies for doing research, in a globalized and diverse capital city of roughly 15 million, on religious experience that is simultaneously—and consciously—both global and local. Not surprisingly, the lives of my informants embodied the contradictions and ironies of the complex environment from which this movement emerged. My fieldwork, perhaps not uniquely, was also riddled with the ambiguities of modern urban environments: how to study, anthropologically, very large and diverse communities; how to understand the notion of "community" that is both imagined through mass media and enacted in small neighborhood groups at the same time; how to define a particular community in contiguous and dense urban residential space; how to access people who commute up to three hours every day and work long hours (as painters, servants, construction workers, vendors); how to pinpoint and describe attitudes and practices that may change daily, sometimes before your very eyes, with a sermon or speech heard on the radio; and, not least, how to cope with the experience—as an observer—of being filmed and observed by *someone else* with cameras broadcasting live on national television. Some of these issues are mentioned in the text of this book; most are not. But all of them color the ethnographic representation I have produced—from my interpretation of events to the overall organization of this work. They also contribute to any shortcomings you may find here.

This book is based primarily on ethnographic data I collected from November 1995 through December 1996 in the Philippines. Most of the fieldwork was done in Metro Manila; secondary case studies were done in four different provinces. I used traditional ethnographic techniques such as participant observation, structured and unstructured interviews, and interview schedules. I also collected limited quantitative survey data both at national rallies and at my primary fieldsite. As well, my research included the analysis of recorded, transcribed, and published preaching texts of Mike Velarde and other El Shaddai preachers and healers, El Shaddai publications, and local media coverage of issues directly or indirectly related to El Shaddai. In Manila, Filipino and English are the languages most commonly spoken. Although my research was conducted in both languages, English was rarely used outside of interviews with relatively well educated informants who were comfortable speaking it. Filipino was most often preferred. Almost all of the interviews and many sermons were taped and later transcribed and translated with the assistance of two Filipino research assistants.

Because the El Shaddai movement is at once a local, national, and even global phenomenon, my fieldwork necessarily ranged between these settings. In fact, I became interested in the various ways in which El Shaddai members form communities (or a sense of community) given the magnitude of their followership and the geographical expanses that often separate them. The majority of my research took place in urban settings in Manila: I lived in a semi-squatter neighborhood for about seven of my thirteen months in the field for this project. This local community, with its particularly high concentration of El Shaddai followers, became my primary focus for studying local manifestations of El Shaddai religiosity. My ties with members of this community began in the second month of this fieldwork period and lasted throughout my stay in Manila. During the months in which I was not actually living in this community, I rented a small apartment in a lower-middle-class neighborhood nearby.

In addition to this local community, I observed El Shaddai at work in eight other local chapters—four in other areas in Metro Manila and four in provincial areas. The four Manila chapters represent a variety of socioeconomic and community characteristics. The four provincial chapters represent different ethnolinguistic El Shaddai constituencies and varying degrees of acceptance and control by local Catholic clergy and diocesan bishops. The Roxas City and Baguio City branches were located in dioceses where the bishop and parish priest had rejected the local El Shaddai groups. El Shaddai chapters in Pangasinan and Batangas were chosen mainly because of my previous contacts with communities in these provinces but also because these two local branches represented opposite poles in terms of El Shaddai independence vis-à-vis local church authority. My fieldwork also involved participating in religious events of a variety of Christian denominations.

Much of my fieldwork was also conducted in national El Shaddai arenas: at national rallies, at the national headquarters where El Shaddai leaders and workers have offices and where some rituals and training took place, and from the airwaves of El Shaddai radio and television broadcasts. I was introduced to Mike Velarde briefly backstage before an El Shaddai rally in Manila. Later in the fieldwork, I personally interviewed him on two occasions at the El Shaddai national headquarters. I also dined with him and several other guests on his birthday in his headquarters office and once backstage after a rally at the Philippine International Convention Center.

I interviewed national religious leaders not only from the El Shaddai movement but also from the Philippine Roman Catholic Church (including the archbishop of Manila and several other bishops), the Catholic charismatic movement, the National Renewal Movement, and various other religious denominations. My interviews also included academics from several universities in Manila, a supreme court justice, and journalists—not to mention the hundreds of El Shaddai members and Manilans of other religious persuasions I spoke to or interviewed throughout my stay. I attended El Shaddai functions at dozens of locations. And, finally, I observed an El Shaddai prayer mass at a Filipino Catholic church in Rome—the parish was composed almost entirely of Filipino immigrants and overseas workers—and interviewed the presiding priest and several participants there. While in Rome I also made unsuccessful attempts in the Vatican to obtain an official church position (or unofficial assessment) of El Shaddai DWXI–PPFI.

For the sake of anonymity, I have used fictitious names for people and places throughout. The names and places associated with public figures and public events, however, have been left unaltered.

CARGO CULTING AND OTHER PITFALLS

Moments of stress can push people to seek out new experiences. Brother Mike once told me that people are more receptive to God when they are weak. Coming from the spiritual leader of El Shaddai, however, this psychological take on religious and spiritual change surprised me. It shares something with the Catholic "Church of the Poor" idea in the Philippines—the idea that poverty has traditionally been a privileged site of God's grace and intervention. But it also resembles the psychologically reductionistic approaches to religious change I have tried to avoid here—functional stress-anxiety and deprivation models, for example, that reduce people to stress-equilibrium mechanisms. God takes many forms in contemporary Manila, and there is an astounding array of options in the religious marketplace. Considering that at least 10 million people have found something compelling about Brother Mike's message and El Shaddai's ideology and rituals, one must ask: Why now? Why El Shaddai? Why this segment of the population? What needs and desires does El Shaddai address that other religious groups do not? Reductionist explanations mask the multifaceted social, political, cultural, economic, and personal conditions in which spiritual choices are made—and in which new religious forms arise and become compelling. A multitude of contexts and factors impact on the religious choices of contemporary Filipinos. Many scholars have recognized the importance of both sociohistorical factors and personal experience and identity in assessing conversion and religious change. (See, for example, Aragon 1992; Hefner 1993; and Kipp 1991.)

Another reduction of the El Shaddai phenomenon that flourishes in journalistic accounts both in the Philippines and abroad is what I call "cargo culting." This tempting explanation focuses on El Shaddai's prosperity theology and its "prayer request" and "seed-faith" rituals through which members request miracles from God. Lamont Lindstrom (1991:1) writes of Melanesian cargo cults that arose in the 1940s and 1950s:

> People turned to traditional or innovative religious ritual to obtain "cargo."... Sometimes the [cargo] concept meant money or various sorts of manufactured goods such as vehicles, packaged foods, refrigerators, guns, and tools. And sometimes, metaphorically, cargo represented the search for a new social and moral order that would ensure

local sovereignty and the withdrawal of colonial rulers. In either case, people worked for and expected a sudden, miraculous transformation of their lives.

Lindstrom has written extensively about cargo cults in the Pacific and notes the peculiar anthropological and popular appeal of cargo cult stories in the West. Stories about cargo cults, he argues, "suggest a kind of forlorn, sometimes mad, state of insatiable wanting. . . . We relish cargo cult narratives because these are parables about our [own] desire" (p. 2).

Applied to El Shaddai (and with comparable fascination), cargo culting offers a facile and comforting answer to the basic questions surrounding the movement—questions such as why do so many poor and marginalized Filipinos give millions of pesos each week to Brother Mike? It reduces El Shaddai enthusiasts to seekers of miracles, both material and social. While the miracle-seeking aspect of El Shaddai religious life is certainly not insignificant, my broader goal is to show there is much more at stake here than appliances, salary raises, jobs abroad, and healing. At stake for many El Shaddai members is their place and identity within society at large; the meaning of their own experiences of poverty, suffering, and oppression; and the relevance of their very notions of God, Christian community, and Christian life.

By avoiding such reductions (whether psychologically functionalist or cargo cultist), by allowing for multicausal explanations, and by emphasizing ethnographically specific descriptions, I hope to avoid several other pitfalls in the study of religious change. One is the tendency to ignore or dismiss or "explain away" spiritual experience. I have tried here to remain open to the possibility that spiritual transformation and experience can sometimes be a significant motivation. I also aim to avoid stereotyping members of the El Shaddai movement and Filipino Roman Catholics. Finally, it is my hope that this ethnographic portrait of the El Shaddai movement preserves the agency of the people involved instead of representing them as mere followers, a mindless mass. They are people with choices, people who fashion and transform ideologies, religiosities, and situations for their own purposes, people who are not mindless at all.

2 | Golden Rules, Miracle Investments, and the Seed-Faith Principle

When I attended my first rally in Manila, I had been in the city for only a week. Immersed in a sea of 500,000 friendly El Shaddai revelers, I was suddenly overwhelmed by a comforting sense of belonging. I felt I was part of something big. It was nighttime, and my foreignness and whiteness slipped away as people grasped my hands, offered me food and precious space on their crowded mats, and called me "sister."

The evening began with prayer and singing interspersed with testimonies by various El Shaddai members. One by one, these individuals took the microphone on the huge, well-lit stage, telling emotional personal transformation stories and giving testimony of miracles—how Yahweh El Shaddai had brought them riches, new jobs, physical healing, and freedom from debt and vices. These blessings had arrived miraculously once they had asked Yahweh El Shaddai for help.

The climax of the rally was the emotional, evangelical-style "healing message" or preaching by the charismatic leader, Mike Velarde. The people around me responded constantly with "Praise God!" and "Alleluia!" as they jumped and waved their arms in unison. They laughed at Mike's corny jokes and at times cried together. They chanted together, repeating Mike's words: *"I am rich! I am strong! Something good is going to happen to me today!"* When he asked them to raise up their bankbooks, passports, job applications, wallets, water, and prayer requests for blessing, they not only raised up these objects but opened them to the black sky—"so that the spirit can come in," a young woman told me, "the flow of the spirit, *daluyan.*" Even Brother Mike's security guards, surrounding the stage, joined in for blessings and prayers.

Throughout the evening, especially during lulls in the program, I saw people sitting quietly, on their own, writing their prayer requests with great care and concentration. Judging from the testimonies of answered prayers I had just heard, most of these requests had to do with basic needs such as relief from asthma or tuberculosis, money for schooling, steady employment, the conversion of a mother-in-law, a mended marriage, a forgiven debt, a place to live, or a job in Hong Kong as a domestic servant. Each of these private requests was put in an envelope—with a cash "love offering" or a "tithe" *(ikapu)*—and dropped into one of the scores of 4-foot-high wooden boxes scattered about labeled "Miracle of Seed Faith Offering." Many people testified that the amount of money they had offered had come back to them later—in the form of their answered prayer request (and often as a monetary reward)—"a hundredfold." On each envelope was printed the words "Be an El Shaddai Covenant Prayer Partner and expect your miracle seeds to yield miracle harvests daily!"

Class and money are central issues not only in El Shaddai practice but also in the ways El Shaddai is viewed by outsiders in the Philippines. The group's treatment of money in both ritual and institutional contexts especially has been the subject of much debate. Concepts of prosperity and suffering are prominent in El Shaddai practice, and the seed-faith principle of giving tithes with the expectation of miracle rewards implies a specific relationship with God. In Chapter 5 we will see how the prosperity theology also opens up a space within which El Shaddai members transform themselves personally. The present chapter—situated in the national context of El Shaddai as opposed to the local barrio context—details the nuts and bolts of El Shaddai's prosperity theology and how it is put into practice.

EL SHADDAI'S PROSPERITY THEOLOGY

El Shaddai's prosperity theology is based on the idea that good things will happen to you if you follow the principles of God, or Yahweh El Shaddai. And among these principles, none is as strongly emphasized as the idea that you must "give your tithes and seed-faith offerings continuously" (Velarde 1993a:33). The El Shaddai member is also expected to follow the teachings of Mike Velarde (and other El Shaddai preachers), the teachings of the Roman Catholic Church, and the teachings of the Bible. There is no codified set of tenets or complex doctrine in Velarde's teachings; El Shaddai officially defers to the church on matters of doctrine. In addition to the emphasis on tithing, Velarde exhorts his followers not to abuse alcohol or drugs, smoke cigarettes, gamble, borrow money, complain, commit adultery, or say bad things about the El Shaddai ministry.

Velarde and the El Shaddai ministry teach that, according to the Bible, gambling and borrowing are against God's teachings and tithing (giving 10 percent of one's income to "the right ministry") is prescribed in the Bible by God. Material rewards come to those who obediently tithe; saving money and striving to improve one's lot are godly. In 1995 Mike Velarde encouraged every El Shaddai member to open a savings account in a bank. In 1996 he recognized Metrobank as El Shaddai's official bank. As he explains:

> Financial and material prosperity is not a sin nor a hindrance to spiritual maturity and well-being for as long as this is acquired and managed according to God's master plan, which is for our own good.... Wealth and success, according to God's plan for you and me, include all our financial, material, physical, and spiritual needs. The Will of God for us is to remain successful, healthy, and strong all the days of our lives here on earth, as well as enjoy Eternal Life in heaven.... This means that God has prepared a *master plan for real success and prosperity* for you and me. [Velarde 1993d:5]

Velarde's prosperity theology is likely to have been shaped by American Pat Robertson's religious talk show/news program, 700 *Club,* and by Kenneth Hagin, another American pastor known for his "health and wealth" gospel. Velarde attributes his own conversion solely to the miraculous healing of heart disease he experienced in 1978. But a Filipino Catholic priest who has been prominent in the Catholic charismatic movement in the Philippines since its beginnings in the mid-1970s and early 1980s—a priest, moreover, who worked with Velarde during his first years in the movement—tells it differently. According to this priest, Velarde told him that he was converted by the 700 *Club* TV program: "So that was the eye-opener [Velarde] had. But then realizing that he was a baptized Catholic, he joined the Catholic charismatic renewal movement."[1]

Velarde's version of prosperity theology is nearly identical to Robertson's message on 700 *Club.* According to Gerard Straub (1986:60), former producer of the TV program, Robertson "sells a 'salvation' that will transform the viewers' life, and a flood of benefits will flow from heaven following salvation: Restored health, healed relationships, career success, monetary rewards, and an improved lifestyle can all be yours if you just say 'yes' to Jesus." Janice Peck describes how Robertson's program raised donations and market ratings by focusing on healing: "From its earliest days, . . . distraught viewers called in their pledges and prayer requests and Robertson healed people on the air" (1993:163).

Velarde's approach was similar. He raised donations and gained listeners by focusing on healing—but also by identifying himself with the Filipino Catholic majority.[2] For the first three years of the ministry, Velarde's radio program did not declare a denominational affiliation and was assumed to be Protestant. A Catholic priest who was in contact with Velarde at the time said: "Well, I saw his leaning. . . . He was not really a well-formed Catholic, and so he was leaning . . . more on the Protestant side, so I told him 'Mike, do you want to deal with the majority of the people or with the minority?' He said, 'With the majority, of course.'" So Velarde declared himself a Catholic and joined the fledgling Catholic Secretariat for Charismatics in Quezon City (Metro Manila), the only one of its kind in the Philippines at the time.[3]

Like Robertson, Velarde emphasized physical healing from the beginning. He himself has long described his sermons as "healing messages." From the movement's very inception as a radio program, physical healing through the Holy Spirit and by means of "positive confession" has been a priority. And, as in the 700 *Club,* Velarde preaches that the benefits of a commitment to God, or Yahweh El Shaddai, are tangible rewards here on earth. In a pamphlet titled "An Invitation to Store Riches in Heaven and Enjoy El Shaddai's Prosperity Plan on Earth Now" (a pamphlet designed to sell shares of stocks of Velarde's Delta Broadcasting System), Velarde's approach is apparent: "Through DWXI Radio (1314 AM) and Islands TV-13 El Shaddai programs, you have heard the Good News of Salvation, healing and deliverance from sickness and afflictions, and the message of success and prosperity. . . . This means an assurance of financial prosperity, good health, and spiritual maturity and stability to them who believe and serve!" (Velarde 1993b).

These themes are repeated in every "healing message" Velarde preaches at rallies, on the air, and in publications. They are reproduced in followers' testimonies as well. The link between donations and God's earthly rewards is just as explicit in Velarde's teachings as in Robertson's. Velarde says, for example: "When it comes to the doctor, we give to him no matter how much it costs. When it comes to the Lord, we do not give him much!"[4] Elsewhere he warns: "Expect your giving to yield a miracle harvest—that is, to produce a miracle healing or a financial miracle for you. The Bible says: *'Do not deceive yourselves, no one makes a fool of God. A person will reap exactly what he plants* (gives)' (Galatians 6:7). If you give nothing, you receive nothing" (Velarde 1992d).

Velarde has the capacity to find biblical support for his message of tithing and offerings in the most unlikely places. At a rally in February 1996, for example, he told those assembled and those listening on the radio and television: "The Lord commanded 'Go and multiply.' That hasn't been changed, that commandment. If the Lord says 'Go and increase in number or multiply,' it doesn't just mean multiplying physically. Our wisdom must multiply. Our donations *(kaloob)* should increase. Amen?"[5] As Velarde put it: "Sometimes others are calling me a preacher of prosperity. But I say that is a wrong notion. I would rather call myself a preacher of generosity."[6]

Eliciting miracles through giving donations to God, as many members think of it, is called the "seed-faith principle" by Velarde. Oral Roberts, also calling it "seed-faith," used the same concept. For Pat Robertson of the 700 *Club* it was one of the "Kingdom Principles" (Bruce 1990:150). In a pamphlet, Velarde explains the principle:

> The *miracle of seed-faith principle* that I have been sharing in this ministry and encouraging everyone to believe and practice *is giving, not as an obligation we have to do, but as a miracle seed we sow.* It is an act of "faith expressing itself through love." The Lord in return, speaking through St. Paul, promised "to meet or supply all our needs according to His glorious riches in Christ Jesus."
>
> *And believe me, God's glorious source of miracle supply in Christ Jesus is not affected by recession, political unrest, inflation, strikes, fire, bankruptcies, earthquakes, and other calamities. Hence anybody who believes and puts into practice continuously this miracle of seed-faith principle, by faith expressing itself through love of God and neighbor, wins God's favor and protection. And as naturally as a seed of palay* [rice] *sown on fertile soil grows and multiplies, so does your seed-faith offering, given to the right mission or ministry, open God's source of miracle supply!* [Velarde 1994:4–6, emphasis in the original]

Velarde goes on to explain that those who have experienced miracles, including himself, have found that the DWXI radio station and El Shaddai DWXI–Prayer Partners Foundation International (PPFI) are the most fertile ground in which to plant the miracle seeds.[7]

Thus people are encouraged to tithe, not necessarily in thanksgiving for miracles or out of obligation, but as a way of eliciting miracles from God. This seed-faith principle was originally developed by charismatic evangelists, including Oral Roberts, in the 1970s. Indeed Roberts had had strands of the prosperity gospel in his theology since 1947 (FitzGerald 1990:74). A Filipino Catholic priest associated with the Church of the Poor described the principle as "a capitalist orientation: nobody will invest unless you get something out of it." The notion of directly initiating an exchange with God that results in God's benevolence is apparent in the title of the first volume of El Shaddai's newsletter: "Miracles by Appointment and Request Only." Furthermore, initiating this process of exchange is a manifestation of belief in God's salvation: "[The Second Step to El Shaddai's Miracles by Appointment and Request]: believe that He is the Only Begotten Son of God Who came to save us and supply all our needs because there is nothing impossible with Him. How do you manifest this belief? By presenting to Him your prayer request for a miracle" (Velarde [1991?]:5).

Robertson's and Velarde's ideas of suffering and its causes are also strikingly similar. As Peck explains: "Unlike [Jimmy] Swaggart, who believes suffering is the lot of a fallen humanity, Robertson sees misery as a temporary state to be overcome through personal and social action. Indeed, it is Christians' duty to deliver themselves from suffering by finding and following God's plan for their lives" (1993:163–164). Velarde's preaching reflects this notion that human actions lead people away from the Lord's will, which is not suffering but rather health and wealth. In the following preaching excerpts, Velarde uses a biblical verse to explain that the cause of suffering is a person's disobedience of God's will or principles:

> Brothers and Sisters, the reason for our suffering and endurance and sadness is that we have not followed the Lord's will. You were already told that something is bad, to gamble in the lotto, yet you still place bets. Amen? [*Amen.*] You have already been told that getting drunk is bad. . . . It is written in Psalms 107:17, "There are those who get ill because of their twisted way of life." Did you hear that? [*Amen!*]. . . . Because of disobedience, what they experienced was suffering and

poverty [*kahirapan*]. . . . You have turned out that way because of your stubbornness. . . . You are in agony. But don't worry. Tonight, if you'll listen, believe, and have faith, we together will call on the Lord. You will rise and be healed by the Lord. [*Yes! Amen!*][8]

Thus suffering and poverty can be alleviated by following God's principles—principles that include tithing alongside abstention from drinking, gambling, and adultery. Furthermore, suffering is not in itself virtuous. Velarde, for example, condemns the Filipino folk Catholic practices of self-flagellation and self-crucifixion practiced in parts of the Philippines, especially in Pampanga province, during Holy Week:

When I was still small . . . I thought that every year [on Good Friday] the Lord would die. [*Laughter.*] Alleluia! That's why when Holy Thursday comes, our faces are so sad. There are people out there who, when Holy Week comes, they carry crosses, they hit their own bodies. That's a big insult to our God! [*Amen!*] Because His own wounds and scars are because of you, so you must stop insulting Him! Stop doing those things! [Applause.] Amen! That's one of the reasons why our nation cannot be freed from suffering and hardships. We insult and continuously insult our God. Those things should not be allowed by our Church! And if you know those who do these things, encourage them to come to El Shaddai so that their minds may be cleared and opened up to the fact that the words of the Lord give life! [*Amen!*] [Applause.] His words that free and heal and can save! Let us praise the Lord![9]

Consider also Velarde's explanation of this classic biblical verse:

The Bible says it's hard for the rich [to enter the kingdom of God]. You know the kind of riches referred to by the Lord—not just money. There are a lot of people without money—no homes, no place to live, those who live on the sidewalk—who cannot enter the kingdom of God. That's why let us not be deceived that the poor will enter the kingdom of heaven. . . . You know why? Because it is hard to enter there, it is really hard, if you are rich in grief [*sama ng loob*]. People who live on sidewalks because they don't want to go home to their parents [for example]. . . . Don't just give up to hurt feelings, to anger, to hatred, and to grudges. Don't acquire this kind of riches because anyone who has bad feelings, anger, hatred toward his or her brothers and sisters is like the rich young man [in the Bible].[10]

Velarde ignores the commonplace interpretation of this biblical story—that the wealthy must be willing to give up all their worldly possessions to follow God since attachment to wealth can prevent one from following God. Instead he turns hurt and anger into the villain and, in an indirect way, the rage and resentment of poverty. No listener should think that because they are among the poor and the suffering of society, they are saved or exonerated. At the same time, the causes of the hurt and anger are not at issue here. The response—the emotions themselves—is the focus.

Velarde teaches that "El Shaddai's Master Plan" for us is prosperity, good health, and success in this life because, ultimately, "He [God] wants us to be a part of His plan to build His Kingdom on earth." (Being prosperous and successful, however, is "not for yourself—but to use it for the glory of God.") The kingdom of God in the long passage quoted earlier is actually God's kingdom on earth. Prior to this passage, Velarde has already explained this:

So I was meditating this morning: . . . "Lord, what should one do to have eternal life? What kind of life is life eternal?" And the spirit of the Lord revealed to me that the life this man [in the Bible] is looking for is an extraordinary life. Did you hear that? Amen. "Extraordinary life." [*Extraordinary life!*] Say that again. [*Extraordinary life!*] Eternal life is nothing but an extraordinary life. There is nothing like everlasting life. There's nothing like it—that's why it's rare. It's difficult to experience it. [Velarde 1993d?]

The message here and throughout Velarde's teachings is clear: paradise is to be achieved here and now, not postponed until after death. This passage is also consistent generally with Velarde's efforts to downplay eternal concerns in favor of worldly concerns. Many would see this as the opposite of some strands of Filipino mainstream Catholic practice and teachings, which focus on the afterlife and which, many say, divert attention away from the individual's physical and material state.

Kenneth Hagin, the American preacher whose booklet *El Shaddai* (1980) was the inspiration behind the movement's name, is another contributor to Velarde's theology.[11] Hagin is the most senior of the "positive confession charismatics" and, more generally, the contemporary health and wealth movement (Scotland 1995:14; Bruce 1990:152). (The health and wealth movement is also referred to as the faith movement or the prosperity movement. For an excellent review of the faith movement and its history see Coleman 2000.) The health and wealth gospel, also called the prosperity gospel, is especially common among the charismatic wing of television evangelists in the United States. It has three distinctive features, all of which are underscored by Mike Velarde in the El Shaddai movement: first, a belief in spiritual healing of physical ailments; second, an emphasis on material prosperity; and third, positive confession (Bruce 1990:153). The idea of positive confession is based largely on Mark 11:24: "Whatever you ask for in prayer, believe that you have received it and it will be yours." This approach has also been called "name it and claim it." We can see this idea at work in Mike Velarde's preaching:

> Now brothers and sisters, the word of faith is right in your tongue. . . . So whatever it is you would like to say or believe, truly those things will happen. [*Amen!*] Amen? [*Amen!*] . . . So if you say "I am still young"—why don't you shout this out? [*I am still young!*] Shout it out loud: "I am still young!" [*I am still young!*] Alleluia! . . . When you go home, you'll see that you are truly young! [*Woo!*] Amen? [*Amen!*] [12]

Velarde often uses positive confession in directly addressing material needs and health problems. At times his approach could be called "positive thinking":

> Say this: Think great! [*Think great!*] Think right! [*Think right!*] Do you understand what "think great" means? [*Yes!*] Just think of things that are remarkable or worth praising. Do not think of your situation. Forget about your situation. Because if we constantly think of our situation, then we constantly think of ourselves, and so Satan overcomes us. Amen? [*Amen!*][13]

According to Nigel Scotland, positive confession, or "faith teaching," began in charismatic circles in the 1960s in the United States as a reaction against teachings by evangelicals that emphasized public confession of sin and crucifixion of the self and, in developing nations, the acceptance of poverty among indigenous Pentecostals during the same time period (1995:38–39). El Shaddai's popularity may be a reaction against similar thinking on the part of the mainstream Roman Catholic Church in the Philippines. Public confession of sins is not currently practiced by Filipino Catholics, but mainstream church officials often urge "taking up the cross"—the idea that there is spiritual value in suffering and hardship. Although Cardinal Jaime Sin, the archbishop of Manila, supports El Shaddai for slowing the flow of Filipino Catholics into born-again groups and the Iglesia ni Cristo (the largest Filipino-originated Protestant church), he criticizes El Shaddai's approach to suffering:

> Mike Velarde has a very particular relationship with the poor. He is able to attract them by his preaching. And they just follow blessings. But . . . he is too excessive when it comes to blessings . . . and he does not say [anything] about the crosses and crucifixes of life. Because Christianity is not only the joyful, but also it has some sorrowful. . . . There is a Good Friday, and there is an Easter Sunday. They [the priests advising Velarde] will tell him about the cross, because you cannot follow Christ unless you deny yourself, take up the cross, and follow him.[14]

Father Anton Pascual, parish priest of the Santo Niño parish in Greenbelt, Makati, assigned by the Catholic church as one of the spiritual directors of El Shaddai, agrees: Velarde's teachings do not entirely represent God's teachings, he says, because Velarde ignores "the wisdom of evangelical poverty" (Samonte 1996). Another Manilan priest understood the emphasis on the positive to be the draw of El Shaddai:

> They're given hope, while if you go to the [Catholic] parish, the priest there is scolding you. And [Velarde] is giving you hope. They'll [the priests] tell you to carry your cross daily, and here the man is suffering from cancer or TB or whatever. And Mike Velarde says, "We'll pray over you and you're going to get well." You see? And he gets well! Now maybe it's from God, but he gets well. So he's for Mike Velarde now! He's not going to go back to his parish priest.[15]

Father Pascual and many others, however, also point out that El Shaddai's theology lacks a concept of social justice.

Velarde has borrowed from other Americans as well: El Shaddai's theme song, "El Shaddai," was written by Kenneth Copeland, a well-known

American preacher. And Velarde refers to members of his group as "prayer partners," just as Jim and Tammy Bakker referred to their P.T.L. members. In a personal interview, Velarde acknowledged these similarities in terms and concepts—such as prayer partners and the seed-faith principle—but dismissed them as coincidence, saying it was the result of having read the same Bible.

Although the issues of saving and borrowing are not as popular as the topics of prosperity and tithing, they do come up occasionally, and Velarde has a coherent teaching on the subject that is known to many of his followers. In one of his instructional booklets distributed to devotees, Velarde states that borrowing and indebtedness violate the laws of God. Romans 13:8, among other verses, is cited to support this view: "Owe no one anything, except to love one another, for he who loves another has fulfilled the law." Velarde writes: "The message of the Scriptures about borrowing is very clear: Do not do it. If you are in it, stop now and get out of it." Otherwise, he says, the result will be financial bondage (1993a:41–42). He continues:

> I made it. You, Too, Can!
>
> See there it is: if you still resort to borrowing money, it's time to stop it and obey the Word of God. And the Lord, Who is the Owner of all wealth, will open for you windows of opportunities that will enable you to pay off your existing loans and liabilities, and set you on course to freedom from sickness, famine and bankruptcy. [1993a:50]

Furthermore, Velarde says that while 10 percent of one's income (including gifts and regardless of debts) should go to tithes, an additional 10 percent should be saved. An accounting guide published in the same booklet suggests the remainder should be divided as follows: food, 20 percent; shelter, 30 percent; clothing, 10 percent; and miscellaneous, 20 percent. Although the majority of my El Shaddai informants did not know about this accounting guide, all were familiar with the allotment for tithing and some knew about the allotment for savings.

Velarde's prescriptions for personal financial management raise the question of whether his teachings have any concrete effect on the way members actually manage their money. Although I did not collect any statistics on rates of saving, repayment of loans, spending, borrowing, and the like, I did ask El Shaddai members if they had learned anything about saving or money management from Brother Mike or El Shaddai Ministries. My informants, generally interpreting this question in the secular sense in which it was intended, said they had not. Nor did they generally report that they had changed the way they handled their finances since joining El Shaddai. Some members, however, mainly men, had stopped spending money on alcohol and cigarettes in accordance with Velarde's teachings against such "vices," which in some cases could represent significant changes in household budgeting. Members used a religious vocabulary to describe changes they felt had happened to them—having increased faith that God would provide for them, having experienced financial miracles, having the feeling that their lives were actually better now than before.

Russell Mask, however, did conduct a quantitative economic study involving El Shaddai members. He looked at the effects of religious affiliation and degree of religiosity on borrowing in three Grameen Banking programs in Metro Manila.[16] Mask found that El Shaddai members who borrowed from the program (despite Brother Mike's cautions against borrowing) were no different from "traditional Roman Catholics," born-again Protestants, and members of other religious groups in terms of borrower performance (on-time loan repayment, business survival, business assets, weekly business income) (Mask 1995:357). In fact, writes Mask, "the economic conditions of most borrowers," including El Shaddai members and regardless of degree of religiosity, "did not dramatically improve during the 18 months of the study" (p. 360).

In the following section we will look at the specific ways in which the teachings of Mike Velarde, and those of El Shaddai generally, are understood and enacted—especially the mechanics of the seed-faith principle—and examine some of the ways in which participants attempt to elicit miracles or try to ensure financial stability and even upward mobility.

INVESTMENTS

"A prayer request is a prayer with money in it," explained a follower at a weekly El Shaddai mass rally. Submitting prayer requests with tithes is the primary way the seed-faith principle is put into practice. But there are other ways of increasing miracles or financial stability: love offerings, the blessing of objects associated with money or jobs, buying shares in

El Shaddai's radio station and foundation, or membership and investment in one of El Shaddai's Golden Rule Company programs.

From Tithes to Prayer Requests

Mike Velarde and his followers define a tithe, or *ikapu,* as a weekly
financial offering of 10 percent of one's income. Although the Bible
specifies that the tithe should be given to the temple, followers understand that the tithe should go to El Shaddai DWXI–PPFI. El Shaddai
followers try to tithe dutifully but sometimes can afford only a "love
offering" (usually said in English)—an offering of an unspecified amount
given (generally to El Shaddai coffers) not necessarily out of duty but out
of love. A love offering can also designate an amount given above and
beyond the tithe. (A Manila priest disputed Velarde's interpretation of
"love offering," telling me that the term is meant to designate offerings to
charitable causes as opposed to tithes, which are meant for the temple.)
Tithes and love offerings together are referred to as "miracle seed of faith
offerings." Neither tithes nor love offerings are specifically required for
El Shaddai members. Nevertheless, the El Shaddai central office keeps
computerized records of the amounts and dates of tithes and love offerings
given by official members.[17] Official members, or "covenant members,"
are El Shaddai followers who have registered at the central office and
have been given identification numbers.

Tithes and love offerings reach El Shaddai headquarters on Amorsolo
Street via a prayer request—a piece of paper on which is written a prayer
in the form of a request. (The term "prayer request" also refers to the
assemblage of the prayer request form and the monetary offering inserted
in an envelope.) There is a space on the back of this paper for signing up
as an official member of El Shaddai. The back of a typical prayer request
form reads:

EL SHADDAI invites you to tune in for miracles on DWXI-Radio
1314 (Khz) AM, IBC-13 and TV Channel 11 and be one among The
El Shaddai Covenant Prayer Partners and experience EL SHADDAI's
miracles daily!

[And below:] Dear Mike Velarde: I have decided to join EL SHAD-
DAI Miracle Seed of Faith Covenant Prayer Partners on DWXI-
Radio. . . . I pledge to support this Ministry with my monthly Miracle
Seed of Faith Offering. Please send me an application form. . . .

If the person is already an official member, she writes her name and ID number on the form or on the envelope. She then includes her weekly tithe or love offering with her prayer request form in the envelope.

Finally, the prayer request (with the money included) is usually "prayed over" before it is submitted.[18] A "pray-over" involves blessings and prayers over a person or object by a preacher or by participants themselves. In mass national rallies, prayer requests are usually prayed over collectively by Mike Velarde toward the end of the event. Followers hold up prayer requests in unison along with other objects (wallets, water for healing) to be blessed. At local prayer meetings, the visiting El Shaddai preacher prays over the requests and other objects.

In the case of a mass rally, the prayer requests are then dropped into one of the many donation boxes and taken in armored trucks to the central office. Seemingly 100 percent of these monetary offerings go to the accounts of the central headquarters, though elders were consistently vague on this subject. In the case of prayer meetings held in local El Shaddai chapters, the prayer requests are gathered by the chapter officers and the money is then divided according to rules specified by El Shaddai authorities. In early 1995, El Shaddai's pastoral guidelines specified that 20 percent of this collection should go to the central office, 50 percent goes to the Catholic parish priest of the local church, and 30 percent stays in the local chapter. (Often part or all of this 30 percent is used to pay the travel expenses of the visiting preacher, who is associated with El Shaddai headquarters in Manila.) When prayer meetings are held without parish church affiliation, the guidelines specify that the parish portion should be forwarded to the central office—making its share 70 percent of the total collection (Velarde 1995:51–53). These guidelines apply to Philippine territory only. El Shaddai officers were obscure and even secretive regarding the accounting of offerings from overseas chapters, which are composed mainly of the substantial foreign currency tithes of Filipino overseas contract workers.[19]

What happens to the actual prayer forms after they are submitted? This is a topic of concern among El Shaddai followers. At mass rallies, after hundreds of thousands of prayer requests are held up collectively by individuals to the sky and blessed, they are solemnly dropped into huge boxes and carried off in white sacks to armored trucks. These trucks take them to the El Shaddai office, where the money is removed from the envelopes and recorded. According to a local chapter coordinator, the prayer requests are then put in a prayer room at the office. For a week, all those who enter the room will pray for the requests. The request papers are then burned by El Shaddai workers. Many followers believe that it is Velarde himself who prays over the requests once they reach the central office.[20] This final stage—the last pray-over by Brother Mike—has significance for many El Shaddai followers. Velarde does not discourage the magical association between himself and the granting of prayer requests. At one mass rally, just before he was scheduled for a monthlong visit to El Shaddai chapters in California and Canada, he announced to cheering crowds that he would personally bring their prayer requests with him to the United States and pray over them there—giving weight to the idea that the papers themselves had somehow become potent catalysts for miracles and there would be extra blessings due to the extra personal care he would show them. Velarde's move suggests the cultural capital of things foreign (within the El Shaddai movement and in the Philippines generally) and the value assigned to El Shaddai's ability to reach a global audience.

When prayer requests are actually fulfilled and the story or testimony is "shared" during a rally or in a publication, an association is usually made between the miracle and either Brother Mike or the tithe. Sometimes Velarde (or his elders) arbitrarily grant prayer requests. Members who submit prayer requests to the El Shaddai central office have had them sent back to them in the mail, rubber-stamped "Request Granted" or "May the Good Lord grant your request" along with Brother Mike's signature. Velarde has told his followers that this means the prayer has been granted.[21] In unusual cases, the El Shaddai ministry may help people by paying for a plane ticket so they can attend a mass rally. This person then gives testimony of the "miracle"—the plane ticket—on stage in front of cameras and hundreds of thousands of followers. This kind of direct involvement is rare, however, and appears to be arbitrary. When it happens, Velarde seems to foster a confusion between the ministry's gifts and miracles coming from God—as can be seen in the following digression in one of his "healing messages" delivered at a rally. Here Velarde is talking about a hypothetical listener trying to get to an El Shaddai rally from Iloilo on another island:

> There's one here who's asking, "Who will pay for the flight?" [Laughter.] You just go there to PAL [Philippine Airlines] and say, "I heard

the good news there on the TV in El Shaddai. Brother Mike said to give me a ticket." [Laughter.] Yes, go over there. Tomorrow, if you have faith, go there to the PAL office. Amen? [*Amen!*] [Applause.] If PAL says, "Where is your payment," just say "It will come." [*It will come!*] [Laughter.] Amen? They will give you that. Then, when they give it to you, it's yours. You can board the plane. When you get here, show me your ticket from the plane and show me, just show me. [Pause.] I won't pay for that! [Laughter.] Alleluia! Praise the Lord! Praise God! But if you come, you will receive a miracle! [*Woo!*] Amen? Alleluia! Praise the Lord! Praise God![22]

The confusion created here maintains both the promise of miracles from God and financial support from El Shaddai Ministries—but does so in such a way that Velarde cannot be held responsible for these promises. Furthermore, the ambiguity blurs the distinction between the benevolence of El Shaddai Ministries and the benevolence of God. In this way Velarde not only supplies "proof" that God indeed follows up on promises of miracles; he also brings a divine quality into his own (and his ministry's) actions. This ambiguity is apparent too in the way he, in rare cases, returns the prayer request envelopes. Although "the Good Lord" is called upon to grant the prayer request (the rubber stamp reads "May the Good Lord grant your request"), it is Velarde himself who has signed the stamp.

In local and overseas chapters, unlike mass rallies, the money is separated from the prayer request forms on site and forwarded (without the forms) to the central office. In this case the requests are prayed over by the local officers, or by the attending preacher, before being discarded. For this reason many followers prefer to submit their prayer requests during mass rallies or take them personally to the central office. Many people think it is more effective to have their prayer request join the volume of other requests and then to be prayed over directly by Mike Velarde.[23] This reasoning sometimes induces followers to send their prayer requests through private channels. One follower told me that her daughter in Hong Kong, rather than submit her prayer requests to the Hong Kong chapter, sent her requests to her mother in Manila so she could deposit them directly in the collection boxes at the El Shaddai central office. A taxi driver told me that although he thinks Velarde is corrupt, using El Shaddai's money for his own personal gain, he still submits money and prayer requests to Velarde at rallies because, he said, that is where the miracles come from. The combination of writing down one's request, the pray-over by Velarde, and the inclusion of money in the form of tithes makes these prayer requests powerful and effective—that is, able to induce miracles. And this begins the request–miracle–testimony cycle that brings potential followers into the El Shaddai community.

Another reason to submit tithes to the central office was expressed by an El Shaddai member in her fifties: "When you drop the tithe at Amorsolo [the main office], of course they will know who you are, so once you're in crisis, they'll send you back the money as a form of miracle." But she continues: "I don't like that. No—why should they return the money? . . . Why did you give, if that's your purpose? Once you give, do not expect anything in return. That's why last September I wasn't able to give because there was no salary yet, and I said to the Lord, 'There's no money yet.' He knows it anyway. But I know the Lord will give it soon, doubled."

While discourse on upward mobility and miracles is intertwined with discourse on redemption and spirituality, the entire rally, which includes Catholic mass, might be seen as a ritual designed to solicit favors, financial and otherwise, from God (and, conversely, to solicit donations from participants). Prayers, in the context of El Shaddai, become prayer *requests*. "El Shaddai," a term used by Abraham to describe God in the Old Testament, is translated and defined in El Shaddai literature, on El Shaddai souvenirs, and in El Shaddai preaching, as "The God Who Is More Than Enough"—implying wealth and abundance. (It is also translated as "Almighty God.") Certainly the emphasis on miracles and financial gain has been a point of contention among traditional Filipino Roman Catholics and clergy. But the draw of the seed-faith principle is not just the prospect of getting miracles. It is the hope and confidence that go along with it. In his preaching, Brother Mike describes what people seem to want for their lives—and through him it seems within their reach.

Blessing Objects

December 19, 1996. It is a week before the El Shaddai Christmas overnight rally. My neighbor's radio is on, blasting the voice of Brother Mike, who is making an announcement about the overnight rally next week. He is listing the items that each person should bring to the rally:

two candles, oil, salt, drinking water, bank savings books, prayer requests "for Christmas," seed-faith offerings, and one *akay* (new recruit). He does not tell us what these items are for, but the implied promise of special blessings seems enticing.

At every rally, participants are requested to bring some sort of prop, such as eggs (raw and cooked), candles, or flowers. In addition, followers bring objects they want blessed—especially those associated with healing and with money and jobs. All of these objects are "raised up" during a certain portion of the rally and blessed by Velarde or, at local chapter meetings, by the attending preachers. These objects may include Bibles, El Shaddai handkerchiefs, bank savings books, passports, visa applications for work abroad, job or school applications, wallets, purses, and bags. Anything that can be opened is opened up to the sky—not only wallets and purses but bottles of healing oil and water, bags of salt, and more. Some of these objects, such as raw and cooked eggs, are used in Velarde's preaching. After being blessed, these eggs, along with other objects such as the water and oil, have healing and strengthening properties when eaten (sometimes raw), according to Velarde and El Shaddai participants.

Most of my informants thought that Velarde's blessing was even more powerful in bringing miraculous results than a Roman Catholic priest's blessing. The blessed water was more powerful for healing than the traditional holy water found in Catholic churches. Miraculous stories abound of jobs obtained overseas after a passport was blessed and windfalls after wallets or bankbooks were blessed. These miracle stories become the subject of testimonies later.

Objects associated with finances or career moves, when brought into the El Shaddai ritual sphere, become catalysts for upward mobility. Using objects to ensure good fortune is not necessarily new in Filipino religious experience—Tagalog fishermen and fish vendors, for example, have long used objects associated with fishing as *anting-anting* (luck charms) (Wiegele 1993). The objects held up at El Shaddai rallies and prayer meetings are not *anting-anting*, however, but direct conduits for God's benevolence. And, unlike *anting-anting*, which are limited in scope, they become conduits for profound life transformation.

Social Services

The social services offered by El Shaddai DWXI–PPFI include consumer cooperatives, livelihood assistance (for natural disaster victims), medical and dental services, disaster relief, educational assistance, and legal help. These services appeared relatively late in the movement's history. The medical and dental clinic, for example, opened on November 15, 1993 (Velarde 1994:20). Patients consult with a medical staff consisting of two doctors, three dentists, two nurses, and volunteers in El Shaddai's central office building. In 1995, the medical clinic saw on average twenty-one people each weekday, the dental clinic on average six per day.[24] Patients pay for doctors' services, which are discounted, and can buy discounted medications at a pharmacy in the building. Approximately 55 percent of the patients in 1995 were card-carrying El Shaddai members ("covenant members"), while 45 percent were classified as nonmembers. (These could be "active members," that is, participants without official El Shaddai membership, or nonparticipants.)[25] Covenant members pay lower rates. Due to limited facilities, however, many patients are not treated at the clinic but referred elsewhere. Indigent covenant members can request financial assistance from the Social Services Department. Indigency is determined on a case-by-case basis and roughly follows the government's poverty level standards. Given that El Shaddai was claiming 7 million active and covenant members at the time and that 80 percent of these followers were indigent (as estimated by the social services staff), the number of patients served in the clinic seems relatively small. Assuming that all patients were El Shaddai followers in some capacity (and that each patient visited the clinic only once), these numbers indicate that only one-tenth of 1 percent (0.1 percent) of El Shaddai followers consulted the medical or dental clinic in 1995.

There could be several reasons for these small numbers. One explanation, offered by one of El Shaddai's doctors, is that El Shaddai members pray over each other and heal themselves. Certainly the location of the office, in the capital's business district, may deter members who prefer to go somewhere closer to home.[26] Another explanation could be the general lack of publicity about El Shaddai's social services. Although the programs of Velarde's Golden Rule Company were heavily promoted on El Shaddai radio and television, from the pulpit, and in publications—and were successfully attracting large numbers in 1996—El Shaddai's social services were rarely mentioned in these public forums. In interviews with the secular media, Mike Velarde seldom mentioned specific services except to say, when asked, that El Shaddai spends much of the money it takes in on social programs. (Velarde has explained that he does not like to boast about El Shaddai's charitable deeds.) Much of the assistance in the Social Services Department, in fact, consists of linking El Shaddai members with government programs or with other charitable organizations. The staff admitted, however, that its efforts to spread the word about social assistance in the form of these linkages "has not been very successful" despite the ministry's extensive media network. My interviews revealed that members who did know about El Shaddai's social services assumed the assistance came directly from El Shaddai itself.

Legal assistance is extended on a case-by-case basis only to the victims of crimes—but not to the defendants in legal cases. Brother Mike, however, has ordered one exception to this rule: those who have been charged with *estapa* (swindling). El Shaddai assists *estapa* perpetrators, according to social services staff, through spiritual counseling and by talking to their victims and "appeasing both parties by reaching a fair settlement." The staff's rather enigmatic explanation for Velarde's exceptional sympathy for swindlers is that "the [El Shaddai] Foundation understands our present economic situation."

A significant form of assistance goes to victims of natural disasters, especially victims of *lahar* (mudslides) in the Mount Pinatubo region, and victims of typhoons. Often this aid has been in the form of capital (usually around 10,000 pesos) for the start-up of small businesses. The foundation has also made donations upon request to Catholic parish churches and Catholic seminaries. And it offered financial assistance (airfare) to Filipino workers in Singapore who wanted to come home during the case in 1996 (a period of strife in which a Filipino domestic worker was convicted of murder in Singapore and executed despite protests and accusations of an unfair trial).

Projects of the Golden Rule Company

The El Shaddai Golden Rule Company, Inc., is a stock and profit corporation headed by Mike Velarde. Although it is separate from El Shaddai DWXI–PPFI, which is a religious organization (a nonstock, nonprofit corporation) in the public imagination, as in the eyes of many El Shaddai followers, the two organizations intermingle and are even indistinguishable. Journalists, too, regularly confuse the two corporations.[27]

The Golden Rule Company was conceived of by Ed Bautista, head of the Social Services Department of El Shaddai DWXI–PPFI. The idea for the Golden Rule Company developed out of the Social Services

Department in 1995. Its primary project is the "Super Bodega" (Super Warehouse), a grocery cooperative for El Shaddai members.

When I interviewed Ed Bautista about El Shaddai's social services, I also asked him how it was that he personally came to El Shaddai. He paused for a long time and then said: "I am a leftist. I was a member of the communist party for twenty-six years." In fact, he was a member of the New People's Army (NPA) for most of that time.[28] In 1994, he got sick and was forced to leave the NPA and come down from the mountains to Manila to recover. For a while, he hid out in a secluded area of Manila, and then his wife told him that El Shaddai was going to hold a prayer meeting nearby. Out of curiosity, he went. After thinking about the word of God for a week, "the power of the Holy Spirit" brought him to the El Shaddai office and he got an appointment with Mike Velarde. After working as a trainee in the office for two months, he went to Velarde and said, "You're lying to the people! You're telling them to pray and raise up their wallets. But their wallets are still empty when they come back down!" Velarde said, "Well, what's your idea?" It was then that Ed Bautista came up with the idea of the Super Bodega—a scheme to eliminate the middleman in the delivery of basic goods. To develop the idea, Velarde sent him to a seminar on cooperatives at a local university. This, says Bautista, is how the Super Bodega began.[29]

The Super Bodega launched its first sale in late 1996, and Philippine President Fidel V. Ramos personally endorsed the project in a statement that is now posted on the bodega's wall. The Super Bodega consisted of a room, about the size of a grade-school classroom, in the El Shaddai office building. According to Bautista, the ultimate goal is to have one store in every province of the Philippines. In 1996, when I visited it, the small store was hardly adequate to serve 7 million followers and is therefore, at best, a symbolic gesture. Nonetheless, El Shaddai is still selling market shares in the Super Bodega project to its followers. The bodega itself is technically open to all shareholders and, according to sources in the office, El Shaddai membership applications mushroomed after the announcement of the plans for the Super Bodega. According to El Shaddai staff, members just feel better knowing the Super Bodega exists. Indeed, my informants said that in times of national financial crisis, when the economy collapses and prices skyrocket, the Super Bodega will be there to save them. These ideas come directly from Super Bodega promotions by Mike Velarde and the elders. One senior elder told me that the Super Bodega will be there for El Shaddai followers during "the End Time," that is, Judgment Day.

Since mid-1996, the Golden Rule Company has also been selling shares in its "Super Murang Lupa't Bahay" program (Supercheap Lot and House). According to promotional pamphlets and El Shaddai officers, a shareholder—who need not be an official member—may have the opportunity to buy a house and lot through a vaguely described lottery system wherein each certificate of stock serves as a raffle ticket.[30] Each participant must have a bank savings passbook in order to join. The concrete houses, once constructed, will each be divided into four small units. As planned in 1996, the houses were to be located on the land outside Manila in bordering provinces. Upon buying shares, participants were asked to choose a site in one of five provinces—all of which are generally inconvenient locations for those working in Metro Manila, not only because of the distance to the city, but also because of the increasingly congested roads and public transport.[31] During the period of my fieldwork, Velarde reported that he was in the midst of business negotiations for land for this program. Every few weeks, stories from these negotiations made their way into Velarde's preaching in the form of inspirational revelations of God's approval of the project.

Although the program in theory has the potential to benefit participants, it was clear that these people were putting themselves at risk. Not only were the logistics of the program vague and misleading in the pamphlet and sign-up form, but ultimately one came to learn that the chances of actually "winning" a house and lot were probably very slim. Yet the grand rhetoric of the promotion, steeped in images of hope, prosperity, and security, was enough to attract many participants—and many new El Shaddai followers. El Shaddai officers reported that the program was highly successful. Since the beginning of the Super Bodega and Supercheap House and Lot programs, according to Golden Rule Company staff members, new membership applications were up to five hundred daily. (The previous rate of new memberships was not disclosed.)

MONEY TROUBLES

Although the amount of money the El Shaddai group takes in during weekly rallies in Manila and worldwide is speculated to be enormous, exact figures are not customarily released by the ministry. On two separate occasions (in 1988 and again in 1996), Velarde was publicly accused of financial crimes related to the El Shaddai Foundation. These scandals were covered nationally in the prominent mainstream English-language newspapers and TV reports, as well as in local tabloids. Both times, after some investigation, Velarde emerged for the most part unscathed. During the first incident in 1988, Cesar Roxas, cofounder of El Shaddai, accused Velarde of diverting some 1.7 million pesos from El Shaddai accounts for his personal use. Roxas brought these charges both to the public and to the authorities (the SEC and the PRCC), but the case remains unresolved (whitewashed by some accounts). Around the same time, Velarde was allegedly arrested (and later convicted) for writing bad checks, nonpayment of a loan in 1983, and failing to deliver the title of some real estate property he sold in 1982.[32] It was also alleged that Velarde used El Shaddai funds to cover postdated checks—an incident that contributed to the separation of Velarde and Roxas in their El Shaddai partnership.

In 1996 various accusations were again publicly launched against Velarde. A group of former El Shaddai members claimed that he transferred 62.5 million pesos in El Shaddai funds to the Golden Rule Company for commercial purposes without informing El Shaddai members—an allegation that prompted a Philippine Senate probe.[33] Eventually Velarde produced evidence that the 62.5 million pesos came from sources related to his real estate business. A senator also filed a complaint at the SEC against two El Shaddai corporations (Velarde's Delta Broadcasting Company and the Golden Rule Company) for duping investors into buying 25 million pesos worth of illegally sold shares in the two companies without SEC approval (Villadiego 1996). Velarde called these shares "Miracle Investments" and instructed his followers to pay him personally for the shares rather than writing checks to the two corporations. Velarde was found guilty of some of the charges—the SEC ruled that although Velarde had not committed fraud, he had sold stocks without a license. He was fined and ordered to stop selling stocks until the companies were registered and licensed, which was subsequently done (Marfil 1996).

Velarde was also publicly accused of collecting donations for an El Shaddai worship and healing center that never materialized and was charged with mishandling funds donated for Channel 11, Velarde's joint venture with Eddie Villanueva, leader of the Protestant group Jesus Is

Lord. These accusations were never legally formalized. It was during this period, in July 1996, that the so-called Poison Letter was anonymously sent to the senator (Nikki Coseteng) in charge of the investigation. This letter, which was then copied and sent anonymously to various religious leaders in Manila, alleges the existence of Velarde's enormous personal wealth and offers documentation of Velarde's bank transactions, weekly collections at rallies, and the land, houses, and cars that Velarde owns and uses. It also claims that Velarde had illicit sexual affairs and that two of his sons were born to women other than Velarde's wife. Furthermore, the letter discloses the amounts paid to various Catholic priests and bishops for appearing at El Shaddai functions. The letter is signed (without names) "Former Elder Disciples of El Shaddai" and other former El Shaddai members. The letter was never published, however, and I cannot personally verify the truth of the information it presents. El Shaddai's public relations man, Mel Robles, describes the letter as simply part of a smear campaign.

Although Velarde lost some supporters as a result of the legal cases against him in 1996, many others were strengthened in their faith and the incident did not significantly affect overall membership figures, which continued to grow. Velarde was in California during the month of sensational press attention in Manila (in June 1996) and presented his side of the story several times via DWXI radio in phone interviews. The Catholic Church was criticized in the press for its silence on the alleged fraud, but Bishop Bacani consistently defended Velarde in public. It was not until Velarde opposed the church in August 1999 over proposed changes to the national constitution that the Catholic Bishops Conference of the Philippines urged Velarde to become "more transparent in the management of El Shaddai funds as these have continuously been the aspect of his ministry most subject to criticism" (Gonzales 1999).[34]

BEYOND PROSPERITY

El Shaddai has attracted many of its predominantly poor followers through prosperity theology and the seed-faith principle. Indeed El Shaddai has the three distinctive features of the prosperity gospel: belief in spiritual healing of physical ailments, an emphasis on material prosperity, and the elicitation of miracles through faithful tithing, positive confession, and prayer requests. Other ways of investing in miracles or increasing financial stability include love offerings, buying shares in El Shaddai's radio station and foundation, or membership and investment in one of El Shaddai's Golden Rule Company programs. The blessing of objects associated with money or jobs is a catalyst for upward mobility too.

The prosperity gospel has been the most controversial aspect of El Shaddai. Its emphasis on worldly over eternal concerns has been a major point of contention with mainstream Filipino Roman Catholics and clergy. Velarde has also been criticized for preying on the needs and desires of a class of Filipinos for whom survival itself is often a struggle. In the eyes of many outsiders, the prosperity theology appears to operate through an economy in which members pay Velarde for the hope of miracles with their donations. In response to some of the criticisms, Velarde has begun a variety of social services for members.

The lure of the seed-faith principle is not just the prospect of getting miracles, however. People are also drawn by the hope and confidence that go along with the prosperity theology in general. As we have seen, Velarde's gospel affirms people's desire for upward mobility and teaches that God's plan for us is prosperity, good health, and success in this life. Paradise is to be achieved here and now, not postponed until after death. Furthermore, suffering and poverty are not in themselves virtuous and can be alleviated by following God's principles, which include tithing and neither drinking, gambling, nor committing adultery. In his preaching Brother Mike describes what people seem to want for their lives, and through him it seems within their reach. As I describe later in Chapter 5, El Shaddai members say that prosperity theology represents not just payment for miracles but rather an opportunity for profound transformations of the self. We shall see in the next chapter, however, that by expanding the ritual arena through mass media Velarde and El Shaddai open up a legitimate space within Filipino Catholicism for the unorthodox beliefs and expressions presented by prosperity theology.

3 Mass Media and Religious Experience

The El Shaddai movement, which began as a radio program, has never constructed an actual physical church or worship center of its own. From its inception the community has been, to a large extent, a mass-mediated community. Even though El Shaddai outdoor rallies and other events are now also experienced live, mass media actually produce this "liveness." It is this predominance of radio and television that differentiates El Shaddai experience from mainstream Catholic experience and helps to create some of its distinctive features—a new form of religious space, new understandings of religious community, and a more personalized relationship with God.

In contrast to the mainstream Filipino Catholic religious experience—where the priest and the church building itself mediate with God and the religious community—El Shaddai members, through experience that is largely mass mediated, feel they have a more intimate and immediate (that is, unmediated) relationship with God and their religious community. And while El Shaddai's members and leadership are determined to maintain their Catholic identities, they define themselves by critiquing what they see as rituals (often Catholic) that are "just traditions" and not authentic Christian spiritual experiences. Although El Shaddai appeals to many of the same desires addressed by popular Protestant groups in Manila, members need not convert to another denomination. Indeed the country's highest church official, Archbishop of Manila Jaime Cardinal Sin, and the church's spiritual adviser for Catholic lay groups in the Philippines, Bishop Teodoro Bacani, publicly support El Shaddai as a "Catholic charismatic movement." Through its use of mass media and open-air rallies, El Shaddai has created a transcendent space, both physical and conceptual, that exists simultaneously within and without the church institution.

REAL ESTATE, RADIO, AND RALLY

Shortly after El Shaddai's beginnings as a radio audience that existed only on the airwaves, it manifested itself as an actual congregation of people. In other words, the mass-mediated community began to materialize as groups of people congregated in particular times and places. As the radio audience grew, so too did the assemblies of people. The physical assembly did not exist independently of the radio ministry but was an extension of it. These assemblies evolved into huge mass rallies. The radio (and now TV) programming expanded greatly as well. Both El Shaddai's radio and TV broadcasts and their mass rallies have become hallmarks of the movement. Local El Shaddai chapters, members of which gather for smaller prayer meetings, have also been formed by followers in Manila and other parts of the country and indeed in Filipino communities overseas.

Mike Velarde described the movement's evolution in the following manner.[1] Brother Mike created a Christian radio program in 1981 and, as well, a monetary foundation that supported this radio ministry. He started this foundation, he said, as a way to channel his own donations into the radio station, DWXI, which broadcast the program. The foundation, DWXI Prayer Partners Foundation, later developed into the movement that is presently called El Shaddai DWXI Prayer Partners Foundation International, Inc. or simply El Shaddai DWXI–PPFI. Velarde explained that his entry into the broadcasting business was just a coincidence. Real estate was his primary business then, and he was forced to buy DWXI because it happened to be located on land he was purchasing. Initially a friend helped him run the radio station. "I encouraged them to use the radio station for evangelization. . . . Never did we know that a movement like this would crop up."[2] Velarde himself started a gospel program that aired only once a week. He continued:

> Without my knowing it, people were listening to my broadcast and were receiving some sort of miracle things. Then they started probing me by means of letters and by coming to my office to request that I go on the air more often. Then I received that letter, which is already published, from one of my listeners, telling me that she was healed of migraines, which she had suffered from for the last seventeen years, just by listening to my radio broadcast. I was encouraged by that letter,

because I never told anyone that I was quitting. In that first mail . . . the person said, "Please don't quit the radio broadcast. . . ."

It encouraged me. So I considered that letter as one of the Lord's confirmations probably of the calling . . . although I really didn't know anything about religion. I was a nominal Catholic. . . . So that started my meditation and prayer for a new radio program.

He had seen the name "El Shaddai" in the title of an evangelistic booklet.[3] Liking the sound of it, he called his new program El Shaddai. He continued:

I introduced El Shaddai on the airwaves. . . . I played the theme song and said, "You know, our God has a name. I have discovered his name. [Whispering.] His name is El Shaddai!" . . . And two or three months thereafter, the program caught fire. It caught fire! So, so fast! I just found myself already in the thick of the crowd. And I forgot all about my real estate business.

Soon listeners were not only writing in with stories of miracles and conversions but visiting the radio station as well. When he invited those who had been "blessed" to a Catholic mass of thanksgiving outside the station, a few thousand came. This Thanksgiving mass soon became a regular occurrence. Each week the multitudes increased, and when the crowds got too big to be accommodated outside the radio station, the group met in various open spaces in Manila. This weekly meeting developed into the rallies that now attract 500,000 to a million people each week. He continued:

And people just kept on coming, even during the rainy days, when the area was muddy, up to knee-deep waters. . . . People were there, dancing and singing, and they go home happy! . . . Up to now, that fervor has not changed. . . . I now find myself traveling frequently because the people are spread all over the world now.[4]

Radio and TV continue to be the first exposure to the group for many El Shaddai followers. A survey conducted in 1995 reported that DWXI was the third most popular AM radio station in Metro Manila.[5] But El Shaddai broadcasts are not limited to DWXI station; the foundation buys air time from other radio stations in nearly every province in the Philippines as well as in other countries.[6] And since 1992 it has been buying broadcast time on several TV stations. In 1995 these included at least eight TV stations throughout the Philippines; most of the broadcasting hours are in Metro Manila.[7] In 1997, Brother Mike, jointly with the leader of Jesus Is Lord, an independent Protestant evangelical group in Manila, bought Channel 11 in Manila. In addition, what the foundation calls its "media ministry" includes the publication and free distribution of the Tagalog-language *Bagong Liwanag Magazine* around the country and internationally, as well as the English version called *The Miracle Newsletter*. These magazines feature gospel interpretations by Brother Mike, reports of large El Shaddai events, and members' testimonies of miracles such as healing, conversion, deliverance from vices, and financial blessings.

The use of mass media, particularly radio and television, gives El Shaddai certain distinctive qualities.[8] The mass rally congregation, even today, is in effect an extension of the radio audience, and the borders between the two types of experience tend to merge. The particular qualities of one's interaction with El Shaddai through the radio (or TV) are evident too in the ritual of the mass rally and in the followers' religious orientations in general. Participants note significant contrasts between these practices, which are particular to El Shaddai, and those of mainstream Catholicism in the Philippines.

TO THE RALLY AND BEYOND

In Manila, the El Shaddai movement operates through three forms of community: the mass-media audience; the anonymous assemblies at mass rallies (with usually 500,000 to a million attendees) featuring Brother Mike as preacher and healer; and smaller local prayer groups.[9] Going to an El Shaddai mass rally on a Saturday in Manila involves bridging the world of the mass-media community with the anonymous but physically manifest congregation of El Shaddai devotees in the PICC compound, the huge open field El Shaddai Ministries currently rents for its rallies.[10] The boundaries between these two communities are blurred both conceptually and spatially.

* * *

I am the last person to arrive at Eddie's dwelling—a two-room section of a house in a cramped semi-squatter area in the heart of Manila in a part of the city I have called Sinag. Eddie's wife, Celia, and their two children are still preparing for the El Shaddai rally, as their neighbor Josie and two other young women wait on the couch. The TV in front of them is on, competing for attention amid the bustle of the rally preparations. On the floor I see a basket of picnic food, bottles of water, small plastic stools tied together, a portable radio, and a bag containing a plastic mat and a bundle of candles. Other personal bags contain Bibles, umbrellas, handkerchiefs, bottles of healing oil, prayer request envelopes, and bank savings books. Josie asks if I have an El Shaddai handkerchief for the journey. When I say no, she promptly produces one for me, telling me I should have it on my body at all times. El Shaddai handkerchiefs are used by participants as protection against evil. Commonly inscribed with Psalm 91, they have become widely recognized markers of El Shaddai identity in the Philippines.

The TV is tuned to the live broadcast coming from the stage at the rally site. The *gawain* (function or happening) has not actually begun yet, but on TV we can see the activity on the stage. A series of people give short, impassioned testimonies of miracles they have received, a choir from a provincial chapter sings religious songs, and an emcee mediates each transition with introductions, announcements, short prayers, and pep talks about the exciting *gawain,* or "Family Appointment with Yahweh El Shaddai," that will begin in a few hours. As the cameras pan the crowds, we see the commotion of hundreds of thousands of followers getting settled in the open-air field for the evening. Peddlers sell plastic mats, food, and other supplies. Ushers keep people from sitting in the roped-off aisles and hand out envelopes for prayer requests and tithes. On the fringes, people wait in line to use portable toilets. As the emcee on stage pauses to lead a short prayer, Josie and the others present in the living room fall silent and listen. Then, in unison with the emcee, they conclude the prayer with an "amen" spoken out loud. Josie joins in, momentarily, as the choir sings the popular song "We Will Serve the Lord." Josie's friend, Nhelin, sits beside her on the couch and writes her prayer request.

When Eddie's family is ready to go, he lowers the volume of the TV and we join hands in a circle for a "binding" prayer with each other. Leading the prayer, Eddie asks Yahweh El Shaddai to bless us and the things we have packed and implores him to bring us safely to the *gawain.* We are then ready to go. Eddie turns off the TV. Although the house is less than a mile and a half from the PICC grounds—in fact, in one of the areas of Manila that is closest to the *gawain*—it will take us over an hour to navigate our way via public transport to our final destination: a spot on the rocky lawn, close enough to see the stage area, but far away enough to be able to sit comfortably, with enough fresh air. "Anyway," Celia says, speaking of the journey, "we have our radio. We can listen to the *gawain* on the way. We won't miss anything." The *gawain* is being broadcast live on DWXI, as it is every week.

Indeed, Celia flips on the radio as we begin the journey. We leave the house, and then the "interior" of Sinag, by walking through the many *iskinita,* or narrow corridors between houses and buildings—the dark urban footpaths that wind around and between the two- and three-story buildings. Neighbors greet us as we pass through the densely populated neighborhood where, according to the local priest, at least 85 percent of the residents live below the national poverty level. By our skirts (Brother Mike encourages women to wear skirts), the things we carry, and the radio broadcast we are listening to, it is obvious that we are "going to El Shaddai." One neighbor greets us with "See you there, sister!" even though she knows she'll never find us in the crowds at the rally. A young man, half-mockingly, hums the first line of the El Shaddai theme song.

After fifteen minutes waiting by a major thoroughfare, a jeepney (public jeep) finally stops and the eight of us get on. As we sit in the cramped jeepney, we listen to a woman's humorous testimony coming from the radio. She is talking about her husband, exaggerating his former bad qualities, and then testifying to his transformation. My companions laugh and say "Amen! Praise God!" as we imagine those in the crowd at the rally are doing the same.

Forty-five minutes and two jeepney transfers later, we arrive outside the Harrison Plaza shopping mall. By now, all the passengers are hot, grimy, and a little light-headed from the humidity, heat, and air pollution. Here we pile out and walk three blocks to a designated spot outside Rizal Baseball Stadium, where enterprising jeepney drivers have formed a new route. All day long, every Saturday, these jeeps run back and forth between the PICC grounds and Harrison Plaza. This route has expanded in recent years to accommodate the hundreds of thousands of travelers going this way to the El Shaddai *gawain.*

We wait in line, along with at least a hundred other people, for space on the next available jeepney. Other people are carrying bags and bundles of varying sizes, just as we are. Radios of various volumes and levels of clarity can be heard throughout the crowd, all tuned to the live broadcast from PICC. There is a feeling of camaraderie among the people waiting in line. With sounds from the *gawain* playing in the background, people greet each other as El Shaddai followers—with the titles "brother" and "sister."

Everyone in the jeepney is going to the *gawain*. Celia turns off the radio because there is a woman aboard with a more powerful boom box blasting out the live transmission. Within ten minutes we are inside the PICC grounds, waiting in traffic, slowing to avoid hordes of pedestrians streaming into the area. Cars and taxis compete with the jeepneys to drop off their passengers close to the stage area, but no one really gets very close. We are dropped off near one of the parking areas and walk the rest of the way.

Outside the PICC grounds, El Shaddai activity extends as far as the highway—a good twenty-minute walk from the stage. On Saturdays (the day of the rally), the area of the city surrounding PICC becomes, in effect, El Shaddai space. Not only are decorated and bannered jeepneys, taxis, cars, tricycles, bicycles, buses, and mobile vending stalls blocking movement and traffic, but pedestrians and vendors adorned with markers of El Shaddai membership—distinctive handkerchiefs, portable chairs, T-shirts, candles, hats, and blasting radios—seem to flow from every corner en masse toward the PICC grounds. Passersby stalled in traffic can sometimes gaze at vending stalls selling El Shaddai religious items: wall calendars, banners, cassette tapes, and ritual items for the day's rally such as eggs and flowers. El Shaddai participants get a small kick out of inconveniencing the unconverted through these huge weekend traffic jams. To them it is a form of evangelism.

As the crowds get thicker and the back of the grandstand area comes into sight, we no longer need our radio—we can hear the live transmissions from countless radios all around us belonging to those sitting here on the fringes. These people cannot hear the broadcast from the stage or even see what is happening. Some people cannot see the grandstand at all because their view is blocked by another building in the PICC compound. Nonetheless, when Brother Mike begins speaking in several hours, these people will listen to the live transmission on their radios and face the center—the grandstand—while going through all the same motions as everyone else, actively participating in the *gawain*. In some areas where large numbers of people are too far away to see the stage, huge video screens have been set up to project the live video broadcast. In these areas, people shift back and forth between facing the actual center and facing its clear image projected on the video screen.

As we head toward the grandstand, the sounds of portable radios are gradually replaced by the sounds coming from the loudspeakers near the stage. Soon we can actually see the emcee on the stage as we squint in the brightly lit area. Now we are part of the live *gawain*. Huge stands with camera and audio equipment block our view of the stage as we get closer. The area directly in front of the stage is blocked off and reserved for the "very sick"—those with terminal illnesses or deformities—so that they can receive the strongest healing power coming from Brother Mike onstage. There is a feeling of excitement, of taking part in history, as a video camera's gaze passes over us and simultaneously transmits our image to people across the country. Josie told me once that she loves going to the *gawain* at PICC, as opposed to the smaller *gawain* in her local chapter, "because it's live!" Were it not for the cameras, the simultaneous broadcast, and the instant playback (after the event is over), this "live" feeling would not exist. In the floodlights and under the camera's gaze, we have come out of the fringes into the spotlight. For a few hours this evening we are, it seems, significant and in a sense demarginalized. Later, as the crowds journey home after the *gawain* around midnight, many radios will be tuned to the playback: a repeat broadcast of the event that has just occurred.

* * *

Radio and TV broadcasts of *gawain,* as well as other El Shaddai radio programs, are often a person's first contact with the El Shaddai community. DWXI announces the upcoming *gawain* all week long, orienting followers to the stage where Brother Mike gives his "healing message." The journey that followers undertake each week—from areas of Manila or from far-flung provinces—is oriented toward Brother Mike, who becomes, in effect, a locus of miracles.

The radio and TV broadcasts extend the ritual sphere of the *gawain* beyond its immediate locale because, before and after the event, radio and TV are played constantly. Since the broadcast is live, one begins experiencing the event even while still at home. Within the PICC grounds, radios serve as links with Brother Mike at the center, focusing attention on Velarde and the events onstage. The mass-mediated community is gradually transformed into the immediate, physical community of the rally. When leaving the rally, the opposite occurs. The rally community is transformed once again into the media audience. Even within the rally context itself, mass media help to create a live feeling. The rally becomes live when participants enter the sphere they understand to be mediated to others—others who may be watching or listening to the live TV and radio broadcasts.

While Velarde is onstage, moreover, he often addresses people he imagines to be listening to the live broadcast at home, even in another city: "There is a woman in Naga City listening right now who is in need of a miracle. She has been suffering from cataracts for several years. Woman, you will be healed, and you will see your son graduating from high school next year!" (Inevitably a person fitting this description will surface later to tell a miraculous story of healing.) Many followers told me they had been healed through radio or television—either from blessings Velarde gave during a live *gawain* broadcast or from one of his radio programs. The following testimony, offered at a local prayer meeting, is typical. This woman testifies that her husband forbade her to go to the rally but she was blessed through the radio:

> You know, brothers and sisters, I cried because you know my heart is with the Lord. But while I stayed at home, the radio was beside me. I prayed too. Even though the rally was far away, the Lord still blessed me, and I was crying. You know what I told my husband? "I love you," and I embraced him. He answered me and said "I love you, too." It was as if our feelings from before came back to us![11]

Another woman outside Manila, in a provincial chapter, described to me how she was cured of a terminal illness after she accidentally tuned her radio to DWXI one day and heard Brother Mike talking. She is now a coordinator for El Shaddai radio broadcasts in her area. Some followers in Eddie's neighborhood in Manila hold up objects to the radio or television to be blessed by Velarde or occasionally by other El Shaddai elders, just as is done at rallies.

The radio and TV, as in the beginning years of the movement, are still channels for blessings and miracles. It is also common for El Shaddai believers to use radio or TV to keep evil spirits away from the house. One woman testified during a local prayer meeting that keeping the radio on in the house (tuned to DWXI) would keep evil spirits from bringing illegal drugs into the neighborhood. Hearing songs of praise in the house (even from the radio), she said, can also cure youths of drug addiction. Others said that keeping the radio or TV on all day repelled the evil spirits that caused them to argue with relatives. A local El Shaddai healer regularly told his patients that the "words of God" from the radio are protection from the devil.

The radio and TV serve as a link to the spiritual power of Velarde and the Holy Spirit. Moreover, Brother Mike not only calls followers to a center of sacred power during rallies through radio and TV but establishes the link to this power even before they approach the rally site—thus expanding the ritual center. The loose boundaries demonstrated here between the mass-media audience and the actual on-site audience create a unique ritual space.

RITUAL SPACE, COMMUNITY, AND THE HOLY SPIRIT

By expanding the boundaries of ritual space through the airwaves, El Shaddai can bring sacredness and ritual blessing into a very personal sphere: the home. El Shaddai prayer and counseling sessions on the radio—and the implication that blessing can travel through the airwaves—allow for a personal relationship with God that is not mediated through traditional Catholic channels such as priests, saints, the Virgin Mary, the Eucharist, statues, crucifixes, or the Catholic mass. In fact, Velarde explicitly criticizes attempts to communicate with God or the Holy Spirit through these mediators: he preaches that people should communicate directly with God (that is, through Yahweh El Shaddai). In an interview, Velarde told me he had a "secret revelation" he had not yet announced: the true calling of his ministry is to "free people from the bondage of religion."[12] Religion, he said, builds walls that block one's relationship with the Holy Spirit. By "religion" he meant "tradition"—specifically, Catholic traditions (such as the mediators mentioned here) that divert people's attention away from meaningful relationships with the Holy Spirit. At the same time, he still supports the sacraments and the practice of attending mass on Sunday and regards the El Shaddai movement as a Catholic movement. At El Shaddai rallies, Catholic mass is said by a priest.

Here we note several key connections between Velarde's use of radio and his ambivalent relationship with the Catholic Church. First, through radio (and also through rallies) Velarde creates a bridge between the listener and the Holy Spirit that bypasses these traditional mediators.[13] He does this by bringing the Holy Spirit, God, or Yahweh El Shaddai directly to the individual through the radio. Second, by locating the channels of sacredness and blessings in radio and TV airwaves and in open-air rallies, Velarde avoids the need to build a physical structure—a church. This is significant because if his group were to build its own church structure outside the Catholic institution, it would no longer need the Catholic churches and cathedrals and would therefore be enacting a symbolic separation from the Roman Catholic Church. Instead, the very nature of mass media allows the group to transcend geographic, social, and institutional boundaries (Babb 1995:17). El Shaddai's coexistence with the Catholic Church, then, is unproblematic on this level because, from its inception, it has occupied a wholly different religious space.

In 1982 (some sources say 1989), Velarde did have blueprints made for the construction of his own church—a "worship center"—which he had blessed by the pope in Rome.[14] Later he even collected investment shares and donations from his followers for the financial capital. But eventually he abandoned the idea, probably realizing the implications of building such a structure—a separation from the Catholic Church. He explained his decision to the public by saying that El Shaddai followers do not need a physical structure because the church resides in each and every one of them—they themselves are the church. And, he added, because they are part of the Roman Catholic Church, they do not need another structure—there are plenty of Catholic churches to use. With these statements he freed El Shaddai Ministries from the Catholic institution in some respects by locating sacredness within the self (a sacredness, nonetheless, to be achieved through a personal connection with God that is mediated by El Shaddai Ministries). At the same time, he adhered himself to the Roman Catholic Church as an institution by deferring to Catholic church structures.

In effect, Brother Mike elevates El Shaddai Ministries to the privileged position of spiritual mediator and relegates the Catholic Church to the position of repository of tradition. While he acknowledges the need for certain traditions such as the sacraments, he nonetheless says that the Catholic Church and its clergy are bogged down with intellectualism and ritual. Velarde himself, as he often points out, is "just a businessman." Having never formally studied religion, he is able to establish a direct link with God. In other words: while the Catholic priest's connection with God is gained through study—and therefore "man-made"— Velarde's connection is "spiritual"—a more authentic connection. When God healed him of heart disease, Velarde wrote in a newsletter, he became "a channel of God's grace and power to heal" and "a channel of countless miracles by appointment and prayer request" (Velarde [1991?]:3). Velarde told me: "This [El Shaddai Ministries] is no longer the work of man. We are just willing vessels. Like me. I have a covenant with God that no man can ever understand."[15] Furthermore, Velarde speaks Tagalog with what many have described as a provincial accent—giving others the feeling that he is "common *tao*," of the masses, as opposed to priests who often speak in both English and schooled Tagalog and are frequently viewed by my informants as having connections to intellectuals and elites.

Through radio and other media, Velarde is able to create the feeling of a personal relationship with the Holy Spirit. Velarde uses El Shaddai in-house publications to establish contact between himself, his readers, and God. In *El Shaddai the Almighty God,* one of El Shaddai's free publications, Velarde writes:

> Do you need a miracle? Would you want me to pray with you? Wherever you may be, this Newsletter can serve as a contact point of our faith for God's miracle power to operate—if you only believe and accept Jesus Christ as Lord and Savior! [(1991?):5]

> I'm excited! I know something good is going to happen to you. Are you ready? Okay, let's do it. Put your hands on this page as our point of contact, as if I am with you. (Did I not tell you that wherever I go, even simply through this El Shaddai Miracle Newsletter, Jesus is with me?) [(1992d?):4]

After each of these passages, Velarde leads readers in a prayer for forgiveness and blessing asking God to "come into my heart right now!" Personal testimonies of the effectiveness of this contact abound in the letters of El Shaddai members (Velarde [1992c?]:2).

> As I was reading the *Bagong Liwanag Magazine* sent to me by a friend, I was filled with great joy and felt the Holy Spirit flowing in me. Indeed, if we receive Jesus Christ as Lord and Savior, He will keep us safe wherever we go. At present I am in this country and have realized

my dream of helping my loved ones with their financial needs. Thank You, Lord!

—Sister Maria Cupan
Dubai, UAE

Recorded voice tapes of Brother Mike, circulated among Filipino migrants and overseas workers, also convey a sense of direct spiritual contact. A Filipina in California testifies (Velarde [1992c?]:2):

While I was listening to the voice tape of a DWXI–PPFI Healing Rally held in the Philippines, I joined in the prayers of Brother Mike for an increase in my working hours which would in turn raise my income. Praise the Lord, a few days later, my employer told me that I would be given more working hours in my job! Thank you, Lord Jesus Christ!

—Sister Linda S. Buquiran
Spring Valley, California

Alay Pagmamahal (Love Offering) is a live radio program that airs several times a week on DWXI. Usually Velarde makes announcements, leads prayers, interprets the Bible, and takes calls from listeners asking to be counseled, prayed over, and blessed. In the following excerpts, taken from a program that aired on February 13, 1996, he is addressing the general listening audience as well as those in and around his office building who have gathered to listen. The program is translated here from Tagalog except for the words in quotation marks, which were spoken in English. Velarde has just asked the listeners to stand up, raise their hands, and bow their heads. Now he tells them:

Praise God. You'll never walk alone. And if you have companions—those standing—your hands are blessed. Put those hands on top of the head of the one beside you. Even those who are outside, downstairs, and all those who are listening to this program, "wherever you may be." The hands you lifted earlier were blessed by the Lord. Don't worry, the hands of Brother Mike and your hands have no difference. "If only I had a million hands, I'd put them on your heads, but there is no way." Your hands have been blessed by the Lord, so offer them to Him. Put your hand on top of the head of the one beside you. Bow and I will pray for your requests. "It's just impossible for me to touch your foreheads." ... Ask now while those hands are laid on you whatever you wish to receive from the Lord. And I believe the hands laid on your heads are the Lord's hands more than the hands of Brother Mike. All those healed are because of the Lord's miraculous and wondrous hands. . . .

Place yourself in the presence of the Lord. "Just continue to meditate right now. It's healing time." If you have brought oil or if you have bottles of oil in your houses, get them out. Bring them out. Lift them up and we will pray over them. After that, rub the oil on the forehead of the one beside you in the name of Jesus our Savior. And on their palms. We're together and one now. The Lord is rubbing your foreheads. Lift the oil and we'll pray. This seldom happens in our program—the Lord's spirit is moving now. He knows all your needs. If you have no doubts, I believe everyone here right now is receiving an extraordinary strength and miracle in their lives. Almighty God and Father . . . right this moment, Lord, it is our prayer that you give them strength, freedom. And heal them from all illness in mind, bones, blood, flesh, in Jesus' name. Open the oil and rub the one beside you on the forehead and palms. Brothers and sisters, that's all you need—not Brother Mike. The Lord is with us now. . . . "Let the weak say 'I am strong.' Let the poor say 'I am rich.' And you will become rich and you will become strong."[16]

This extract not only demonstrates a personal relationship with God but formulates an El Shaddai community that crosses geographic boundaries. Not only is the community implicit in the mass-media audience but Velarde asks them to imagine the community, for example, when he says, "We're together and one now" and "If only I had a million hands, I'd put them on your heads."

By blessing his listeners in this way, Velarde is shifting sacredness and the power to heal away from traditional ritual space (the church, for example, or that designated by the priest through his presence, his ritual dress, or incense) to Velarde's hands, which become God's hands, which then become each and every individual's hands. "I believe the hands laid on your heads are the Lord's hands more than the hands of Velarde," he says. The blessing and the Holy Spirit, as in the newsletter, seem to flow from Velarde, through the radio, into each person's home, into each person's own hands, and in this case into the healing oil. One's body and one's home become sacred, and ordinary people are empowered to handle God's power and blessings—to enact grace and blessings themselves. Through the radio, Velarde is able to bring "the Lord's hands" to people. Yet his own hands are still there to mediate this process.

This laying-on-of-hands is done at rallies, too. While this practice is common at Catholic charismatic rituals—and is occasionally done in mainstream Catholic contexts such as mass—apparently it is always associated with specific ritual spheres (inside the church, for instance, or during a prayer meeting) and with the priest or a lay leader as ritual specialist. Performing the laying-on-of-hands and the blessings over the airwaves releases these ritual practices from traditional religiosocial contexts such as a church. Hence mass media, in mobilizing religious symbols and practice in this context, transcend social distances of status and class. El Shaddai followers repeatedly mentioned this absence of social distinctions as a significant difference between El Shaddai rituals and "ordinary Catholic" ones that occur in the church. At El Shaddai rallies, for example, it is constantly pointed out that status and wealth are irrelevant ("an engineer stands next to a maid"), that one need not get dressed up to attend a rally, and that "everyone is equal" in the eyes of Yahweh El Shaddai. One of Velarde's favorite stories tells of an illiterate man who became an El Shaddai preacher. This annihilation of social difference (between each other and with the priest) creates a feeling of comunitas that participants find transforming and empowering.

Followers regard the open space of the airwaves and the open-air rally context as conducive to the free movement of the Holy Spirit. The Holy Spirit is at the rally, they say, because of the open space. Informants consistently associated the rally with God as spiritually manifested; the church was "just tradition" devoid of the efficacious presence of the Holy Spirit. As one El Shaddai member put it: "At church, God is near. At the rally, he is actually there." They say they can "feel" God at the rally in the open space—as energy, as heat running through their veins, as rainwater on their skin (when it is not raining), or as wind (when no wind is blowing). Moreover, they say the feeling of God's presence follows them into their everyday lives. Going to church, by contrast, is seen as limited in space and time: "You go in, you go out" or "After one hour, it's over." A fifty-five-year-old woman from Sinag understood it this way in an interview:

[The Holy Spirit] said to him [Velarde], "Here build me not a church but a wide place where the people can go, attend, and know me. Because they do not know me at the church." In the church, they leave, come in, and just sit down, while here they listen attentively. That is what he [Velarde] did, he did not make a church. Then it was "El Shaddai" that was said to him. When he was asked, he said "I do not know that, it was just told to me." . . . He communicates with the Holy Spirit.

The priest's education and religious training are thought to limit his ability to communicate with or be a channel for God as the Holy Spirit. He is there only because of his training. But Velarde and his preachers, precisely because they lack this formal religious training, are held to be more effective conduits for the Holy Spirit.

Gaining access to the Holy Spirit through the radio is also seen as a direct and pure path bypassing the use of distracting mediators, such as saints, by those who are "just Catholic." Simply by turning on the radio, followers become part of a community through which they can receive constant reassurance and hope all day long. The medium of radio lends itself well to Velarde's style of talking—conversational, direct, never losing track of the person who is listening. This style is even more apparent when Velarde does counseling on the air. Listeners who call in with personal problems can receive personal advice on the spot. Often their stories are emotional, revealing feelings and experiences that might not normally be disclosed to neighbors. This intimate atmosphere contributes to an image of a community that is close to them and familiar. The advice, counseling, and pray-overs they receive in response are personal as well. El Shaddai members contrasted this feeling to the impersonal atmosphere of attending mass in a Catholic church. Aside from feeling little personal connection to the priest or indeed to God during mass, El Shaddai followers said that many of the standardized prayers and rituals are not even fully understood by those who practice them. Through the medium of radio, by contrast, they were able to share their problems with others and get a response; during Catholic mass, they neither spoke nor were spoken to directly. Even if one never phones in during an El Shaddai radio program, hearing others do so creates an atmosphere of intimacy. As at the rally, where participants feel connected to others when they enter the sphere of the movie cameras and spotlights, a sense of intimacy emerges when radio listeners feel connected to other listeners.

Scholars have often noted how television creates a feeling of intimacy between performer and viewer. In American religious programs such as 700 *Club,* this intimacy is based on an "illusion of face-to-face relationship with the performer" (Horton and Wohl 1976 in Peck 1993:101). According to Janice Peck: "The immediacy and intimacy of television that brings televangelists into people's homes creates an 'evocative relationship' between the viewer and broadcaster, according to Horsefield [1984]. Evangelical programming utilizes and capitalizes on this capacity by both addressing and appealing to viewers' personal concerns" (1993:101–102). El Shaddai's simulation of intimacy through the radio is especially powerful because of the possibility of "real" intimacy—that is, an actual conversation on the air by phoning in. This intimacy can be manifested in a different form when one goes to a rally. Far from passively receiving a one-sided message, El Shaddai members are active participants in mass media use and interpretation—simultaneously consuming and coproducing the content and meaning of El Shaddai broadcasts. El Shaddai integrates participation in religious programs with other forms of religious practice and indeed with religious life as a whole.

Miracle stories are a consistent feature of all of El Shaddai's mass media: radio, television, and printed publications. They are also a key feature of rallies—both the mass rallies and the local prayer groups. Personal narratives on the radio foster a feeling of familiarity with the personal lives of others who are at the same time part of the larger community. Radio, publications, and live TV broadcasts of rallies are by nature conducive to such language-based rituals and help create an imagined community that is both anonymous and intimate at the same time.

EXPANDING THE SACRED SPHERE

The religious experience of the El Shaddai follower depends to a large extent on spaces of congregation, sacredness, and community—spaces that are expanded and transformed through the use of mass media. Mike Velarde and the El Shaddai group, by reformulating religious space through mass media, create forms of religious experience that are very different from those of the mainstream church. Most notable are the ways in which El Shaddai followers see their relationships with God and with others in the religious community, their experience of ritual, their emphasis on the spiritual manifestations of God, and their orientation toward Velarde as a conduit to God. And by using mass media and open-air rallies, Velarde puts El Shaddai Ministries in a strategically favorable position with the Catholic Church—allowing El Shaddai to remain both independent from the church and under its wing at the same time. This position gives El Shaddai a perceived distance from Catholic orthodoxy while allowing it to capitalize on the sense of legitimacy that derives from its Catholic identity.[17] This ambiguity also opens up a space for El Shaddai practices and belief that diverge significantly from mainstream Filipino Catholic religiosity—such as El Shaddai's prosperity theology, its emphasis on financial and material gain through tithing and miracles, and its disapproval of mainstream Filipino Catholic mediators. Likewise, the fact that El Shaddai religious practice occurs mainly outside Catholic buildings makes it easier for church officials to overlook unorthodox practices. At the same time, church officials see El Shaddai as an effective way to keep these millions of enthusiastic devotees within the Catholic Church—and away from the increasingly popular Protestant groups in the Philippines.[18]

Through the use of narratives and language-based ritual, moreover, mass media allow for the construction of a community that is more personal, comforting, and omnipresent than the community of mainstream Catholicism practiced in Manila. Mass-mediated religious practices are conducive, too, to a more intimate experience of God and the Holy Spirit. El Shaddai members' use of religious programming, combined with their participation in mass rallies, extend sacred and ritual space beyond the immediate locale into the radio listening sphere, the home, and the body, blurring the boundaries between mass-mediated religious experience and more temporal forms of religious practice. El Shaddai's combination of rallies and live programming orients followers toward the conduit of miracles and blessings—that is, Brother Mike.

Finally, El Shaddai participants, through mass media, are able to comprehend their religious identities in new ways. Mass media and their derivative open-air rallies are associated with an emphasis on spirituality over Roman Catholic tradition—making it possible to relegate tradition to the church institution and spirituality to the realm of El Shaddai.

4 | Urban Spaces of Community and Congregation

In the open air of mass rallies, and over the airwaves of mass-mediated space, El Shaddai carves out unique forms of religious community and spaces of congregation. Who are the people who form this community, and where do they come from? What does it mean for them to enter these mediated spaces? In the following pages I describe the physical and geographic setting of this study and my efforts to discern a community in contiguous urban space as a workable area of ethnographic focus. Briefly I outline the living conditions there, profile the inhabitants, and then explore the urban context within which this community is situated by discussing the recent political and historical geography of the spaces El Shaddai occupies and showing how people's movement through urban spaces expresses attitudes toward class and recent political history.

A VIEW OF MANILA

Neferti Tadiar, a scholar of Pacific and Philippine culture, offers this provocative view of Manila:

> I have always experienced Metro Manila as a generally flat city. Ostensibly because of flooding problems, it has no underground transport system, nor do the majority of its houses have basements. With the exception of commercial office buildings, hotels, and condominiums, most of its structures are no more than a few stories high. Moreover, there is no single public monument from which a view of the entire metropolis can be seen. As such, most people have no access to an aerial perspective. I, like most residents, maneuver around the city

without a mental aerial map (without, even, a sense of North, South, East, and West); instead, I get around with images of seriality, that is, particular pathways. This is the kind of fluency one develops in a congested, view-constricted space like Manila. One might call it imaginary urban tunneling, except that all the tunnels are aboveground. And when one moves through this saturated space, submerged in the inundation of people and matter, it is like swimming underwater in a shallow metropolitan sea. [1995:285]

As pathways become established, moving around in the city becomes easier. These pathways *become* the city. Once a workable path is learned, one is not likely to risk hopping on an unfamiliar jeepney or cut through unknown streets in the hopes of finding a shorter path to one's destination. My housemate, for example, a nursing student, constantly complained of her daily thirty to forty-five minute jeepney ride home from the hospital. The jeepney route—actually two routes since she had to make a transfer—was one that she was already familiar with, for it went near her university as well. She went some thirty-five blocks each day on the jeepney, then walked another three blocks to our house. Once I learned which hospital she was coming from, I told her that this hospital, in absolute terms, was only five blocks from our house. She was shocked; she had no idea how close it was. She had no mental concept of an aerial view of the city: she knew Manila only by familiar jeepney routes.

My knowledge of Manila, however, perhaps like many natives' and like Tadiar's, is based largely on bus and jeepney routes. Jeepneys and buses move through the city on hundreds of mazelike intertwined routes that are subject to spontaneous change due to congested streets, construction, the whim of the driver, or too few or too many passengers. Jeepneys, however, unlike buses, are able to cover small circuitous routes profitably and to wind through narrow and obscure side streets. When I started looking for a place to live in Manila, I was equipped with a jeepney route map I had bought on a previous trip eight years earlier. The map proved somewhat useless, though, because most of the current routes were not on it, many of the routes it showed had since changed, and some of the routes on the map were simplified to the point of being inaccurate, excluding details of tiny streets, showing only the major thoroughfares. Even so, this map was one of a kind and there was no new edition.

How to navigate the city via public transport, then, is privileged native knowledge. Tourists and foreigners in general are expected to travel in taxis or private cars. Although each jeepney has a placard in the windshield with a name roughly corresponding to the area covered by the route, the only way to find out where a jeepney really goes is to get on it. On one occasion I was offered money for my jeepney route map, however inaccurate and tattered, by Western tourists who were disoriented and mystified. While the jeepney is the most common mode of transport in the city—and, in fact, a symbol of Filipino identity—many American expatriates I met had never once boarded a jeepney. They worried about the lack of established stopping points, the mystery of what seemed to be secret, puzzle-like navigational plans, and the inability of natives to tell them exactly where the jeepney would go.

I learned how to "swim underwater in this shallow metropolitan sea" by getting on jeepneys daily. At the same time, however, I retained the desire to trace portions of the routes I learned in different colors on the map of the greater metropolitan area posted on my bedroom wall. This gave me a certain feeling of mastery. Once in the jeepney again, I would try to imagine my position on the map, often unsuccessfully. Furthermore, once I entered the "interior," the unmapped footpaths, I was again disoriented both in terms of cardinal points and in terms of reckoning points relative to major thoroughfares—those that divide the interior neighborhoods. My orientation shifted to landmarks along the footpaths and alleyways.

Moving between these perspectives—between underwater swimming and aerial gazing—is ultimately what an ethnographer is expected to do: to map a phenomenon such as a social movement both through generalizing and through fluent navigation through particulars on the ground. I became conscious, however, as I tried to grasp a larger view of the city and also the El Shaddai movement, of the problematic nature of describing or even beginning to understand the totality. In writing one always becomes aware of the way, as Timothy Mitchel (1991) says, "a framework appears to order things, but also to circumscribe and exclude." He writes:

Among European writers who traveled to the Middle East in the middle and latter part of the nineteenth century, one very frequently finds the experience of its strangeness expressed in terms of the problem of forming a picture. It was as though to make sense of it meant to stand back and make a drawing or take a photograph of it. . . . [Even writers] wanted to portray . . . the same optical detachment. [p. 22]

Herman Melville wrote of wanting to withdraw from the "maze" of streets [in Cairo], in order to see the place as a picture or plan. . . . He expected there to be something that was somehow set apart from "things themselves" as a guide, a sign, a map, a text, or a set of instructions about how to proceed. [p. 32]

But . . . there were no names to the streets and no street signs, no open spaces with imposing facades, and no maps. The city refused to offer itself in this way as a representation of something, because it had not been built as one. It had not been arranged, that is, to effect the presence of some separate plan or meaning. [p. 33]

Likewise Manila, as Sally Ness says of Cebu City, "would be impossible to represent in its empirical totality, so varied, so numerous, and, often, so minute [are] its material constructions, which [are] in many cases quite temporary or transient" (1992:33). As Neferti Tadiar puts it, once again referring to Manila, "attempts to represent the city with any single monument invariably fail. A greater collective signifier might be the experience of moving through the thickness of the city, through its crowds and traffic, its dirt and pollution, and its relentless assault on one's senses" (1995:308).

A COMMUNITY IN THE INTERIOR

In the latter half of my fieldwork, I focused my attention on a small community in the heart of Metro Manila: in part of a *barangay* (neighborhood) I call Sinag and in part of the adjacent *barangay* of Bandong. (To preserve the anonymity of this community and its inhabitants, I have created the fictional names Sinag and Bandong.) *Barangay* are officially delineated divisions of municipalities, each represented in the municipal government by *barangay* captains or heads.[1] Technically the boundary between these two *barangay* (Bandong and Sinag) also forms the boundary between the City of Manila and Makati City: Sinag is part of Makati City; Bandong is part of the City of Manila.[2] This boundary is invisible to an outsider, as there are no obvious signs that one is leaving Bandong and entering Sinag, and vice versa. This small community, as I will define it, is my subject here.

I was introduced to the Bandong-Sinag community not by any grand plan but through a series of serendipitous events. Shortly thereafter, in the second half of my fieldwork, I moved my residence about a mile and a half—into Sinag itself—to avoid the daily hassle of finding jeepney rides to and from my fieldsite and to get more closely involved in the lives of the people who lived there. Since none of us (neither myself nor my informants) were connected by phones, any sort of communication among us was difficult.[3] According to elders in the El Shaddai central office, the area I chose as my focus lies within the section of Metro Manila that has the country's highest concentration of El Shaddai members.[4] This area is close (thirty to sixty minutes by public transport) to the open fields along the coast of Manila Bay where El Shaddai holds weekly and special overnight rallies.[5] In addition, the El Shaddai office is relatively nearby (thirty to forty-five minutes), although it is in the business district of Makati City where clean, wide streets and modern high-rises give the feel of another world. I rented a small section of a house in a lower-middle-class neighborhood in an adjacent area—an area bordered by squatter-and-shanty neighborhoods and two busy national highways. I then began attending functions at various nearby El Shaddai chapters. Each chapter was distinctive in its style of prayer meetings, community involvement, size, and affiliation with the local Catholic parish.

In densely populated contiguous expanses of urban space, it is no easy task to define a "community." Using *barangay* to define communities can be extremely impractical. More important, *barangay* may not realistically represent the flow of social life for locals. Here I begin by describing Bandong and Sinag as *barangay* in municipal terms. I then narrow the focus to a smaller community—that is, an area within the *barangay* that crosses both *barangay* and municipal boundaries but has a common center of activity and social life. Bandong, which covers 1.5 hectares of land, had a population of approximately 5,000 people in 1995,[6] and the adjacent Sinag, covering 9 hectares, had around 10,000 people.[7] Therefore, in terms of acres, 5,000 people live on less than 4 acres in Bandong, or around two-thirds of a standard American square block. Some 10,000 people live on 22.5 acres in Sinag, or less than four square blocks.[8] Even for the City of Manila, which has the thickest population density in the entire metropolitan area—indeed in the country—this is fairly dense.

Not surprisingly, according to a local parish priest, around 85 percent of the people in his constituency (the Bandong area and beyond) are below the national poverty level.

Most households in Bandong are located in concrete or wooden multiple-family houses or in makeshift shanties.[9] The entire *barangay* contains around 350 houses of various structural designs. Most houses contain several distinct households (anywhere from one to seven) that could be considered apartments. Household sizes vary dramatically, but I found they average from five to seven people each.[10] Although Sinag as a whole is more economically diverse than Bandong, the section of Sinag in which I worked could be similarly characterized. Wealthier residents, however, can also be found in this community in Bandong-Sinag. It would not be unusual to see a child with roller-blades and kneepads skating in the same lane where other children, barefoot and with torn clothes, float toy rafts made of candy wrappers down the open sewage canals.[11]

The community where I worked covers an area of roughly seven to ten "blocks"—clusters of dwellings separated by paved alleys (not to be confused with an American block, which is much larger in area and differs in shape and character as well).[12] The area, as I have said, crosses the Bandong-Sinag boundary. Those who attend the local (Bandong-Sinag) El Shaddai prayer meetings come from a slightly larger area than the one I focus on here. The area I designate as a "community" surrounds two centers of activity, or gathering places within Bandong-Sinag, which are located almost back to back. One is a miniature paved and lit basketball court; the other is a tiny wooden *barangay* chapel. The basketball court is bordered by houses such that a loose ball could bounce into one's doorway or window (and often does).

Although the Bandong-Sinag border technically passes between the chapel and the basketball court, these two areas, together, function as a meeting center for all sorts of community activities, both formal and informal, such as the Halloween party, religious meetings, sewing cooperatives, games, and official *barangay* meetings. During the Bandong *barangay* fiesta, for example, a mass wedding (that is, involving a group of couples) was held outside the chapel. The chapel was large enough to shelter the priest and the altar but too small for the dozen couples to fit inside, so they sat on benches set up on the sidewalk. For the wedding reception, portable tables and chairs were set up and decorated in the basketball court behind the chapel, where the couples (but not the guests) had refreshments. The basketball court is now used for local El Shaddai prayer meetings that are attended by both Bandong and Sinag residents.[13] Since the public address system that serves Bandong can be connected to microphones in the basketball court, events there can be broadcast all over Bandong and parts of Sinag (much to the annoyance of certain residents).

Residents on either side of the basketball court and chapel not only know each other but are involved with one another daily. It is an area where cooperative work, gossip, and just hanging around take place. In this neighborhood, indoor space merges with outdoor social space. A similar spatial and interpersonal intimacy has been noted in many first-hand accounts of squatter or semi-squatter areas throughout Metro Manila.[14] The chapel/basketball court area is also a well-used passageway between the two *barangay*. Small though it may be, it is the only open space where community members can congregate in groups. People also meet to talk or play games in walkways—especially in front of *sari-sari* stores (small variety stores usually in the front of houses)—but larger groups generally congregate on the basketball court.[15] Open spaces are hard to come by in these neighborhoods. In a *barangay* less than a half-mile from Bandong, I attended a blessing ceremony for a space—not larger than a two-car garage—that had been recently paved with concrete to form a community meeting place. Members of the community attended the blessing, which involved a local priest and the mayor of Makati City.

THE PEOPLE OF BANDONG-SINAG

Many of Bandong's residents emigrated to Manila from the island of Leyte after World War II to work in shipyards and other industries; others are the descendants or spouses of these immigrants. Manila experienced a period of rapid industrialization from 1949 to 1962, due partly to import and exchange controls instituted by the Philippine government (Caoili 1988:62). Under these controls, not only did importers and exporters surrender part of their profits to the Philippine government but American investors in the Philippines were forced to reinvest their profits in the country:

The industries that developed during the era of controls were conveniently located in Manila and its suburbs because of their central location, availability of port facilities, skilled labor and other considerations. The industrialization in the Metro Manila Area [MMA], coupled with agrarian unrest and rural underdevelopment, contributed to the heavy in-migration of rural population during the postwar era. This rapidly increased the slum and squatter population of the MMA, as a direct reflection of the "primacy" of the area. [Caoili 1988:63]

The second largest group came to Bandong from Samar Island, which is next to the island of Leyte. Together these two large islands form a region of the Philippines (the Eastern Visayas) that is among the poorest in the entire nation (UNICEF 1987). Migration from this region into Bandong has continued since this initial wave.

Residents from 60 percent of Bandong households I interviewed report that Waray (a native tongue in the Leyte/Samar area) is the primary language spoken in the home. If one adds to this sum the households who reported speaking Tagalog primarily and Waray secondarily, the number goes up to 75 percent. And if one includes in this number other Visayan languages (besides Waray) spoken as the primary or secondary language in the home, the total increases to 87 percent. In other words, only 25 percent of the households surveyed in Bandong spoke no Waray in the home, and 13 percent spoke no Visayan language in the home. Clearly the predominant ethnolinguistic group is the Waray of Leyte and Samar. Nonetheless, all residents I interviewed reported Tagalog as either a primary or secondary language in the household. Rarely did I find any resident, except occasionally very old people, who did not speak and understand Tagalog fluently.[16]

Bandong is named after a small town in Leyte where many of my informants still maintain connections with family members; some even retain land and other property there. Many of these people still visit their hometowns in Leyte and Samar when they can afford to do so. Moreover, Bandong residents from a certain small town in Leyte form the core of a civic and religious association whose primary function is to organize a fiesta for residents of Metro Manila who hail from this town. This fiesta, which coincides with a festival in the Leyte hometown,[17] is held in a central Manila location, but not usually in Bandong, since there is no space large enough for the dance. Bandong also celebrates its own *barangay* fiesta.

Sinag, a much larger *barangay,* developed earlier than Bandong. Its population is more ethnolinguistically mixed: migrants from a wider variety of regions, more Tagalogs, and more people who consider themselves natives of Manila. The area of Sinag bordering Bandong where I conducted fieldwork, however, is also home to many Waray-speakers.

The majority of the male residents in the community of focus are laborers: painters, carpenters, security guards, shipyard workers, owners or tenders of mobile vending stalls, managers of small businesses, motorized tricycle drivers, deliverymen, seamen (laborers on ships), janitors, bartenders. Notably, many of them were underemployed or unemployed at the time of the interviews. Many of the women prepare rice cakes and other dishes to sell at food vending stalls; others do hired work as dressmakers, laundrywomen, maids, hairdressers, and nurses' aides; a few were known prostitutes. As the *barangay* captain put it, referring to Bandong residents, "very few are office workers."

Many households have family members who work abroad in places such as Japan, Saudi Arabia, Hong Kong, or Singapore and regularly send money home. They work as "entertainers" (hotel musicians, escorts, dancers), domestic workers, and skilled and unskilled laborers. Many others who have not yet found overseas jobs aspire to do so. Of my surveyed informants, 85 percent had relatives working abroad; of those, 43 percent said these relatives were directly supporting them financially.[18] Most adult residents have only an elementary school education (sixth grade). The next largest group has had some high school education, followed by those with high school degrees. Very few have attended college. Around one-third of those I surveyed reported at least one child who was currently in some kind of postsecondary school or in college or had graduated from such a school; around two-thirds said at least one of their children had plans to attend college.

EARTH, WATER, AND AIR

From atop a local four-story concrete apartment unit—the tallest building in all of Bandong and Sinag—one looks over a sea of rusty corrugated iron rooftops patched in all ways imaginable, with wood or linoleum, weighed down with tires or stones. From here the narrow walkways between houses are indiscernible. Laundry lines hang from every corner; cats saunter along rooftops; wafts of smoke rise up between houses from barbecue stands, occasional cooking fires, and burning trash. Although there are very few cars in the neighborhood (the sidewalks and corridors are too narrow), the major thoroughfares that border this interior section are jammed with honking jeepneys, buses, cars, trucks, motorized tricycles, pedicabs, pedestrians, and vending stalls. The smell of diesel and other exhaust permeates the air even at the fourth floor. Radios and TVs can be heard blasting above the morning traffic.

Looking across the expanse of these precarious rooftops, my view of the skyline is hindered not by trees or buildings but only by scattered TV antennas and Manila's morning smog. Here and there churches and cathedrals break the surface as well. But from here, looking toward Makati from the edge of Manila (on a clear day), one can see the capital's main business district approximately 2 miles away. A few dozen highrise buildings sprout up in an isolated cluster on the horizon. The posh hotels, apartment buildings, department stores, office buildings, banks, and malls attest to the wealth concentrated in this financial center—which from this vantage point seem surprisingly near. On public transport at ground level, the distance between these sections of the city seems much greater. Near the western edge of this cluster on Amorsolo Street is the El Shaddai DWXI–PPFI headquarters—a relatively modest nine-story building owned by Brother Mike himself. El Shaddai members simply call this building "Amorsolo." Beyond the financial district—in a walled subdivision full of mansions with expansive green lawns, pruned trees, expensive cars with drivers, bodyguards, and (relatively) clean air—is the main residence of Brother Mike and his family.

Bandong and Sinag residents do not feel they have it so bad, however. Though they see themselves as poor, they say, there are others worse off. While people in a nearby Sinag alley are squatters (some local El Shaddai followers live there too), living illegally on land that is not theirs, many of the houses in the Bandong-Sinag area are rented or owned by locals. According to one resident, the head of the local homeowners association and a community organizer, the houses in Bandong stand on land that is available for purchase by its legal tenants from the National Housing Authority.[19] Because these families have occupied and developed this land since the 1940s or so—and in fact have been documented tenants since the national census of 1982—they are eligible for first-priority status in the purchase of land on which their houses rest. While the majority of homeowners in Bandong have not yet been able to buy their land, they have worked hard to preserve the right to do so and resent the term "squatter."[20] Not only do these people have the opportunity to own their land at some point in the future, but most of them are able to pay for electricity—unlike some in nearby neighborhoods who get their power from an illegally tapped street lamp that supplies the entire alley with enough current for a light bulb or two per cramped household. Because the connection is illegal, they live with the knowledge that it could be cut off at any time (as indeed it is periodically).

Sinag and Bandong have a fairly regular water supply as well. Some of their neighbors, by contrast, must share illegally tapped water from a nearby source, bringing it into their alley with a single garden hose that serves the entire area. In Bandong and Sinag there is either a water faucet or an occasional deep well on the street for every three to five houses. (Each water source is shared by ten to fifteen households.) Both those with faucets and those with wells pay the municipal water department for the water. For most residents (those who depend on faucets) this water is available only three or four hours a day, usually beginning at around 9:30 or 10:00 P.M. and lasting until the early morning hours. Entering the barrio at 10:30 P.M., one can see women and young girls sitting with basins and buckets on the pathways, doing laundry by the light of street lamps. Sometimes, however, this water does not flow at all. Most residents are equipped with a myriad of sizes and types of containers for collecting water for bathing, laundry, and cooking. Those few with deep wells are fortunate to have water more regularly. According to a *Chicago Tribune* report in December 1997, the water situation in many sections of Manila was especially bad that year. Indeed, neighborhoods in Manila similar to Bandong depended on water sold for cash on the spot by commercial water companies for those who could afford it. This water arrived sporadically in huge trucks parked just outside the interior (Schmetzer 1997).

During several months of my fieldwork in 1996, water sources in the Bandong area and elsewhere were contaminated with cholera—presumably due to water pipes broken by construction crews. Some people from the community were hospitalized, and newspapers reported the deaths of children in neighboring areas. My informants did not seem overly concerned about the cholera outbreaks, however. Some boiled their drinking water to deal with the waterborne disease, but many did not. Some believed that the contaminants would settle to the bottom of water containers; others thought that blessing the drinking water in the name of Yahweh El Shaddai would purify it for those who believed. I boiled my own water at home. On several occasions, however, sensing that rejecting the water would offend them, I drank blessed but unboiled water at the houses of my informants. I was fortunate on two counts. First, I did not get cholera. Second, I later found out that offering blessed water to a newcomer can be a litmus test. If the person turns down the water or disparages it (saying it tastes bad or warm), some believe the person is being controlled by the devil.

Most residents bathe in the street (especially the children) or in makeshift enclosed areas, wherever drainage is possible. Although most households I visited had access to water-sealed toilets, open sewage canals, one or two feet across, line every pathway. The brown-green sludge has a distinct odor and is a likely breeding ground for rats, roaches, and mosquitoes. Thankfully, most of the pathways in Bandong and Sinag are paved. Just a step away, in an adjacent *barangay,* however, residents must wade through mud (sometimes mixed with sewage) to reach their dwellings during the rainy season. During the heavy rains of the monsoon season, Bandong-Sinag residents get their share of flooding. With each rain, large portions of the *barangay* are knee-deep in water and cut off from major interior thoroughfares—forcing residents to go long distances out of their way to reach their house from another direction. As Manila experiences major and minor typhoons every monsoon season, this is a common occurrence. Many households remain dry inside because their houses are elevated slightly or they live on the second floor. Those on the ground level get one to three feet of water and mud in their houses at times. For this reason, most have either dirt floors or plain concrete floors.

With five to seven distinct households within each house, the area is extremely densely populated. This density leads to a crowded but vibrant and intimate atmosphere—as well as excessive air pollution and noise. Smoke from garbage or cooking fires clouds the air; fumes from sewage and smoke-belching vehicles are everywhere. The weather is hot (in the eighties and nineties) and very humid year-round. An electric fan is an essential item in every household. Nearly every household also has access to a TV and a radio. It is not unusual to hear many radios, TVs, and karaoke machines playing simultaneously from a given location—not to mention the screams and laughter of children playing, dogs barking, vendors calling, neighbors talking, and the various sounds from miscellaneous activities such as sewing, mechanical repairs, house repairs, and more. These busy alleys are usually a mere step away from one's dining table.

Neferti Tadiar's "tunneling effect" best describes the feel of moving through this community. Narrow, complex alleyways separate the blocks of houses. Smaller passages that go around individual houses, leading to households, are often part of the households themselves. Now let us take a closer look at this interior space. It involves a trek to the household of Theresa, a friend who lives with her parents and four unmarried brothers in Sinag. Theresa is active in the local El Shaddai chapter and works as a *barangay* health care volunteer. The size and location of her household (part of a multihousehold structure) are typical of this community.

* * *

It took me several visits before I could find Theresa's residence on my own without asking for directions. Upon walking down the narrow street, the first step was to locate the "entrance." The landmark is a small yellow sign advertising Knorr Instant Soup put up by a local *sari-sari* store. (There are too many such stores for one to be used as a landmark.) I enter at the gate that directly follows the sign. The gate opens into a dark corridor with an uneven path of stones and pieces of concrete.

The first being I encounter is a barking dog that is quickly called off. As my eyes adjust to the dim light, I can see, in the middle of the corridor, an old woman doing laundry in numerous basins on the path. The corridor is lit by sunlight peeking through small gaps in the patchwork roof. After greeting this woman, I ask if Theresa is home and she gestures me onward. Over her laundry I step, through puddles of soapy water, following a turn in the path, ducking to avoid banging my head on various parts of the low roof structure. The next thing I encounter is a plastic shower curtain draped across the corridor. I call out *"Tao po!"* to announce my presence. From behind the curtain a voice shouts *"Sandali!"* (Just a minute!). In seconds the curtain is drawn by Theresa's brother, who greets me as he stands in shorts and plastic slippers, completely wet from head to toe, interrupted in the middle of his bath. We are both embarrassed, but only slightly, as this is a regular occurrence when I visit Theresa in the morning.

Stepping over more puddles and a soap dish on the concrete floor, I duck through the small doorway into Theresa's house. It is a stuffy yet cheerful room lit by an electric light and a tiny window. Two dogs sprawled on the floor make it nearly impossible to enter, however, for the entire room is only ten to twelve feet square. The household consists of just this room plus a sleeping room upstairs of roughly the same size. Attached to the living room is a kitchen area, resembling a tiny passageway, and a small closet enclosed by a curtain. The room is cramped with a shelving unit and a kitchen table and chairs. A TV sits on the table. Various framed diplomas of the children decorate the walls. I am greeted by Theresa's parents and invited to sit on the wooden bench lining one wall. They turn on the electric fan for my benefit.

GHOSTS, MARTYRS, AND MOVING ON

The field of the Philippine International Convention Center (PICC) where weekly national El Shaddai rallies are held is one of the few spaces in Manila that gives you at least a *feeling* of perspective. The PICC refers to a huge open space—a piece of land that juts out into Manila Bay. For El Shaddai members, the PICC also refers to the group of buildings on this land that comprise the Cultural Center complex. This is prime property, on the seafront facing west, offering what the postcards and tour books say is the most stunning sunset in Southeast Asia. As one resident of Manila put it: "This is the only spot you can stand where you realize that Manila is really a harbor city, and not seemingly a landlocked jungle as is the atmosphere even in the Ermita and Malate sections now [which are near the bay], a sprawling horizontal mess where you cannot distinguish the landmarks from the present living habitats of its people."[21]

The PICC area is relatively close to Manila's tourist district. It is also reclaimed land (landfill)—that is, this area was once part of the sea but was filled in with earth to extend the coastal land area in the 1970s as one of the extravagant showcase projects of Imelda Marcos, former first lady and wife of the late dictator Ferdinand (Pinches 1994:30). According to earlier maps, there had been plans to reclaim the land for some time. A U.S. Army map, for example, shows plans for a national airport in this space ("Philippine City Plans" 1945). According to a later map (Varias 1953), Filipino officials proposed a public recreation zone that included a beach, a children's play area, a pool, a beach park, aquariums, and a playing field. Within a few decades, plans for the use of this space had changed drastically once again. A 1979 map shows a proposed financial center, central business park, the Philippine Plaza Hotel, and a cultural center ("City Map of Manila and Suburbs" 1979). Imelda Marcos built the Cultural Center complex to attract artists, performers, and guests from all over the world, bringing pride and international recognition to the country. As Michael Pinches writes: "Both functionally and symbolically, this whole complex seemed to address the affluent West as a statement of progress, national identity and state power under the regime of Ferdinand Marcos" (1994:14). The elegant Cultural Center of the Philippines (CCP), devoted to Filipino cultural events, stands on this land, as does the International Film Center, the Folk Arts Theater, the International Convention Center, and a hotel.[22]

The International Film Center—a huge imposing modern concrete building—has been abandoned since the 1991 earthquake and is reputed to be haunted. For Filipinos it represents the greed, cruelty, betrayal, and lavish spectacle that Imelda Marcos embodied. The story of its construction is legendary in the Philippines. As the story goes, Imelda pressured the construction workers to work at an inhumanly rapid pace in order to finish in time for the Manila International Film Festival in 1981. Because the workers were forced to labor under slavelike conditions, a makeshift scaffold collapsed inside the building and more than a hundred workers plummeted to the unfinished floor inside. Some were killed, and some were trapped alive under the fallen debris. When word of the event reached Imelda (in Germany at the time), she refused to delay construction while the workers were rescued. Instead she ordered her manager to hire more workers and continue with the project—that is, continue pouring cement in the building's foundation, burying the workers, dead or alive.[23]

Reportedly the Film Center is still haunted with the spirits of these workers, and people seeking to persuade the spirits to move on conduct group seances in the abandoned structure to this day. In 1996, for example, two attempts were made by Spirit Quest, a group from Ateneo de Manila University.[24] The spirits in the Film Center reportedly told them they would not move on until Imelda Marcos made reparations for her deeds. At El Shaddai rallies the crowds often stretch across the open fields all the way to the Film Center. Sometimes rally participants sit on the massive steps of the Film Center, watching the stage nearly a half mile away across the grassy field, as they listen to their radios. The Film Center, regardless of the position of El Shaddai's movable outdoor stage, always seems to be a visible backdrop from one angle or another during El Shaddai events.

The reclamation area is now a cultural, convention, and business zone (de Guzman 1996:C1). Parts of the reclaimed land have been sold by the government at various stages to private businesses such as the Philippine National Bank and the extremely posh Philippine Westin Plaza Hotel, which takes advantage of this unobstructed view of sea and sunset. A lunch for two at this hotel in 1996 could cost an average lower-class Manilan half a month's salary or more.[25] Indeed, access to most of the PICC–CCP artistic and cultural events, due to their cost, is restricted to members of the upper echelons of Manila society.

The extravagance of the reclamation area and the PICC–CCP complex —in contrast to Manila's overcrowded urban slums—embodies the Marcos' attitude toward the urban poor in general. After the imposition of martial law in 1972, notes Neferti Tadiar,

> in its bid to join the international community of advanced nations, the Marcos regime launched a program of economic development that was export-oriented and foreign-capital-dependent. To attract foreign investments, it built five-star hotels, an international convention center, a cultural center, specialized medical centers, and numerous other "beautification projects." . . . "The efforts of the First Lady have been focused on making Manila a center for the 'jet set' and the 'beautiful people'" [Doherty 1985:25]. This meant the eradication of unsightly structures such as slums. Consequently, every international visit or event held in Manila resulted in the eviction of squatters or the relocation of their shanties from the site of the event or the routes to be taken by Imelda's guests. Hence, although the city was Imelda's personal domestic showcase, it was "beautified" for the eyes and pleasure of foreigners and to attract the flow of foreign capital. In her vision, Manila was to be "the city of Man," the practical definition of which excluded the urban poor.

The urban poor, however, help to sustain the very same economy in behalf of which they are marginalized. [Tadiar 1995:290][26]

These so-called beautification projects continued under the democratic governments of Corazon Aquino and Fidel Ramos. In the months leading up to the Asia-Pacific Economic Cooperation (APEC) summit held in the Philippines in November 1996, for example, the Ramos government "beautified" the routes the international delegates would take to reach the summit in Subic Bay. According to the *Philippine Daily Inquirer*'s Donna S. Cueto (December 3, 1996), a local human rights group, Karapatan, reported:

> More than 783,000 families of peasants, urban poor, and indigenous people were affected by demolitions and dislocations nation-wide. . . . Demolitions of squatter shanties alone in Metro Manila affected 10,000 families because of beautification and cleaning up programs intended to make the capital free from eyesores for the APEC delegates' benefit. . . . This is the result of the government's rush for economic super-liberalization to put itself at the head of the APEC's member-economies. . . . *Karapatan* also said that politically motivated arrests and detention increased in the APEC month of November.

Other sections of the reclaimed land south of the Cultural Center are occupied by semipermanent squatters who live in shanty towns along the coast. These squatter areas are periodically razed by government demolition crews for beautification purposes or when parts of this land are actually developed. Rizal National Park (also known as Luneta Park), named for the Philippine national hero José Rizal, a large, clear grassy area north of the Cultural Center along the coast, is home to many homeless people who sleep there overnight. The marginalization of Manila's poor in the world capitalist system and in the Philippines' quest to modernize is written into Manila's geography (Pinches 1994; Tadiar 1995).

Ironically, some of my El Shaddai informants feel that life was better under Marcos' martial law. Brother Eddie, for instance, a local healer and municipal worker, when asked why he preferred martial law to the current administration, expressed his ideas in terms of public space. He said that during martial law at least he could bring his family to Rizal Park to sleep (at times when they were homeless) and criminals would not disturb them. Now, he said, one risks being robbed when sleeping there. For some of my informants, public spaces such as these are safety nets during times of economic destitution, especially when family relationships fail. Another resident of Bandong, an El Shaddai member, told me that she slept for several months in Greenbelt Park in Makati when her siblings kicked her and her family out of their house.

The El Shaddai group has occupied increasingly larger spaces in the city since the mid-1980s. The history of the movement itself was narrated to me by more than one El Shaddai elder as a chronicle of the numerous spaces it has occupied. Before the group moved to the PICC, for example, the rallies were held in nearby Rizal Park. Some El Shaddai rallies, such as the smaller Tuesday night gatherings, are currently held at the Rizal Baseball Stadium, located in the same general part of Manila. *Asiaweek* begins its cover story on El Shaddai as follows:

> No church can contain the El Shaddai congregation. Soon, perhaps, no urban space will either. Its legions have already outgrown a football stadium and overrun a public park. Now they gather every Saturday in a field outside the Philippine International Convention Center beside Manila Bay. The first arrive the night before to claim choice spots in front of the stage. The next day, thousands of others appear, covering more than 66,000 square meters of lawn. [*Asiaweek,* September 20, 1996, p. 36)

Public spaces in many cities are sites of struggles for power. One reason the El Shaddai rallies moved away from Rizal Park to the PICC, apart from their size, was that proprietors and customers of the nearby Manila Hotel, one of the oldest and most prestigious hotels in the city, complained. The weekly traffic and noise created by the group were considered an inconvenience.

One can see why El Shaddai followers enjoy the rallies in the open space at the PICC on the coast and "feel God" there. One emerges from cramped, tunnellike streets and neighborhoods to a rare, wide-open space with a view of the sunset and, on the horizon, a partial view of the Makati skyline. Fresh air, sea breeze, open space, stars—all signify a different, liberating sort of existential state to many of those who come to spread blankets on the PICC grounds. In this space El Shaddai members get a perspective not only of the city but of themselves and their own critical mass. They are able to express the force of this mass to outsiders by disrupting the city and its imposed "order" and by occupying, even reclaiming, public spaces. They create massive traffic jams at unusual times and take over the clean, posh segments of the city. In the interior barrios, El Shaddai's mass is dispersed and unseen. But a rally crowd is a totality that can be seen and felt. As part of this collectivity that is simultaneously broadcast on national TV, El Shaddai members are in a sense demarginalized. Seeing El Shaddai's impressive assembly—especially from atop the steps of the Film Center or through the TV cameras above the stage—gives participants a sense of significance, even empowerment. This view of "the numbers" makes El Shaddai seem awesome to outsiders as well.[27]

Emerging from the barrios, El Shaddai members also enter a space where mediation with the elites and power brokers of Philippine society seems possible. People in the rally audience are courted by politicians and candidates who appear on stage, address them directly, and banter with Brother Mike. As one observer put it:

> However these weekly meetings may have affected their political consciousness or will, I don't exactly see a social revolution forthcoming from these . . . masses. Whatever may come of their participation, it would be change in the immediate, personal realm—the family circle or friends—because that's still the brunt of the message of God changing their lives. As for political enlightenment or however it makes them connect to Velarde's hidden political endorsements and stimulates their sense of irony of the powers that be, I don't know. In spite of the press they get every time the elections come around, and seeing every campaigning politician jump to Brother Mike's every utterance, the followers see more entertainment and hypocrisy in the "visitors" courting their favor than in their own plaid head-honcho.[28]

It is a well-known axiom in Bandong that any candidate for political office—be it for mayor, senator, or councilor—who actually comes to the barrio and visits the folks there will automatically receive votes from the residents simply by virtue of his visit. Perhaps it is because people imagine that this candidate has put them on his map; they now *exist* for the candidate. In El Shaddai/PICC space, formerly invisible people now exist for the nation—they are on the national political map and in the national consciousness. Not only do politicians, candidates for political office, high officials of the church, and prominent businessmen regularly visit them, conferring a sense of importance, but these visits reach a national audience through mass media. It is not surprising, either, that El Shaddai followers from other provinces make long trips to take part in these national rallies. Even for those who see hypocrisy in the words and actions of their visitors, the visits are important to them because, as some have put it, these politicians "need our prayers." In other words: "they need *us.*" Just by being at the rally, these politicians will receive the word of God and be blessed. And this, they say, can only be for the good.

While El Shaddai occupation of this space may be read as the urban masses' reclamation of the area, it is still full of bitter irony. The El Shaddai group, through devotees' tithes, must pay rent on this land—land that rightfully should be public—to hold their weekly rallies. And despite the painful history of the PICC–CCP complex, and the Film Center within it, I found it intriguing that not once during my fieldwork did I hear any reference to the irony of having El Shaddai, composed primarily of the urban poor, occupy this space on a weekly basis. The closest I came was hearing a member of Manila's elite liken Brother Mike to "a cross between Imelda Marcos and Oprah Winfrey"—implying that Brother Mike is continuing the grand betrayal of the urban poor that so characterized the Marcos regime (and, as many say, the administrations that followed him). As one Manila journalist put it:

> These people at the El Shaddai rallies are really the masses to their very last Filipino blood. They aren't bothered by the ghosts of the Film Center simply because the people who died there building what Imelda wanted were in a sense martyrs to them. These people who haunt the Film Center are also your El Shaddai devotees. [And yet] they will not think of it in political terms because they go there to be spiritually stimulated first and foremost, and Brother Mike will be the last person to even hint at the political implications and the ghosts they break bread with every week there.[29]

RECLAIMING SPACE?

Bandong-Sinag offers insights into the broad social and political contexts from which El Shaddai members in Manila emerge. Although it is difficult to find a typical El Shaddai member, the people and conditions described here would likely be familiar to a vast majority of the El Shaddai constituency. Thus the bulk of my ethnographic investigations into local El Shaddai experience takes place in this community.

The El Shaddai members I became familiar with for this study dwell in a world of contested spaces—from the cramped interior city slums where they live to the open spaces onto which they emerge to praise and petition their god, Yahweh El Shaddai. Most residents of Bandong-Sinag live below the poverty level in tough conditions while struggling to retain their claim to the ground on which they have built their homes. And as part of the El Shaddai congregation, each week they occupy land that embodies the history of marginalization of their class—land their sacrifices helped create, land for which they must now pay rent.

Yet ironically it is in this PICC space where members seem to discover the power of their own critical mass and assert themselves, in some way, in a society where they are otherwise invisible. Furthermore it is here, not in a church, where they feel they directly encounter their god: a god that both transcends and directly confronts the harsh realities of their existence. Through their presence, El Shaddai members transform this land each week into a powerful site of mediation—in ways those who originally reclaimed this land from the sea never intended or even imagined.

In the next chapter I continue to explore issues of class and identity by examining how El Shaddai members, including many in Bandong-Sinag, interpret prosperity theology and the seed-faith principle. Their reflections express transformations in self-perception that help to explain why El Shaddai ideology resonates with so many members of this segment of Manila society.

5 | Stories of Transformation and Desire

El Shaddai's prosperity theology affirms the desire for upward mobility and emphasizes the personal elicitation of miracles through tithing and "positive confession." Simplistic interpretations of prosperity theology, however, fail to grasp the significance of class and class perceptions (both inside and outside the organization) for understanding El Shaddai identity and transformation. El Shaddai members are generally defined in terms of class in Manila—specifically as belonging to the *masa,* or masses, which in local contexts means the lower and lower-middle classes, that is, the working classes. Yet in El Shaddai circles, class as a concept of societal critique is avoided or even denied—even while members, as El Shaddai followers, construct themselves as subjects within a particular socioeconomic stratum. El Shaddai members in fact participate in a discourse that replaces, reencodes, and resists prevailing attitudes and perceptions of wealth and class, a discourse that becomes personally transformative. Some of these new attitudes are contested, both nationally and locally, within the broad cultural milieu.

Through prayer requests, testimonies, and the practice of seed faith, El Shaddai members express and bring about a more profound type of personal transformation than is normally attributed to them by outsiders. Although they are criticized for their focus on the individual's commonplace desire for health and economic security, this perception of El Shaddai goals is only partial, for it fails to perceive the significant changes that members have expressed to me. Understanding these personal changes paints a more complex picture of followers' motivation while bringing to light the consonances and dissonances in the public's perception of El Shaddai experience.

A CLOSER LOOK AT CLASS AND CRITIQUE

According to Ed Bautista of El Shaddai's Social Services, approximately 80 percent of El Shaddai members are below the national poverty line and 15 percent are what he called the "petty bourgeois."[1] My own nonrandom survey of 259 people at several El Shaddai rallies in 1996 (conducted with the cooperation of El Shaddai officials) supports Bautista's rough estimates. The vast majority we surveyed had blue-collar occupations; only a small percentage were white-collar workers. Common occupations for men were laborer, carpenter, and driver, while women listed occupations like dressmaker, vendor, and housewife. A lesser percentage operated small businesses, such as those who owned a taxi or jeepney. Although the survey did not ask about level of employment, some respondents volunteered that they were unemployed or underemployed—a factor affecting income level and hence poverty rates.[2]

Umbrellas Full of Blessings: The Outsider's View
Mike Velarde has been nicknamed by outsiders as, among other things, "The Prophet of Profit" *(Asiaweek)*, the "Tollmaster to Salvation" *(Manila Standard)*,[3] and "The Man Who Has More Than Enough," a play on his translation of "El Shaddai" as "The God Who Is More Than Enough" *(Philippine Daily Inquirer)*. Money is at the heart of most debates in the contemporary Philippines surrounding El Shaddai. Outsiders criticize Velarde for his handling of El Shaddai funds, for his personal wealth, and for his trafficking in a system where people seem to pay money for miracles from God, a system where the goals are often financial and material.

In Manila, El Shaddai is almost exclusively conceptualized in terms of class when spoken of by outsiders (nonmembers and nonparticipants). In the local press and Manila society, it is characterized as a movement of the *masa,* or common people—which includes the poor *(mga mahirap)* and what could roughly be called the lower-middle class or the blue-collar workers.[4] The tabloids, which generally pitch stories to the *"masa* market" in Tagalog or Taglish (as opposed to the major news journals, which are written in English),[5] are known to jump on any story that deals with El Shaddai. Since facile use of English generally signifies a higher social (and often economic) status, the fact that these stories are big sellers for the tabloids is evidence, according to El Shaddai's public relations man, Mel Robles, that El Shaddai draws from the *masa*. Manila's Catholic clergy also typically describe El Shaddai's constituency as "the lower classes" or "the poor" or *"mga mahirap"* in their hierarchies of charismatic and transparochial communities. Both the English and the Tagalog labels are used in Manila.

It is a common perception in Manila that Brother Mike takes advantage of the poor. He is seen as offering false hope to them while persuading them to donate their last pesos, promising miracles in return. Velarde's "net trust rating," according to the independent research group Pulse Asia, was −4 percent in the Philippines in 1999. For comparison, Velarde fared only slightly better than Imelda Marcos, who received a rating of −8 percent from the Filipino general public (Doronila 1999).[6]

Explanations for El Shaddai's persistent popularity are full of class overtones. Some say, for example, that people attend rallies because they are "free entertainment" or that followers are attracted to the free Catholic sacraments El Shaddai sometimes provides, such as mass weddings, in which there is no fee for the priest. Others say that it is a sort of emotional outlet—a catharsis for people burdened by heavy financial problems. Another common explanation is that desperate people are easily duped. Some add that because Mike Velarde preaches in Tagalog (indeed with a provincial accent—he is from Caramoran, Catanduanes), as opposed to English, and uses stories and simple teachings, he appeals to the poor and uneducated.

Many people cartoonize the El Shaddai follower as a person holding an umbrella turned upside-down, toward the sky, waiting to catch blessings from heaven. Indeed this picture is drawn from reality—at times, during mass rallies, Velarde asks those assembled to do just that. During one rally I attended, as the followers held up their inverted umbrellas in what they thought was just a symbolic gesture, blessings actually rained down on them in the form of official El Shaddai handkerchiefs (signed by Velarde) sprinkled over the crowd from helicopters, each handkerchief anchored with a miniature orange. The chaos this created transformed a meditative crowd into hordes of screaming revelers hungry for an official blessed handkerchief that might bring them miracles. This scene was, in typical fashion, caught on film and published in major Manila newspapers the next day.

One Catholic priest explained the group's popularity this way:

It is an answer to the poverty of the people. It's giving them hope. Let's put it this way. It gives them hope that they will better their lives. So it's raining and he tells them to close their umbrellas, and they close their umbrellas. Tell them to jump, they jump. Tell them to dance, they dance. You see? . . . Yes, they're very good speakers, very charismatic, very good leaders, they easily persuade simple people. . . . So that's why he gets . . . the ordinary crowds. He's giving them hope.[7]

Even the positive evaluations of the movement from outsiders see El Shaddai in terms of class or economic aspirations: El Shaddai, they say, gives poor people a positive attitude, something to hope for, and teaches them to save their money, not to gamble, and to be responsible.

Critiques from within the *masa* focus on the financial and material ethics of El Shaddai as well. Vic, thirty-three, who drives a tricycle (a motorcycle with a side-car used for short distance public transport), is a former El Shaddai member from the Bandong-Sinag area. He articulated a common reaction against El Shaddai:

The people are giving money in order to receive. More capital, more return. Velarde is motivating the people to give more. Does the Lord ask for payments? . . . And if the prayer request is granted, they give testimony (*patotoo*) and then make another prayer request, this time with more money, and it goes on and on. There is no more pure offering to the Lord. It's like the more you offer, the more you receive . . . . People should offer up to God what they have accomplished for the whole week. A real offering is service for the people.

Vic feels that El Shaddai followers' material aspirations and the seed-faith principle, motivated by the desire for returns, have polluted what he sees as an authentic relationship with God. A "pure offering," he says, is not a payment with an expected return; it is service to others.

People with Needs: The Insider's View

"The rich don't need El Shaddai. Why would they put up with rain, heat, and smelly outhouses?" This was the question posed by a follower at a weekly rally. Indeed, many followers I met, like this woman, observed that rallies are attended overwhelmingly by the poor. But they are not the "very poor" who, they say, cannot afford the expenses of going to the rally and giving offerings. These "very poor" may be those with no steady income whatsoever, the chronically homeless, or the beggars on the street. But even in the area in Bandong-Sinag where the residents were described as being worse off than those I worked with, there lived some El Shaddai members and an El Shaddai chapter coordinator and healer. It is hard to imagine living in conditions worse than this, though the economic status of the residents here is variable and fluid.

Although rallygoers generally describe themselves as "the poor" when forced to place themselves in socioeconomic categories, many are quick to point out there are those at the rallies who have "made it"—who now own cars or businesses or have gone abroad to work. Many point to the number of cars parked on the perimeter of the massive gatherings. One woman said that in earlier days there were not so many vehicles and this is proof that Brother Mike is right—that life is improving for those who are faithful and tithe. Some outsiders say these cars are an indication that El Shaddai draws from the middle classes as well. Many of these vehicles are taxis and jeepneys—the livelihood of their owners and drivers who attend the rallies. Even so, it is difficult to draw demographic conclusions from their presence. The ratio of cars to people seems very small and hence does not contradict earlier socioeconomic estimates that a proportion of El Shaddai's followers, probably between 5 and 20 percent, could be called middle class. Although most told me they were poor or *tao lang* (common people), some said they were middle class. I have no means of confirming a change in the group's socioeconomic composition over time, however.

When asked what type of people are attracted to El Shaddai, rallygoers often described the group in terms of desire: "the poor," they said, "because the poor have the most needs." Implicit in this statement is the idea that El Shaddai is an answer to the needs of the poor. If there are rich people at El Shaddai rallies, followers say, they are there only for the healing. Unlike the poor, they do not need El Shaddai for material aid. The rally, followers say, "is where the common people find solutions to problems." Such comments express a desire for economic security—a desire that then becomes part of El Shaddai identity and demographics. But both the rich and the poor sometimes give other reasons for going to rallies. Some say they see changes in their lives like physical healing and positive transformations in family relationships. Others say they go "because it's Catholic."

In their own hierarchies of religious groups, El Shaddai members often consider Protestants to be rich: one has to wear "nice" clothes, they say, to a Protestant service. Their perceptions of Catholics are more varied: some see Catholics as just ordinary people like themselves; others, thinking of prominent members of their parishes as quintessential Catholics, say that the rich are mostly Catholics. For many, a socioeconomic hierarchy exists among Catholic lay groups that can lead to competition within parishes. (Couples for Christ, for example, is one of the Catholic lay groups that many of my informants saw as being "for the rich.") Early after the San Marco El Shaddai chapter was formed, for example, its weekly *gawain* was held in the nearby Catholic church itself. Another (unnamed) Catholic lay group complained to the priest that the El Shaddai chapter was not only noisy but was idolizing the oil, the salt, and the handkerchiefs used for healing. El Shaddai members thought the complainers belonged to a certain prominent family. The coordinator of the El Shaddai chapter told me that both groups met together with the priest: "They did not listen to our side. They were well dressed, of course, while some of us were even wearing slippers." The priest then asked the El Shaddai group to hold its *gawain* outside the church compound, so they moved it to the *barangay* sports complex, an open court near the elementary school. They maintained their official relationship with the parish, however.

Despite this sort of socioeconomic mapping of religious groups, Velarde and his retinue emphasize the lack of social class distinctions in El Shaddai gatherings. Brother Mike often points out that at rallies "you can see an engineer standing next to a domestic worker" and says that one of El Shaddai's preachers was illiterate when he joined the group (but learned to read while training to become a preacher). Many El Shaddai followers express the belief that "we are all equal in the eyes of God." One woman at a rally, for example, when asked about the composition of the huge assembly, expressed this ideal ambivalently: "Here at the rally we are all from different walks of life. No one is rich or poor in the eyes of God. But I see mostly the poor ones here." A recently unemployed lower-middle-class woman, who travels up to nine hours from Baguio City to Manila for the rally every weekend, spoke of her first rally experience: "I felt something I can hardly express, the feeling I had. . . . Because I felt that I was one of those people—that I was already in the community. They don't mind who I am or what I am." While she may have been feeling an identification with her own kind, this feeling is most often expressed as being in an atmosphere where social and class distinctions disappear.

Thus while everyone seems to acknowledge that El Shaddai is particularly appealing to "the *masa*," insiders find it inevitable that the group attracts people "with more needs." Both El Shaddai members and Brother Mike downplay the group's demographics. As we shall see in the next section, they resist identifying with any specific class or any class-oriented ideology (such as Marxism or liberation theology).

Health, Wealth, and Struggle

"Why do these journalists keep focusing on money? This isn't about money, it's about renewal of the church!" We are in Mike Velarde's office. As he speaks, I quickly peek into the envelope he has just handed me. Inside I see cash, which later I count to be 10,000 Philippine pesos (about U.S. $400 at the time)—a gift from him, he says, in honor of his fifty-eighth birthday.[8] The other visitors who have been invited into his office for lunch—some, like me, impromptu—have presumably received the same, as there were no names on the envelopes. The small gathering in his office includes Mike Velarde and his wife, two priests (one Canadian and one American),[9] a Filipino "born-again Christian" TV personality, and a Philippine consul from a city in California.[10]

As we eat, Velarde continues. He rarely gives interviews, he tells us, because the journalists always want to talk about money. "Indeed, they should mix with the followers—the people—as Kate here does, if they want to know the real stories about how people have changed. It's not about money, it's about miracles in people's lives," he says. His speech flows smoothly into one of his favorite miracle stories of a woman who was stopped from committing suicide after hearing him address her—directly—through the TV. To demonstrate how outsiders misperceive his group, he jumps up to retrieve a letter from his desktop. Although the letter is from a prominent Filipino novelist and left-leaning intellectual, Brother Mike stumbles over the name as if unfamiliar with it. He says the letter has been on his desk for several days and he does not know how to respond to it. He reads the letter out loud to us.[11]

In it the writer says that he is the only one among his friends—the intellectual elite of the Philippines—who is not completely cynical about El Shaddai. Every Saturday, the writer says, he walks through the field where El Shaddai rallies are held and observes that most of the followers are poor people. The writer then goes on for two pages describing how Velarde could do something good for the poor since he can offer them what they really need: health and wealth. Velarde, he says, is the only one in the country who has enough economic power and influence to do this. In fact, he has a duty to do this for his loyal followers. He suggests a variety of socialized programs Velarde should start: hospitals and medical schools for the poor, their own banks and cooperative insurance programs, even their own political party, led by Velarde. He suggests it should be called something like "the People's Party," leaving out references to religion to avoid excluding the unconverted.

Brother Mike looks up from the letter, expecting us to share the same disbelief his own face reflects. With matching astonishment, the TV star, a longtime friend of Mike's in the charismatic movement, reacts first: "He's trying do it *his* way, not God's way!" In the ensuing flow of exclamations, they agree: "This is not who we are! We are here to do God's work! We are not here to accomplish our own goals. We respond to God's calling, not the calling of *men*." Returning to his original theme, Velarde points out that this letter is yet another illustration of the world deteriorating with the obsession for money. Later, in a personal interview with the letter's author, I discovered that he did not know that El Shaddai had recently initiated some of the social services described here. Eleven years into the movement, partly in response to criticisms that he was exploiting the poor, Velarde had created the Golden Rule Company.

While some of the Golden Rule Company's projects such as the cooperative store seem to express socialistic ideals, the El Shaddai foundation (Velarde, elders, etc.) rejects identification with the left and with leftist social, political, and economic ideals in the Philippines. Ed Bautista, a former communist insurgent and now head of social services in El Shaddai DWXI–PPFI, for example, stated that "the Lord will use El Shaddai to eliminate subversions." Bautista said he disagrees with forceful struggle but believes only in "wealth from heaven."[12] Mike Velarde has a similar message: "Let us not blame one another. Let us not blame the church or our government. Our country needs us—the people whose hearts and minds Christ Jesus has changed! . . . God . . . would like to perform a miracle for the Philippines. He would like to perform an economic miracle for all of us."[13]

Neferti Tadiar (1995) argues that the Catholic Church in the Philippines has taken over the symbolically significant geographical spaces of the 1986 People Power Revolution (also called the EDSA Revolution, named for EDSA, the street in Manila where thousands of people gathered in a protest that led to the toppling of President Ferdinand Marcos).[14] In the same way, El Shaddai commonly relabels "People Power" as "God's Power." The revolution in this context becomes a "miracle" rather than a triumph of the collective power of the masses or even a military coup. This conceptualization is not unique to El Shaddai; in fact it is a somewhat common revision of historical events in other religious groups in Manila. Mike Velarde, in the message he delivered to those gathered at a monument on EDSA commemorating the revolution on its sixth anniversary (many of whom were El Shaddai members), said: "And every 25th of February, the God's Power people, the children of El Shaddai, will gather in this place to thank and glorify Him for the miracle at EDSA . . . to proclaim to the ends of the earth that what happened in this place seven years ago was not the result of people's power, but of God's Power—the power of the Living God—Yahweh-El Shaddai." (Velarde [1993c]:16)

Unfortunately, tapes of Mike Velarde's preaching and radio programming during the revolution were not available in the El Shaddai Ministries office, although many from other years were. El Shaddai certainly existed at the time of the revolution, but Velarde's attitude about the political events of February 25, 1986, is as elusive as tapes of his preaching that week.[15] The letter just described, however, shows that El Shaddai speaks to similar needs addressed by various progressive organizations in the Philippines. One Catholic priest, making the same observation, complained about El Shaddai's prosperity theology, the communists, and liberation theology in the same breath:

> Mike Velarde is a very fine man . . . honest and sincere, but . . . he told me one time, "God is interested in prosperity, not in suffering, in death," and so forth. So that's why I could not believe in what he's saying because I don't think Christ came to bring us material prosperity. He came to set up the kingdom of God, not to give money to every person who gives 50 pesos so that it will come back as 500 pesos. So to me that's all hogwash, you see. And so these poor people . . . are expecting to get something in return. . . . It sounds more like the teachings of the communists, you see, like liberation theology,

that Jesus came to liberate us from poverty, from injustice. . . . Indirectly, yes, but not directly. He did not come to do that.[16]

El Shaddai's solution to poverty and suffering is oriented to the individual, whereas leftist solutions aim for social and structural transformation. Velarde and his preachers rarely, if ever, address social or economic injustice.[17] When Velarde talks about improving the nation (never the main focus of his preaching), it is in terms of individual, not collective, change: "Our country needs us—the people whose hearts and minds Christ Jesus has changed." Marxist-influenced theologies and ideologies —including the Catholic Church's own Basic Christian Communities–Community Organizing movement (BCC–CO) espousing a type of liberation theology—also emphasize that transformation begins with the individual.[18] Indeed, Bishop Julio Labayen, O.C.D., a major figure in the development of the Catholic "Church of the Poor" movement in the Philippines (of which BCC–CO is a part), inscribed his book (Labayen 1995) to me with these words: "The heart of the revolution is the revolution of the heart!"[19] Nonetheless, their ultimate goal is the transformation of society. The Catholic BCC–CO movement, according to Catherine Coumans, sees as its Christian duty "the transformation of social, economic, and political relationships and structures in the Philippines in favour of the country's poor majority by organizing and 'conscientizing' local communities so that these would be able to mobilize and take counter-hegemonic social action on their own behalf" (Coumans n.d. (a): 5). Kathleen Nadeau (2002:ix) writes:

> The BECs [basic ecclesial communities] are the context out of which emerged Liberation Theology, called *Theology of Struggle* in the Philippines. Also known as Basic Christian Communities, BECs are organized by nationalist intellectuals and Christian activists seeking to develop a post-capitalist society based on sustainable production modes and new social relationships. BECs . . . [have a] multilevel focus on issues of class, gender, culture, and ecology.[20]

El Shaddai, by contrast, takes a strong position against forceful struggle and "subversions." Typically Velarde aligns himself and his group with the state: authority is God-given, he says, and must be respected. A local Filipino BCC–CO document summarizes that movement's perspective in the phrase "Man's cause is God's cause."[21] El Shaddai's antithetical position is evident in Velarde and his companion's astonishment at the letter described earlier: "We are not here to accomplish our *own* goals. We respond to God's calling, not the calling of *men*." Yet Velarde and his group are criticized (or lauded) for focusing on people's material concerns, and Velarde would be the first to say that "God wants us to prosper." An article on El Shaddai in *Asiaweek* (September 20, 1996) reports that "Velarde is doing to Philippine Catholicism what [President] Ramos is attempting on a national scale: focusing energies on development and material well-being." What Roger Lancaster (1988:67) has written about the liberation theologists in Nicaragua—that they insist "the classical distinction between the spiritual and the material, the religious and the political, is contrary to authentic Christianity"—is true also of El Shaddai, except that Velarde, while aligning himself with the state, insists that his group is apolitical. And, as noted earlier, El Shaddai focuses on individual transformation while liberation theologists emphasize social transformation.

Although commonplace desires and the promise of miracles do attract many followers and inspire them to tithe, to reduce El Shaddai devotees to these desires is to paint an incomplete picture. Reports in Manila newspapers that depict El Shaddai members as "a mindless mass" deny them agency. Though Velarde's preaching is often seen merely as religious rhetoric that justifies material goals such as healing and good fortune, in fact the relationship between El Shaddai devotion and the occurrence of "miracles" often represents a profound self-transformation.[22] A transformed view of the self and one's life makes the occurrence of these miracles not only possible but inevitable. This change in self-perception also contests readings (from secular, liberation theologist, and mainstream church sources) of El Shaddai subjects as members of a specific class or oppressed group. Rejection of class identification, in fact, is central to the profound transformations in identity and desire that characterize El Shaddai conversion. This becomes apparent when, following Velarde's advice to the journalists, one stops focusing on money and instead listens to people's stories of transformation.

By focusing exclusively on money and class, outsiders fail to understand one of the key aspects of El Shaddai's appeal—that in accepting Velarde's prosperity theology, members alter their self-perceptions and redefine their class situation. These deliberate choices of identification not only resist but recast the very notions of poverty that outsiders use to characterize them.

STORIES OF TRANSFORMATION

"Let the weak say 'I am strong!'" At nearly every El Shaddai gathering I attended, those around me sang with enthusiasm these words from a popular Christian song.[23] Mike Velarde explains to a rally congregation the transformation these words express:

> Many are coming to me saying, "Brother Mike, for four years my husband and I lost our jobs, and until now we cannot find jobs." And I ask her, "How many are your children?" She says four. "What are they doing?" "They are studying." Then praise God and be thankful to God because for four years you had no job, and yet your children are able to go to school and until now you are still alive. [Applause.] Praise God! Alleluia, glory to God! These are the things we cannot see. We cannot see the goodness of the Lord to all of us because our mind and soul was blinded by the spirit of darkness so that we would not see the greatness and love of God for you and for me. Brothers and sisters, this is where new life begins, so that it will grow and be strong, so that the evil spirit will not defeat you anymore. . . . He can drive away the spirit of hunger, He can drive away the spirit that robs you of your work.[24]

Velarde is speaking here of transformation as a change in outlook—the way people view events in their life. The woman who is now jobless is told to re-view her life for the past four years and see blessings where before she saw hardship. "We cannot see the goodness of the Lord," he says, because we were "blinded by the spirit of darkness." "This," says Velarde, "is where new life begins."

In the same way that El Shaddai and other religious bodies have recreated political history by telling the story of the EDSA Revolution in the language of Christianity, El Shaddai members' stories of transformation involve the retelling or reevaluation of their life using the language of El Shaddai and prosperity. Their testimony, as is true of many Christian conversion narratives, is not solely or even primarily a story of something that occurred in the past. It is the creation of something new: the reinvention of one's past, present, and future (Stromberg 1993:3).[25] Religious discourses and narratives within them may constitute a reality that resonates with some aspect of one's present reality. Full engagement with El Shaddai's prosperity theology involves choosing an apolitical and ahistorical interpretation of inequality emphasizing personal action and faith over other ideologies—such as those emphasizing structural, social, or historical causes and solutions to problems of poverty and sickness (or, conversely, those that accept suffering as an aspect of spirituality). How do El Shaddai members try to fit their experience into the interpretive framework of prosperity theology? And when this framework fails to describe their lives, how do they negotiate these competing interpretations?

Terry Eagleton (1991:14–15) writes that although ideologies can "actively shape the wants and desires of those subjected to them," in order to be effective "they must also engage significantly with the wants and desires that people already have, catching up genuine hopes and needs. . . . [They] must be more than imposed illusions, and for all their inconsistencies must communicate to their subjects a version of social reality which is real and recognizable enough not to be simply rejected out of hand." Clearly Velarde has found a fit between his theology and many Filipinos' desires. His understanding of this link may be summed up in a statement he made while dining with a small group of friends after a rally one Saturday: "People are more receptive to God when they are weak." Velarde tells his followers that prosperity is God's plan; that faith and tithing will bring about miracles and prosperity; and that speaking and affirming certain ideas ("I am rich!") will make them true through the power of Yahweh El Shaddai. But people whose lives have not improved materially in any obvious way are still convinced of the transformative power of Velarde's teachings. For many it is because they now see blessings where before they saw suffering—the way they view their lives has changed. This change may also have positive effects in other areas of their lives, which can in turn confirm the validity of the transformation.

Vangie, an El Shaddai member from Sinag, compares El Shaddai to other religious groups she has attended—for example, the Bread of Life group. She tells me:

> Those in the other groups do not preach about prosperity, unlike Brother Mike. . . . But for me, I like that prosperity. At least I can see if I'm prospering, while instead they say, "I'm so poor." The Lord doesn't have children who are poor. You want to have it, but you just don't want to rise from poverty. The Lord has given you to rise, but you are the one who doesn't want to. You will not really prosper if you

will not work. But in prosperity, I know the Lord is giving prosperity to us. He did not create a person to become very poor.

Vangie has been with El Shaddai for six years and belongs to the core group of the San Marco chapter. Like many others, she believes one must work in order to be prosperous; in fact, Velarde preaches this. But to Vangie, prosperity is about more than work. After all, she says, "the Lord is giving prosperity to us." As one El Shaddai preacher said: "If we strive hard to earn money, we should acknowledge the one whom that money comes from because it all came from him. We should thank him." All financial success, even when it results from personal effort, comes from God. What Vangie describes here, however, is also a new self-image: "At least I can see if I'm prospering, while instead they say, 'I'm so poor.'" The others still speak of themselves as poor, but "the Lord doesn't have children who are poor." The problem lies in their outlook: "You just don't want to rise from poverty. . . . You are the one who doesn't want to."

Luz, an El Shaddai member and newspaper vendor in her early fifties from Sinag, has a chronically ill husband and has been homeless in the past. Responding to my question "What kind of people are drawn to El Shaddai?" she said: "The poor, because the poor don't know God. They think that because they are poor, they'll remain poor. But the Lord doesn't want you to always be poor. He also wants you to progress." Seeing oneself as poor signifies a state of distance from God—of being "blinded by the spirit of darkness," as Velarde puts it. A person who "wants to rise from poverty" is seen as being closer to God. When God blesses this person, as Velarde says, "good things are going to happen." Later Luz said that she tithes to the El Shaddai Foundation because "it is good to give to the poor." Although her neighbors would describe her as poor, she no longer thinks of herself that way. She has embraced a religious language that allows her to articulate her needs and desires while opening up space for an alternative identification. Luz' poverty now represents potential—a miracle or blessing waiting to happen. Thus her poverty becomes temporary and personal rather than determining. Here it becomes apparent that El Shaddai's prosperity theology shares much with liberation theology, development, and other discourses on "culture" in the Philippines that identify an infamous "culture of poverty"—an attitude of hopelessness and fatalism—which in their view prevents the poor from rising up, organizing, or striving for upward mobility.

Brother Eddie, the coordinator of the San Marco chapter, uses his story of transformation during his healing and counseling sessions, especially when preaching to non-El Shaddai members. During one such session I witnessed in Sinag, referring to himself by name, he explains the changes in his life to a nonmember with an eye infection he has been called upon to heal:

> When I had no money, we would quarrel. . . . I would wake up in the morning, "Lord give me this, Lord give me that." I would live always asking, and not knowing how to give. . . .
>
> Now I wholeheartedly give thanks to the Lord. A person can bear it even if he has no money in his wallet. As long as you know Jesus Christ, you are already happy. Brother Eddie doesn't need money now. That is true. Before, Brother Eddie kept working and working just to look for money. And he had not saved anything. Now Brother Eddie doesn't look for anything. Now Brother Eddie doesn't look for money; it is money that comes to Brother Eddie from the hands of Yahweh El Shaddai. Because someone will be used, and will give to you. As long as you know the Lord, the richness in heaven will be poured out to you.

Brother Eddie is articulating a transformation of desire or a change in the way he desires—from a state in which he "would live always asking" to a state in which he "doesn't look for anything" because it comes to him "from the hands of Yahweh El Shaddai." Thus his self-concept has changed, too, as desire is partly constituent of the self. This change resonates with one of Mike Velarde's accounts of his own personal transformation—one precipitated by the miraculous healing of his heart disease by an angel. In the *El Shaddai the Almighty God* newsletter he writes: "EL SHADDAI, the Almighty God, did perform a very special heart transplant in me! From that time on, my desires and ambitions changed. The Word of the Lord that He planted in my new heart bloomed. I was transformed overnight from a fisherman of dollars and pesos to a fisher of men for Jesus" (Velarde [1991?]:3).

Shirley, thirty-six, a married Bandong-Sinag woman with children, told me about a change in the way she approaches financial anxieties since joining El Shaddai:

KW: Does El Shaddai make women stronger in the family?
Shirley: Yes. Because first, from a financial viewpoint, there we are

weak. . . . But every day you hear from the Gospel that you have changed. Before, I'm always short on cash. Three days before pay-day, when I have only 200 pesos, I get mad. I would start talking nonsense and get mad. But now it's different. I always say "God will provide." That's because of faith and hope. Always be positive.

KW: So this is one way for women to be stronger?

Shirley: Yes, it's faith. Because if there is faith, you won't be afraid. Because the hindrance of people *(tao)* is being afraid. All those worries that you're afraid of and everything. Before, I'm always afraid of those things. But now I just say *"bahala na si Lord"* [It's up to the Lord]. Before, it's as if you are just alone. And before I was also afraid to die, but not anymore. Whatever his will, it will be done.

What she describes is primarily a change in outlook: she now approaches her difficulties with faith that God will provide. Shirley listens to El Shaddai radio constantly while at home. When she has problems with her mother-in-law, who lives in her house, and her sister-in-law, who lives next door, she raises the volume to drown out her bad feelings and reinforce her new outlook because "every day you hear from the gospel that you have changed."

Nina, fifty-eight, a devoted El Shaddai member from Sinag whose alcoholic husband is a chronically unemployed painter, documented her prayer requests on a list and checked off each one that was granted. She says: "You must keep a list of your blessings so that you can really see that your life is getting better." For El Shaddai members, documenting the positive events in their lives is part of the process of transformation they describe as characterizing their initial commitment to the group. This ongoing process includes writing prayer requests with faith, waiting for blessings and miracles, and then testifying about them to others. Since the Tagalog word *"nagpatotoo"* (to testify) comes from the root *"totoo"* (truth), a testimony "confirms" or "makes true." In many ways, testifying about blessings from Yahweh El Shaddai "makes true" the miracles and in fact the self-transformation. It transforms events into miracles and makes a testifying self a changed self, as the act of testifying is part of the transformative process. In this way discourses—and the narratives (or testimonies) within them—constitute reality. One's faith in Yahweh El Shaddai is then continuously reaffirmed by giving testimonies of further blessings either to other individuals or to a group at an El Shaddai *gawain*. "Testifying" has been common in Pentecostal groups and is central in contemporary charismatic religious practice worldwide; Roelofs 1994:220.) Many consider giving testimony to be a sign that a person is a full member of the El Shaddai group (a "true child of El Shaddai") insofar as it is not only an informal rite of passage but also evidence of one's faith in God. The fact that someone is "now testifying" is a sign that they have experienced some change in their lives due to their faith in Yahweh El Shaddai. And faith is central to one's new outlook—believing that "good things are going to happen" if you tithe with faith and request with faith.

Through written prayer requests, conversion, and miracle testimonies *(patotoo)*, El Shaddai members redefine their own suffering and, in doing so, are able to reinvent their own pasts and futures. Writing a prayer request, as we have seen, involves writing one's desires on a sheet of paper that is then submitted (along with an offering) and prayed over by El Shaddai ministers. In writing their prayer requests, members articulate and define their needs and, consequently, sometimes their suffering. When miracles or blessings occur, El Shaddai members may begin to see their life in terms of before and after meeting Yahweh El Shaddai—thus differentiating the past self from the present self. Sometimes this process of differentiation happens suddenly; sometimes it is realized gradually over time. (See also Stromberg 1993.)

Prayer requests and *patotoo*, together with the prosperity theology, have a transformative power that members tell me is absent from mainstream Catholic practice. (See also Chestnut 1997.) Furthermore, it is a particular ideology of transformation of the individual and not society. As a narrative of hope, prosperity theology can inspire or reinforce the desire for change and alter the way in which one desires. The prayer-request-plus-testimony process documents positive change, making it visible and spiritually significant, making miracle stories possible within the interpretive framework of prosperity theology. For the most fervent El Shaddai followers, almost any positive change is seen as a blessing from God or even a miracle.

Loretta, for example, testified that her son was cured of a rash one week after an herb doctor had put ointment on his legs. Since she had written prayer requests asking that her son be healed, she testified that Yahweh El Shaddai had answered her prayers and given her a miracle. As

Gerard Roelofs writes: "Charismatic Christians do not confine their religious activities to particular times and places. . . . They are continually
living in an 'expectant atmosphere' (Samarin 1972:54) that prepares
them for happenings to which they can attribute religious meaning"
(1994:220).

Successful prayer requests that become testimonies constitute a mode
of knowing personal history—a mode that recontextualizes suffering,
success, pain, illness, and ongoing events in life. These narratives are
constantly emergent as men and women learn to interpret and reinterpret life events in terms of the impact of the Holy Spirit, or Yahweh El
Shaddai, on their lives. Some of these stories grow larger than life when,
for example, they are told for mass audiences, reproduced through television and radio, or published in El Shaddai newsletters that are then
distributed to members all over the world.

Prayer requests and stories of miracles take on a recognizable narrative
form similar to those found in other charismatic Christian groups. The
model for El Shaddai testimonies is provided by Brother Mike's "life
story," which is well known to his followers. As it is told and retold, on the
radio, in magazines, at rallies and prayer meetings, it affirms or "makes
true" Brother Mike's vision of a God who keeps promises—and gives
financial rewards to the faithful and the generous. Velarde redeems himself
again and again through the retelling of these stories. As he says, he came
from a family of modest means and was, at various times in his life, rich,
then bankrupt, on the brink of death, a gambler, and a business swindler.
Wealth, health, and success came as rewards at various epiphanic
moments when he decided to give himself and his money over to God.
Because he has testified to these prior failings—because he admitted his
sins and accepted God—he is considered redeemed and forgiven. His current prosperity is a reward from God for his good deeds and generosity.
"If you follow the teachings of the Bible," he tells his followers, "you will
be rewarded as your servant leader, Mike Velarde, has been rewarded."

In some of his accounts, Velarde's turning point came in 1978; in others, it was 1986. In 1978, Velarde was in the Philippine Heart Center for
Asia when he was visited by an angel and, as mentioned, miraculously
cured of heart disease and "transformed overnight from a fisherman of
dollars and pesos to a fisher of men for Jesus." His most often told story,
however, is one in which he was bankrupt and 200 million pesos in debt
as a result of the financial crisis that hit the Philippines in the early

1980s.[26] Later, in 1986, Velarde committed 10 percent of his income to his new Christian radio station; by 1990, all his foreclosed properties had sold "miraculously" at sky-high prices, making him a millionaire.[27] El Shaddai "opened up His windows of opportunities for me," he says, as a result of God's grace and his own repentance and commitment to tithing (Velarde 1992a; 1992b; 1993a; 1993b). He supports his story with an Old Testament passage in which God tells the sons of Jacob that their nation will be cursed because they have robbed God of his tithes and offerings, but if they bring all tithes to the storehouse, blessings will be poured out upon them.

These real estate prices were likely affected by political events: the People Power Revolution; the end of the Marcos dictatorship in early 1986, and the subsequent hope, financial and otherwise, inspired by the turnover of power. But Velarde and his elders' own mode of knowing history—the history of El Shaddai, for example, and their own personal histories—is apolitical and makes virtually no reference to these political and economic contexts. These histories are built upon accounts of miracles and grace, which are related to one's personal commitment to God, often in the form of tithes. Subsequently this narrative form blocks any critical discussion of El Shaddai's institutional history from within the group. It is the stories of tithes, miracles, and grace that make the history. As Karla Poewe (1994:12) writes:

> Charismatic Christianity reverses emphases that we have taken for granted: the centrality of the rational, of calculated doing, of articulate verbal skills, of doctrine, and of things Western. It does not deny or reject these things. Rather it comes to *them* in unexpected ways. A charismatic Christian comes from the nonrational to the rational, from happening to doing, from experience to talk, from sign to metaphor, from spiritual gifts to utility, from receptiveness to action, from demonstration to theology.

In a similar way, Velarde's and El Shaddai adherents' modes of knowing personal and institutional histories—evident in their testimonies—privilege experience, demonstration, the nonrational, and the happening over rational, intentional, calculated, and opportunistic doing. Even while miracles and grace come at least partly as a result of intentional action such as tithing, prayer, and faith, these acts make one *receptive* to miracles as in the seed-faith principle: "Good things are going to *happen.*" Velarde and his spokespeople continuously shifted the focus of my questions about "decisions," "actions," or "plans" within the El Shaddai leadership structure to the grace, will, guidance, and inspiration of Yahweh El Shaddai. As they continually insist, none of this is ever planned. And although El Shaddai members seem to attempt to elicit miracles through seed-faith offerings, they stress, somewhat contradictorily, that one cannot give with the expectation of return.

Velarde's example—his personal testimony, which becomes a way of constituting and knowing historical truth—is mimicked by El Shaddai members. They accept, variously, the language and epistemology that make their own poverty and suffering redeemable—here and now—through faith and tithing. They also accept the story structure. I met Rodolfo and Loretta, a couple who had been with El Shaddai for three years, at a rally in Manila. When I asked Loretta about the relevance of choosing one religious group over another, she responded: "As long as you are blessed . . . as long as you are graced or prosperous in the religion of your choice, then that's all right."[28] Her answer reflects the notion that religion provides the context and language for realizing "prosperity." Rodolfo later described some of the changes he experienced after joining El Shaddai:

> *Rodolfo:* Before I would really be out of control. I would fight with my parents, never give in to them, understand them. Now, ever since I went there [gesturing toward the rally], when that happens to me, I know how to endure it, to control my temper, to deal with those around me. Of course, people would tease you, make fun of you [for being a member], that's just there. But if it was during my old life that they did that, I would not be able to give in to that, to let it go, because I would still be living in a world that is filled with the whole mind-set of being human—
> *Loretta:* —where you don't allow anyone to oppress you—
> *Rodolfo:* —yes, like that.

Rodolfo speaks of his old life in a world filled with a human mind-set. Now he no longer aggressively resists people who bother or "oppress" him. He has learned to control his feelings, to let it go and trust God. He and Loretta explain:

KW: What has El Shaddai given you that just being Catholic couldn't give you?

Loretta: Here with El Shaddai I really saw there was a feeling of cooperation. If your house burns down, for example, you have someone to turn to. Like us. We don't have our own house and lot. Brother Mike has offered a "Super Mura Lupa't Bahay" (Supercheap House and Lot). That's a big help to us. It's not—well, it's also our money. With the church, okay, you go to mass and that's it. You receive communion—that's it. But you're still the same. You are still poor.

Later she continues:

Loretta: You see, if you're only in church, when you're there, yes, you're all quiet and it seems like you're so blessed. But when you get out, in your house, that's where the problems are.

Rodolfo: It's still the same.

Loretta: It's still there. What the priest has said, you can't apply at home. But when you attend here, listen to it on the radio, at least you can believe or whatever you want.

Mainstream Catholicism, in their view, does not address the immediacies of poverty: "It seems like you're so blessed," but "it's still the same." In fact the mainstream church tries to correct El Shaddai's focus on financial blessings by emphasizing that suffering is an important part of spiritual life.[29] But after going to church, says Loretta, "you are still poor." They continue:

Loretta: . . . When we joined El Shaddai, we learned to stand on our own feet. We learned to save money, how to handle money, how to work on our own.

Rodolfo: . . . Even if your wage or salary is small, and you think you won't be able to set aside enough money for a house, if you do it with trust, confidence, and faith, you will be able to do it. You'll be able to live on your own.

Loretta: . . . You see, Rodolfo used to be a security guard, but he had a bigger wage then. Twelve hours at 4,000 every fifteen days. That was when he still wasn't with El Shaddai. But we couldn't save money then. Everything just sort of "went out." I didn't have a job then. But when we started to attend here, at El Shaddai, he only earned 2,000 every fifteen days but we were able to save money. We were able to put money in the bank. As for me, even if I'm just at home, I still earn a little money. . . . That's the big help El Shaddai has given us. Money for us used to mean nothing—as long as we could spend it. But now, even if we don't have money, it comes to us. That's the thing. . . . Now we understand why we should tithe, even if we're short on money. It's not like before we joined El Shaddai. We would be short on money and we would fight. . . . Now, even if we don't have money, we're okay. We're able to understand one another. Yes, we still have little arguments, but not like before.

El Shaddai may indeed teach people to be financially responsible, to open savings accounts, and the like. Yet unlike Rodolfo and Loretta, members seldom acknowledge learning how to save in their stories. When they describe a positive event—say, the family received some capital to start a business—the practical details of their windfall are often subsumed in their testimony of blessings and miracles from Yahweh El Shaddai, which came as a result of their faith and offerings. With Rodolfo and Loretta, these two interpretations—miracle from God versus learning how to save—periodically erupt, but the El Shaddai before-and-after story is primary. Later in the interview, for example, they say that everything they have, including their livelihood, comes from God alone. They also mention several instances of miraculous healing of their children that resulted from prayers and faith. At another point they say there is a relationship between giving tithes and being blessed. And Rodolfo, in the passage quoted earlier, says that faith is essential in saving money. Later in the interview, we asked Loretta and Rodolfo if they tithe regularly. They replied:

> *Loretta:* To be truthful, I'd like to be honest with you. [Pause.] We are sinning against the Lord. But deep inside, we are really sorry about it. We really have so many shortcomings. Brother Mike says that we're stealing from God. That's our biggest trial.
> *Rodolfo:* Yes. That's in the Bible—
> *Loretta:* —that we should really give. But it's just that we really lack money—

Rodolfo: —to tithe.

Loretta: But if you are really physically touched by Brother Mike, you'll really give tithes, because your conscience will really bother you.

What I find most interesting in this conversation is the contradictions in how they assess their financial situation. Although they consider themselves blessed, Rodolfo is now making half what he used to earn and they are so strapped they are unable to tithe. (Two thousand pesos every fifteen days puts them below the national poverty level. We do not know how much Loretta earns.) The circumstances surrounding this change— and the fact that Loretta now earns "a little money"—are never explained except to say that "now, even if we don't have money, it comes to us." Before, the money "just went out." They have reinterpreted their financial situation by marking a dramatic change before and after joining El Shaddai. And yet it is unclear whether they are actually doing better financially in the sense of making more money to live. Apparently they are not.

Rodolfo and Loretta have remade their own past and present through their story of transformation. Although they are now in a more difficult financial situation, they describe their current state as more prosperous and characterize their previous situation as a time of shortages and fighting. Telling this story in the language of El Shaddai also brings them into the El Shaddai community, which makes them feel supported. Even while acknowledging that they must work for this support, they now have confidence in their ability to make it on their own. Their newfound closeness to God comes to signify a release from suffering or misfortune—a state of hope that is constantly renegotiated with their (often contradictory) present reality. Their acceptance of prosperity theology may even effect changes in other areas of their lives such as family relationships and spending patterns.

THE GOD WHO IS MORE THAN ENOUGH

Outsiders tend to view El Shaddai's prosperity theology as a simple appeal to the material desires of a poor—a group with overwhelming social and economic needs who hold up their umbrellas to catch blessings from heaven. El Shaddai members, however, tell of internal transformations that complicate these simplistic interpretations. In writing their prayer requests, El Shaddai members define their own suffering and in doing so create the potential to transform the way they interpret events in their lives. Each time they write a prayer request and testify to its fulfillment, they are affirming a particular version of their present reality and transforming perceptions of themselves as members of a particular class, as one of "the poor" and oppressed. One is no longer a victim of alcoholism, for example, but a catalyst for change within the family. Their misfortunate is no longer simple suffering but meaningful—part of an intentional story. It is not the story of "spiritual poverty" or "carrying one's cross." Nor is it a story of struggle against the powers-that-be in society. It is a story of personal faith and transformation. In mainstream Catholic theology, suffering and poverty are part of God's plan. But this Catholic experience, in the view of many El Shaddai members, lacks the transformative power of El Shaddai.

El Shaddai reframes deterministic class-based cultural models implied in development, liberation theologist, leftist, and other progressive discourses in the Philippines. Even in the face of the group's demographics, with 80 percent below the poverty line, El Shaddai members resist class labels, choosing instead an alternative identification. Using Brother Mike's life story as a model, they emphasize individual faith and action while rejecting structural, societal, or historical understandings of inequality as well as those that accept suffering as an aspect of spirituality. For many followers, to see oneself as poor is to be blinded by the spirit of darkness whereas to see blessings is to see the truth—to trust in God and thus be closer to God.

One Catholic priest observed that Velarde is merely offering hope to his El Shaddai followers. But what critics view as an expensive placebo blinding followers to the actual causes and nature of their suffering is seen by insiders as a simple recognition of God's generosity and grace. For many of my informants, the changes they see in their lives since becoming "children of El Shaddai" are much more real than the results of the BCC–CO movement, which remains unpopular in the local parish church, and more real than the unmet expectations of the EDSA Revolution, which many feel did not significantly alter their living conditions. Placebo or grace, they feel that "something good is happening." Thus their umbrellas may go up empty, but they come back down full

of blessings. A change in self-perception, in desire, and in their understanding of God's intentions for them, affirmed with prayer requests,
tithes, and testimonies, makes these blessings real. Formerly emblems of
an oppressed class, their needs and hardships are now catalysts for blessings, points of contact with "the God who is more than enough."

FIGURE 1. *Praying at an El Shaddai rally. Photo by Ben Razon.*

FIGURE 2. *A woman wearing an El Shaddai handkerchief accepts Holy Communion from a Roman Catholic priest at an El Shaddai rally. Dozens of communion stations such as this are set up throughout the crowd. Photo by Ben Razon.*

FIGURE 3. *Brother Mike preaches on stage at the El Shaddai twelfth-anniversary celebration in August 1996. Photo by Ben Razon.*

FIGURE 4. *Writing a prayer request at an El Shaddai rally at the Philippine International Convention Center (PICC). Photo by Ben Razon.*

FIGURE 5. *An El Shaddai volunteer supplies envelopes and prayer request forms to members while guarding one of the many collection boxes on the afternoon before an evening rally. Photo by Ben Razon.*

FIGURE 6. *The El Shaddai faithful hold up eggs to be blessed by Brother Mike during a rally at the PICC grounds. The blessed eggs, eaten both raw and cooked, are believed to heal illnesses. Photo by Katharine L. Wiegele.*

FIGURE 7. *Vendors display handkerchiefs for sale the morning before a rally. The handkerchiefs show support for Brother Mike, who has just returned to Manila from California during the money scandals of 1996. Photo by Ben Razon.*

FIGURE 8. *The Film Center at PICC as seen from the El Shaddai grandstand area. Photo by Ben Razon.*

FIGURE 9. *Two children on an interior Bandong street. The wealth difference represented here is a familiar sight in the community. Photo by Ben Razon.*

FIGURE 10. *The basketball court is a center of activity and a meeting place for community members. Local El Shaddai prayer meetings are held here on Friday nights. A public address speaker can be seen upper right. Photo by Katharine L. Wiegele.*

FIGURE 11. *The* barangay *chapel in Bandong, freshly painted for the barrio fiesta. Photo by Ben Razon.*

FIGURE 12. *Doing laundry at a pump in front of a home in Bandong.*
Photo by Ben Razon.

FIGURE 13. *An* iskinita *(interior walkway) in Bandong-Sinag. A sewer drain runs alongside the walkway. Photo by Katharine L. Wiegele.*

FIGURE 14. *Following Brother Mike's instructions, El Shaddai national rally participants extend inverted umbrellas to the sky to catch "blessings from heaven." Photo by Ben Razon.*

FIGURE 15. *Brother Eddie blesses water during a counseling session in a second-floor Sinag home. Photo by Katharine L. Wiegele.*

6

Local Religious Life

Local El Shaddai practice differs in many ways from what is practiced and professed by Brother Mike, El Shaddai elders, and participants at the weekly mass rallies. Local expressions of El Shaddai are hugely variable—as variable as local Catholic religious practice—and are influenced by the socioeconomic nature of the community, the El Shaddai chapter's history, and the chapter's relationship with the local Catholic parish.[1]

THE MARKETPLACE OF HEALERS

Religious life in Bandong-Sinag is fiercely competitive due to the many brands of religion vying for converts in the area: both new and established religions (especially various Christian denominations and television-based groups), mainstream Catholicism, and practices and ideas brought by migrants from other areas of the Philippines and from Filipinos returning home from abroad. While the presence of many established denominations is felt in the community, the Catholic Church is the predominant religious institution. There is no singular cohesive belief system in Bandong-Sinag because of the complexity of this urban situation—both in terms of migration and in terms of competing ideologies from various organized religions that have been brought by deliberate evangelization or dispersed by local adherents themselves. El Shaddai ideology and practice exist within this complex and fluid web of beliefs, supernatural beings and forces, rituals, and religious authority. Although El Shaddai often presents itself in opposition to other religions, some people combine El Shaddai practices with other ones and consult El Shaddai healers along with other practitioners; yet others deal with El

Shaddai exclusively. Moreover, ambiguity regarding spiritual matters combined with the constantly shifting religious landscape makes El Shaddai experience quite different in this urban neighborhood compared to national contexts and creates an atmosphere where contestation comes to the foreground.

Everyday religious practice is often created within a public arena of competing religious discourses. Likewise, rituals and contexts of supernatural mediation in Bandong-Sinag become the arenas in which the fault lines in everyday life are debated. Richard Lieban, for example, noticed that accusations of sorcery in urban versus rural areas of Cebu, Philippines, reflected the different issues at stake in the two sites. In the rural areas, most sorcery cases involved disputes over landownership; in Cebu City, disputes focused overwhelmingly on courtship or marriage—specifically, problems of social control of sexual relations (Lieban 1967:127–132). In Bandong-Sinag, the fault lines are most often and not surprisingly related to general survival (poverty and illness), to gender roles and family relationships, and to ambition, upward mobility, and differences in wealth. As well, there are conflicts over spiritual matters such as the appropriate relationship to God (especially concerning reciprocity and exchange with God) and the discernment between good and evil spirits, religions, practices, and objects.

Incidents caused by *kulam* (witchcraft), possession (by both good and evil entities), mischievous *duwende* (invisible dwarfs), *asuwang* (vulture-like creatures that assume different forms and harass people at night), and the control of persons by the devil and various *kulto* (cults), among other things, are commonplace in Bandong-Sinag. How to classify and resolve such incidents and the everyday problems of existence is debated in Bandong-Sinag in conversations, ritual contexts, and situations of crisis. People search for rites, healers, and ritual specialists that can explain and rectify problems. Sometimes this search involves converting to a new religion or joining a group that offers a more comprehensive worldview addressing, in whatever way, the multitude of conflicting beliefs and practices—a group like El Shaddai. At other times the search involves combining elements from various sources. Even among people embracing the more comprehensive religious ideologies, there is great variation in doctrine and practices. Actions and stated beliefs may be based on guidance from religious authorities or on one's own experience. Among the spectrum of religious specialists who can help with physical and spiritual problems are *hilot, yakal, albularyo, mangkukulam, spiritista,* leaders of religious denominations, ritual specialists of various *kulto,* and El Shaddai healers.

The *hilot* is typically a midwife who also sets broken bones through massage. In this Bandong-Sinag community there is a *hilot,* a seventy-year-old woman called Ninay, who also cures people possessed by spirits, does massage for the lame, and heals cases of sickness caused by the invisible dwarfs known as *duwende* (also called *lamang lupa*). For this reason she is also called *manggagamot* (healer/doctor). Ninay is a devoted Catholic in that she goes to mass each week, gives donations to the Catholic Church, and recites the rosary nine times a week. She has donated candles and eggs to the local parish ever since Monsignor Tomas, the parish priest, helped the community deal with a land dispute. For healing she uses oil (blessed at least occasionally by Brother Mike via television), snakeskin soaked in oil, an egg-shaped stone (bought from a Muslim), a round flat piece of wood, and Catholic prayers. Occasionally she allows herself to be prayed over by El Shaddai healers for help in healing people. Ninay sees the El Shaddai healers as Roman Catholic.

Before healing she prays in front of the *rebolto* (statues of saints) in her house for help. She believes her healing power comes from God by means of the statues. The statues are also used at times in rituals. When a neighbor was possessed by a wicked spirit, for example, Ninay placed statues of Santo Niño (the child Jesus) at the front and back doors of the woman's house before using the oil, stone, wood, and prayers for healing. In her own house, Ninay has statues of Our Lady of Perpetual Help, "Lourdes," "Mama Mary," Sagrado de Corazon, and three Santo Niño statues. She bought the Mama Mary statue from a friend in order to help her with the expenses needed for a trip home to Leyte. The friend insisted the statue was good luck. Within days, Ninay won more than double the cost of the statue in *ending* (a gambling game). Giving food to the poor has also brought her good luck in the lottery—which helped her to build her house, she says. According to Ninay: "When you do something good for others, you will be blessed in return." She does not charge money for her services but occasionally accepts small gifts.

Albularyo are people who heal with herbs. There are several *albularyo* near Bandong-Sinag, but none in the neighborhood where I worked. They are known to use religious images such as *rebolto* and, like the *hilot,* they work alone. The *yakal* is similar but is not known for using herbs.

One informant described a *yakal* who transforms into "Immanuel Five"—the Santo Niño in five different forms, each representing the child at different ages. The *yakal* uses divination, too, and can exorcise evil spirits. Although there were no *yakal* in the immediate community, residents knew of one nearby whom they consulted on occasion. *Mangkukulam* are generally witches or sorcerers. Stories of witchcraft and witches in the community surface from time to time.

Spiritista are healers known to work in places that resemble community medical clinics. They wear white doctor's robes, have offices and receptionists, and charge patients a fee for doing what is often known as psychic surgery. Some *spiritista* reportedly have *rebolto* present during the healing. Although some residents consult with *spiritista,* many are suspicious of their claims, questioning both their effectiveness and their high fees. There are no *spiritista* in Bandong-Sinag, but residents have traveled to consult with them in other sections of Manila. Various other groups, such as the one known as Sacrifice Valley, draw followers from this community. Sacrifice Valley, which has a worship center in the mountains outside Manila, centers on a woman who claims to be a prophet, a healer, and a channeler for the Virgin Mary. The group advances an extremely conservative gender ideology: women are encouraged to serve and submit to men always; at the worship center, women must wear dresses or skirts and cover their face and hair with veils; men and women are separated for worship and other activities.

Finally, two El Shaddai healers associated with a local chapter are well known in the community for healing, exorcism, deculting, and counseling. Each of these healers goes on house calls together with a core group or "choir" of half a dozen or so El Shaddai members. Every Friday night, the El Shaddai chapter associated with San Marco parish holds *gawain* in the basketball court in the center of the community where healing, prayer, and worship take place.

LOCAL CHAPTERS

Nationwide, the local chapters of El Shaddai DWXI–PPFI used to exist both inside and outside parishes—that is, they were supported by the main El Shaddai office on Amorsolo Street whether or not they were affiliated with local Catholic parishes. In 1995, however, in an attempt perhaps by both El Shaddai DWXI–PPFI and the Catholic Church to gain more control over local chapters, Brother Mike announced that independent, non-church-affiliated chapters would no longer be formally recognized by El Shaddai Ministries. In theory this meant that Amorsolo's portion of a chapter's monetary collection could no longer be forwarded to the Amorsolo office unless the chapter was forwarding a portion to the parish as well. As a result, independent chapters either attached themselves to parishes, dissolved, merged into other chapters, or continued to exist without official support from Amorsolo. From the chapter's perspective, the crucial aspects of this support are monthly or weekly visiting preachers from the Amorsolo office for local prayer meetings and sometimes funds for a small office. Preachers are normally rotated from chapter to chapter—staying at one location for several weeks in provincial areas and rotating weekly in Manila locations.

Some El Shaddai chapters in the Philippines were in fact denied affiliation by the local diocese or archdiocese of the Catholic Church for various reasons—most notably the bishop's disapproval of the local chapter's sectarian tendencies or El Shaddai theology. In December 1996, five bishops had denied affiliation to El Shaddai groups within their diocese, all outside Manila. My research involved two of these five dioceses. In Baguio City, the local chapter had continued to function without support from El Shaddai headquarters by utilizing the talents of local volunteer preachers. The Roxas City chapter, however, continued to receive support in the form of visiting preachers and possibly funds from El Shaddai headquarters even though they were banned by the local bishop from meeting within any Catholic church. Members of the group met for weekly *gawain* elsewhere. Those I interviewed generally resented the ban but continued to attend Catholic mass on Sundays and said they prayed for the bishop's change of heart.

I observed El Shaddai religious practice for varying lengths of time in nine local chapters in all—four in provincial areas and five in Manila. My longer case studies involved two chapters in Manila: the chapter associated with the Holy Trinity parish church and the chapter associated with the San Marco parish church. (Both are fictional names.)

Holy Trinity and San Marco are the two parishes attended most often by my informants. Although Holy Trinity is closer to the section of the community I have focused on in this book and is more involved with the Catholic ritual elements of community life—barrio fiestas, novenas, and the like—the El Shaddai chapter associated with San Marco church is vastly more active and serves the group of people in my study. Most of my ethnographic data on local expressions of El Shaddai, therefore, comes from the San Marco chapter. Let us briefly diverge, however, with a look at the Holy Trinity chapter, which is in conflict with the local Catholic Church and whose future is uncertain. The San Marco El Shaddai chapter will be taken up extensively in Chapter 7.

CONFLICT WITH THE PARISH

The Holy Trinity church was my first introduction to Bandong-Sinag. According to a priest in a nearby parish, in Holy Trinity I would find a vibrant El Shaddai chapter and a religiously active community because, he said, "it is a poor parish." Moreover, he said, the young priest there, Monsignor Tomas, was trying to create Basic Ecclesial Communities (BECs) in his parish.[2]

Holy Trinity parish, according to Monsignor Tomas, serves a constituency of roughly 500,000 people in its surrounding *barangay* (one of which is Bandong)—a large number even for Manila. Most of the people active in this church, he said, come from the 85 percent of his constituency "below the poverty level." The parish itself is home to numerous lay groups called "cell groups," including five charismatic groups (El Shaddai, The Lord's Flock, God's Love, The Lord Is My Shepherd, and Pax Christi), fourteen Biblia cell groups, mandated Catholic organizations such as the Legion of Mary, Catholic Women's League, Mother Partner's Guild, Knights of Columbus, and other groups such as Eucharistic Ministers, Marriage Encounter, Cursillo, and Couples for Christ. As Monsignor Tomas pointed out, there are even subgroups within these groups. Recently, ten new special ministries were created within the parish—each consisting of people who organize responses to special needs (such as the "healing ministry") or other efforts within the parish (such as the "livelihood ministry"). The El Shaddai chapter in Holy Trinity had only been affiliated with the parish for a short time. Formerly an independent chapter, in 1995 it was required to affiliate and give a portion of its offerings to the parish. This meant that the parish priest might exert more influence over the group.

When I arrived at the Holy Trinity parish church in February 1996, I discovered that its El Shaddai chapter had been dissolved by Monsignor Tomas six months before. In fact, he had temporarily dissolved all cell groups in the parish. The focus of this decision, however, was the charismatic groups, of which El Shaddai was the largest. The priest felt that the charismatic cells were becoming too competitive and acting as "a breed of their own." To support his position, he showed me the "Acts and Degrees of the Second Plenary Council of the Philippines" published in 1992 by the Catholic Bishops Conference of the Philippines. Though the document states that parish priests should welcome the various "movements of renewal" (including the most prominent, the Catholic Charismatic Renewal, of which El Shaddai is a part), Monsignor Tomas directed my attention to the following paragraph:

> Members of such renewal groups should realize that the Spirit has raised them up to renew the local Church. Movements of renewal are not only for their members but for the whole Church. Movements of renewal with similar charisms should network for stronger impact locally, nationally and globally. However, when they develop loyalty to their leader or group loyalty stronger than their loyalty to the wider Church, they become sects. [Catholic Bishops Conference of the Philippines 1992:206]

During our conversation Monsignor Tomas said that the various renewal groups in Holy Trinity parish, including El Shaddai, were becoming sects and were too independent. (According to some El Shaddai members, however, it was the monsignor who was "cold" to them, not vice versa; they felt unaccepted.) To encourage the charismatic groups to network and to "work for the benefit of the entire community" (especially focusing on BECs), each group was dissolved and then regrouped six months later as one large, aggregated charismatic group. This group was then asked to meet weekly for prayer meetings led by Monsignor Tomas—a sort of substitute for the various prayer meetings and weekly *gawain* that had been discontinued as a result of the breakup of individual groups. The El Shaddai chapter was one of the charismatic groups that held regular weekly *gawain* prior to the dissolution.

The new combined charismatic *gawain* began with great anticipation, but gradually the meetings diminished until very few people were coming. The donations were diminishing, too. Part of the problem seemed to be that it was Monsignor Tomas himself who determined the format of the prayer meetings and led them. The charismatics complained that the preaching style and the meetings were boring—even though Monsignor Tomas tried to include typically charismatic elements such as joyous singing, pray-overs, and sharing (testifying and witnessing). "If the same person is always talking, it doesn't click anymore," said one who compared these *gawain* with the El Shaddai practice of rotating preachers from the main office each week. Moreover, Monsignor Tomas did not announce the Bible passages he was using. The charismatic congregation, used to specific biblical references (and echoing a popular Protestant critique of the sermons typically delivered in Catholic mass), complained they could not follow along in their own Bibles. Monsignor Tomas added a full Catholic mass to the *gawain,* as well, along with what the charismatics called "an old thing" (an old Catholic prayer), making the service too long. "With these long prayers, the people are too lazy to attend because it goes too late. Their husbands are scolding them," said one woman.

Informants, especially El Shaddai members, also mentioned the lack of familiar ritual and prosperity-focused elements such as the blessing and offering of prayer requests, the display and blessing of El Shaddai handkerchiefs, the El Shaddai theme song, and the emotional mood of the *gawain.* Comparing the atmosphere of the new Holy Trinity *gawain* with the El Shaddai prayer meetings at PICC, one woman said: "At PICC it's like a reunion, it's a family appointment. They see each other, brothers and sisters. . . . They feel closer there." Moreover, the priest did not have "healing power"—the ability to heal and to cast out evil spirits. Ultimately the heavy-handed design of Monsignor Tomas failed to inspire them. Not surprisingly, most El Shaddai members gave up and attended the PICC mass rallies instead. Monsignor Tomas' audience dwindled.

Many El Shaddai outsiders thought there was some truth to the priest's complaint that the El Shaddai group functioned "for themselves." Although El Shaddai (especially the San Marco chapter) has healing and counseling "outreaches" in which they go on house calls, they do not do any community organizing. Residents can call on El Shaddai healers, who then call on the Holy Spirit for healing or exorcism, but the residents themselves are not organized for community or church service. With El Shaddai, people become empowered only insofar as they connect with the Holy Spirit through the healers (or through faith and positive confession). In the Holy Trinity church, which seems almost secular in comparison, people are encouraged to organize for the benefit of the community—due in large measure to Monsignor Tomas' efforts to establish BECs. Direct mediation with the Holy Spirit is not required in order to effect positive change, and the priest works in the community in contexts beyond the spiritual. Monsignor Tomas' concern for social justice is absent in local El Shaddai work.

As mentioned, the most active El Shaddai chapter in this community (the one affiliated with San Marco parish) will be the focus of Chapter 7. For now, let us return to our discussion of religious life in general in Bandong-Sinag.

OTHER CATHOLIC ACTIVITIES

Despite its rocky relationship with the charismatics, the Holy Trinity parish church is still strong, vibrant, and involved in community life. Monsignor Tomas helped Bandong residents, for example, in a long legal battle to defend their right to buy their own land when the *barangay* captain tried to negotiate an illegal sale outside the community, and for this he has won much respect. Other locals have organized community projects through the church—such as an ongoing effort by Vic, a tricycle driver, to provide free transportation at night for sick people and Nellie's program that organizes *hilot* services (midwifery, bone setting, first aid) for people who need them.

Outside the parish's cell groups, there are numerous Catholic organizations in the Bandong-Sinag community whose connections to the parish are varied and at times less official. Prominent among these groups are those associated with the Virgin Mary, popularly referred to as Mama Mary. Most of these groups aim to promote devotion to the rosary and Mama Mary or to encourage community members to participate in Catholic sacraments. One such group is Kahit Bata May Nagagawa (Even Children Can Accomplish), composed of children who take an image of Mama

Mary from house to house and say the rosary. Several groups (including the Legion of Mary) encourage unmarried couples ("live-ins") to have the sacrament of marriage in the Catholic Church. These efforts often result in "mass weddings," often with outside sponsors (such as campaigning politicians from the area) who donate expenses for ritual items such as the marriage rope and candles.[3] El Shaddai groups have made similar efforts—bringing couples instead to be joined in mass weddings officiated by Catholic priests at national El Shaddai rallies.

Another Mama Mary group is called the Block Rosary. According to residents, local members of Sacrifice Valley (also known as Apo) started the group, but it has been taken up by non-Apo members. All year long a statue of the Virgin Mary circulates from house to house. When the statue arrives at a house (brought in a small procession), the residents involved say the rosary. Stories of miracles are associated with the statue that is now circulating in Bandong. Miraculous healing and financial blessings—such as new jobs and winning lottery tickets—are said to have been experienced by people during the statue's visit. *Malas* or bad luck is said to be experienced by those who refuse to have the statue in their house. Once a well-meaning family decided to replace the statue with a new one. They buried the old statue, which had become chipped, broken, and worn, in their yard and began circulating the new image of Mama Mary. Shortly thereafter, according to my informants, the family had a string of bad luck including several deaths. When someone advised them to dig up the statue and continue circulating it, they did so and their bad luck ceased.

Other church-related practices and rituals are numerous: fiestas celebrating each barrio's patron saint, the birthday celebration of Mama Mary (which involves a parade and the release of a rosary constructed entirely of balloons), the celebration of the Immaculate Conception, the long celebrations in May and October in honor of Mama Mary, and the major Christian holidays (Christmas, Easter, and the like). Most residents have statues of saints in their homes that are used in various rituals and celebrations, including processions, healing, and prayer. Although not all residents participate in church events or even attend mass, those active in the parish church have calendars full of church activities aside from mass on Sunday. To completely separate Catholic activities from other traditions would be misleading, however, as Catholicism is woven into both the religious and secular lives of all community members.

MAMA MARY AND IDEOLOGIES OF GENDER

As can be seen by the many Catholic and lay organizations in Bandong-Sinag dedicated to her, Mama Mary is a popular figure of devotion and intercession not only in the community but throughout the Philippines. She is a controversial figure, as well, and even a site of struggle over gender relations and roles. I was told, for example, that Rosita, a Bandong resident, had once been possessed by Mama Mary, causing her to scold and shout at her father. As the story was retold to me by her husband, he expressed doubts that it was really the Virgin Mary. "Would Mama Mary scold her father?" he asked.

While for many Mary is a symbol of obedience, suffering, and passivity, there is also much support for the idea that Mary is actually a symbol of strength, justice, and resistance to oppression. Mary's position is debated in Bandong-Sinag as well as in national contexts. The following story represents a larger, more complex discourse on the position of Mary in the Catholic Church in the Philippines and on gender roles in Philippine society.

* * *

Nellie lives with her friend Dulce and Dulce's father in Bandong, just one house down from the chapel of San Roque, the miniature *barangay* chapel next to the basketball court. Dulce's father is now an old man. When he retired years ago, he won an award from the U.S. embassy club known as Seafront (a recreation club for U.S. diplomats and other officials) for his faithful service to the Americans and for not missing one day of work in his forty-some years on the job as a security guard. Every day he had made the hot, dirty bicycle journey of several miles on city streets from the barrio to the American club.

Dulce's father is one of the few in Bandong who owns his house fully—a rickety three-room wood and bamboo hut on stilts. The outhouse is several steps from the door, as is the water pump. The small space in between is decorated with plants potted in coffee cans and stepping stones made of concrete chunks placed in the often muddy path. Underneath the length of the house, a heap of garbage 3-feet deep has accumulated. The cats stay in the house and on the wooden ladder leading to the door, seldom venturing beyond for fear of oversized rodents, according to Nellie.

Nellie moved here from her mother's concrete house down the street to help Dulce with her aging father. Nellie and Dulce are close friends. Both women are unmarried, energetic in their mid-forties, and dedicated to service in the Holy Trinity parish. Currently they run a small business together making hamburger patties and delivering them to an elementary school across the city each morning. Both are active in the Legion of Mary, an old Catholic Church organization. To be a devotee of Mama Mary is to be a feminist, says Nellie. The night before the People Power Revolution in 1986, she had a dream that Mama Mary was running toward EDSA Highway carrying bullets and guns.

Nellie is the kind of person whose life seems to be a constant unfolding of dramatic stories—a woman whose wit, defiance, and intelligence turn tragedies into triumphs of character. As a child in Leyte, for example, Nellie was "loaned" by her mother to her aunt and uncle. There she spent her childhood as a virtual slave to a family that abused her and denied her kinship to them. As an overaged high school student, she organized her classmates in protest against mandatory labor at school. Among many other jobs, she has worked as a cook in a brothel, sold encyclopedias, mixed ice cream for vendors, and attended nursing school for a time. She has been courted by a doctor, a first cousin, numerous seminarians, and even an Aglipayan priest who was also believed to be an *asuwang* (a notorious Filipino mythical creature).[4] Nellie is known, as well, for her occasional psychic and spiritual powers, including her ability to prophesy through dreams and exorcise evil spirits. Although neither Nellie nor Dulce are El Shaddai members or charismatic Christians, Nellie also has the ability to perform "slaying in the spirit."[5] Occasionally she reprimands and advises priests on spiritual, theological, and administrative matters.

One day Nellie told me with great animation that Dulce had become an official "catechist"—meaning that she would be responsible for teaching catechism to children at the Holy Trinity parish church, a position that paid a small stipend. There was some competition among community members, mostly women, for these positions. Dulce had wanted to do this ever since she had been a schoolteacher in her twenties in the province—ever since she had fought a long battle with regional authorities to allow her to teach prayer in school. (She had won this battle but was so upset that she never taught again.) After failing several times, she had recently passed the written exam, successfully delivered her "sample teaching," and been appointed a catechist. "This is a dream come true for her," said Nellie.

The sample teaching had not been easy, however. Struggling to prepare for it, Dulce had been waking up early for a week. The night before the exam, she still worried about teaching the sample lesson. It was supposed to be about Mama Mary and how she is a classic example of obedience. In making the lesson relevant to the children's lives they were also given a "human situation" to use about kids obeying their parents. At 3:00 A.M. on the morning of the sample teaching, Dulce woke Nellie complaining: "I don't know how to teach this lesson!" So Nellie helped her with the "human situation." She told Dulce: "It's good for kids to be obedient, especially in those wealthy families in nice neighborhoods where they don't have serious problems at home. But here in the squatter area, being obedient may not always be the best thing." Nellie suggested that Dulce should change the "human situation." Instead she should talk about how the kids need inner strength to face their problems, knowing that Mama Mary is always strong and steadfast and will always be there for them, even if a time comes when they cannot trust their parents anymore. Dulce agreed and gave a sample lesson based on this alternative view of Mary. Although the other candidates were upset because Dulce had diverged from the lesson plan, she was accepted as a catechist and began training. When cross pendants were given to the new catechists during mass, Dulce was the only one crying. Afterward, walking home, Dulce instinctively wore her cross inside her shirt, as she always did, rather than outside. But Nellie said: "No, Dulce. You are a catechist. You can wear it on the outside now."

* * *

Dulce had committed to a locally relevant meaning of Mama Mary—a meaning that provided a more empowering stance for herself and her young Catholic students. The church institution, represented by the parish priest, had accepted the modified "lesson." Catholic religious practice in local settings supports a variety of interpretations of the figure of Mary, which are also represented in theological discourses in the Philippines. Certainly the Virgin Mary has been the subject of much scholarly religious writing. Sister Hilda Buhay, O.S.B., for example, in her article "Who Is Mary?" echoes a common trend in Mariology when she challenges her readers: "Can we situate the Christian Filipino's image of Mary in the urgent task of liberating women from male domination as well as being in solidarity with the Filipino people's struggle for national sovereignty?" (Buhay 1992:55). Sister Hilda represents Mary as a person of "commitment to the social destiny of her people" who had "solidarity in struggle with the poor and the oppressed" (pp. 58–59).

Brother Mike and El Shaddai devotees, by contrast, like many Protestant groups in the Philippines, criticize what they see as an overemphasis on the Virgin Mary in the mainstream Catholic Church, and excessive popular devotion to her image. Rather than mobilizing Mary's image for social causes, they choose to focus on God alone—deemphasizing both Mary and the saints as images of devotion, admiration, and intercession. Preaching at a combined Mother's Day El Shaddai national *gawain* and the Catholic Church's celebration for Our Lady of Fatima in Manila, Velarde outlined his position on the proper treatment of Mama Mary. While in line theologically with the church's official position on Mary (she is "highly favored by God," like the saints she prays for people in heaven, but she is not God), his views challenge popular Filipino sentiments and practices that have been encouraged or at least accepted by clergy and Catholics alike in the Philippines. Catholics should not pray to Mary or the saints, said Velarde, but directly to God. He downplayed the rosary: "Praying the rosary will not save you, but only the words of God can save you."[6] Outlining the traits of Mary that made her "highly favored by God," Velarde portrayed Mary's character as humble, docile, submissive, and obedient—submissive and obedient to authority, to the word of God, to her husband, and "to everything her husband desired." Velarde used this moment as an opportunity to reiterate his views on gender roles in the family:

> All government on earth is according to the will of God. . . . Men as husbands are like the government inside the home, amen? The authority in the family in the household is in the man. That's why if in a home it is the other way around that happens, and it is the woman who dominates the family and not the man, that family is going to have problems. Because that is not according to the will of God. If in a home it is the woman who works for a living and the husband does laundry, that household has a lot of problems. The Lord will not bless that home because it is against the will of Yahweh El Shaddai. Glory

be to God, glory be to Christ Jesus. So that is where we see that Mary has a special trait which made her highly favored by God.[7]

Although he is careful not to contradict official Catholic Church theology, Velarde is perceived by detractors and followers alike as being to a greater or lesser degree "anti-Mary"—or, more accurately, anti-Mariolatry. And, as we have just seen, he and El Shaddai Ministries have been explicitly conservative on questions of gender. Not only does he follow the church on issues of abortion and ordination of female priests (and El Shaddai preachers), but he teaches that women should submit to men and wives to husbands. This teaching is so clear that nearly all of the hundreds of El Shaddai members I spoke to, when asked directly whether women should submit to men, answered yes without hesitation—and many pointed out they had learned this from Brother Mike. Nonmembers, by contrast, especially women, were much more likely to express ideals of equality and women's strength of character.

Members saw Brother Mike's notion of gender roles as beneficial to their relationship with spouses. Women in El Shaddai often described their relations as more peaceful because they had learned to stop "nagging" and talking back to their husbands during arguments.[8] In cases where the husband joined El Shaddai along with the wife, many couples described improvements in the husband's behavior—stronger dedication to marital fidelity, for example, and renunciation of alcohol, cigarettes, and gambling. (It was not clear whether El Shaddai membership had any effect on the level or consistency of employment.) Such behavior is encouraged by Brother Mike and by peers within the El Shaddai group; it may also improve household finances, as many reported, because less money is spent on these vices. El Shaddai members felt that mainstream Catholicism provided no such explicit directives on gender roles or even offered guidance on common problems such as alcohol use, cigarette smoking, or gambling.

Although a wife has less authority within the family according to this ideology (for example, an ideal wife should forgive her husband for such misdeeds without scolding him), men who join El Shaddai are expected to take a more responsible approach to their role as head of the family. Thus there may be some truth to Elizabeth Brusco's argument that the conservative gender ideologies of evangelicals in Colombia may on one

level lower women's status but on an everyday level may actually benefit women and families if the husband joins the group (Brusco 1986;
1993). Conversely, women who take the lead in family breadwinning
may be made to feel guilty—and this, for obvious reasons, has incurred
disapproval from feminists in the Philippines.

RELIGIOUS COMPETITION AND
SHIFTING AFFILIATIONS

It is not uncommon for Bandong-Sinag residents to have gone through
several changes in religious affiliation or to attend more than one religious (usually Christian) group simultaneously for short periods—what
we might call group-hopping. Some employers suggest or even require
that their employees join a particular religious group (with unstated but
understood rewards of promotion and privilege). Manila and Bandong-
Sinag offer a diverse marketplace of religious options. Perla, a Catholic
woman in Bandong, thinks the sheer number of religious options in
Bandong-Sinag is confusing:

> Now my sister is here. Sometimes they're joining El Shaddai, then the
> "born again." She will go wherever she is invited. That's why the
> daughter is telling her she has no backbone, she has no conviction.
> She'll get confused and crazy going all around. She should go where
> she is happy, where she believes. I myself am not an El Shaddai mem-
> ber. I have no time, though I entertain them too when they come to
> the house. I think it is a matter of belief and how you accept their
> explanation. There are those whose explanations are against my belief
> —and I'll tell them if their approach makes me mad. Once there was
> a *Sapatista* healer who told me to look after my death. I told him: "I
> will not look after my death, I will look after my life, how to uplift
> it! Everybody dies, so why should I look after my death?" So I told
> him to get out and don't explain to me anymore. And then there are
> Mormons who go house to house. And people are getting confused
> with so many religions! Anyway, it is said in the Bible that there will
> come a time when there will be a lot of people who are sweet-talkers.

Perla—more hostile than most to religious solicitors—reflected that dis-
unity over spiritual matters causes family strife. She told me of a relative

whose husband had become "born again" while working in Saudi Arabia, most likely through a Filipino overseas group. When he returned home to Bandong-Sinag, his wife, a devoted Catholic, had a statue of the Virgin Mary in the house as part of a neighborhood rotation. Because of his new religious convictions ("born-again" groups in the Philippines are notoriously opposed to the use of these religious images), he wanted to break the statue into pieces, but his wife stopped him and they quarreled. Since then, according to my informant, he has been proselytizing in the neighborhood—"carrying the Bible, disturbing our activities," she said. "But you see what happened to his family? They are a broken family. One of his sons is in a rehabilitation center. It is difficult if the family cannot understand each other." Perla was not the first in Sinag to warn me about the dangers of a family without religious unity.

Many Filipinos returning from work or extended stays abroad (*balikbayan*) come home with new religious affiliations. Some of these *balikbayan* become aggressive evangelizers upon returning. The Baguio City chapter of El Shaddai was established in this way when a woman returned from Hong Kong having "met" El Shaddai there. She then founded the Baguio City chapter. Marlene, an active member of the San Marco chapter who worked in Hong Kong as a domestic worker on and off for several years, also "met" El Shaddai while abroad. She related a portion of her religious history to us in the following manner. The JIL (Jesus Is Lord) and INC (Iglesia ni Cristo) churches she mentions are both Filipino-originated Protestant churches. Eddie Villanueva heads JIL, much in the same way El Shaddai is headed by Mike Velarde.

Researcher: How long have you been in El Shaddai?

Marlene: Since I was in Hong Kong. It was there I learned about El Shaddai. When I was still here in the Philippines, I joined first the charismatics in our place in the province. When I applied in Hong Kong, the first *gawain* I attended was—of course there are a lot of *gawain* that encouraged me, there's the JIL, INC, and the Mormons. I stayed a long time in the JIL, almost two years, but I wasn't baptized. They always encouraged me to be baptized. I was happy, but I didn't like it totally because the born-again is different. When you're baptized you are no longer a Catholic.

Researcher: So you're a Catholic?

Marlene: Yes.

Researcher: And born-again is not Catholic?

Marlene: No, because there are two kinds—Pentecost, and I think Oneness as they call it. Oneness, they only worship Jesus Christ. But the born-again I attended there is—the Holy Spirit is included and God the Father. That's Catholic, like charismatics. So I attended the JIL by Villanueva—no rosary, no images of saints. They were having me throw away the images. So I said I didn't want to throw them away or my rosary.

Researcher: Which group did you attend first?

Marlene: JIL. But I didn't attend Jehovah. They were visiting me before. But because I wanted to know the differences, I entertained people who would come and I joined their *gawain.* I attend the INC because my companion before was INC. Every time there were Bible expositions, she would bring me along. But I stayed a long time with the JIL until, maybe because I'm a Catholic, I admitted to the Lord that though I graduated from a Catholic school, I don't know about the rosary, praying, like that. When I joined the JIL I felt happy because there is testimony, sharing. When you have problems, there is someone who listens to you. So I was with the JIL for almost two years until my contract in Hong Kong was about to be finished.

Although Marlene attended JIL as a member for two years, she never converted officially. At times she would attend both Catholic mass and the JIL *gawain* on the same day, and eventually she had conflicts over the images and rosary. She joined El Shaddai after a healing incident in Hong Kong. In the park where Filipino domestic workers gather on their day off, her cousin's friend, an El Shaddai member, healed her of a uterine cyst that day by praying over her. Later, when she returned to the Philippines, she discovered that her boyfriend had already joined El Shaddai. He encouraged her to attend regularly and apply for an El Shaddai identification card. After another trip to Hong Kong, she returned home again and they were married in an El Shaddai mass wedding. Marlene also had an offer from another Catholic group at the time: Couples for Christ. "They were encouraging us to marry there, but I didn't agree. Even my family, they were encouraging them, but they are all joining the charismatic. But that is Catholic too."

Marlene's story is not entirely unusual, even for people who have not worked abroad. Switching affiliations does not necessarily mean official conversion. I met a young woman at a San Marco *gawain* who had recently migrated to Manila from Mindanao (the southernmost major island of the Philippines) and was staying with relatives in Sinag. She had been a member of a Protestant born-again church in Mindanao. While walking down the street in Sinag one evening, she heard the El Shaddai *gawain* from a distance and, recognizing the song they were singing, joined the prayer meeting. She then began attending regularly. She said: "Anyway, it's just the same as the born-again. The songs are mostly the same, and I like the *gawain*."

Religious life in Bandong-Sinag can be dramatic. With each shift of affiliation, one has to become familiar with the new group's position on religious matters. People would change their beliefs or learn new ones even before my eyes. Luz, another Bandong resident, attended several groups before joining El Shaddai. In the middle of an explication to me about *duwende*—small invisible dwarfs thought to cause illness in humans if their homes are disturbed or they become jealous—she was corrected by Marlene:

Luz: There are good *duwende* and bad *duwende*.
Marlene: No, that's not it. Because they are all bad. Brother Eddie
   [the local El Shaddai healer] says they are all evil.
Luz: Really? Oh, I didn't know that.

The following week, Luz told me in an interview: "I thought there were good and bad *duwende*, but Brother Eddie says they're all bad. Now I see it that way, too, because my family gets sick." Luz had altered her belief based on what Brother Eddie had said. Note that Brother Eddie did not deny the existence of *duwende*; rather, he defined all *duwende* as evil. Danilo, who worked as a carpenter in Saudi Arabia for a few years, is a local El Shaddai member living just two blocks from Marlene. About *duwende*, Danilo had this to say:

Danilo: Before, I did not believe in *duwende*. But it's like I believe now.
Fely (research assistant): Why?
Danilo: Because in El Shaddai, Sister Marina is taking care of *duwende*
   and she gave a testimony. . . . I only heard it on DWXI. I don't
   know the real story but she is really taking care of *duwende*.
KW: Are there good and bad *duwende?*

Danilo: There are. Because for Sister Marina, it's the white one she takes care of. The black ones are the bad ones.

Danilo's belief in *duwende* had been altered by what he heard on DWXI, El Shaddai's radio station. Sister Marina may have been an employee of El Shaddai Ministries (not a preacher, since only men may be preachers), or perhaps she was just a caller to the station. But her appearance on DWXI carried enough authority to make Danilo reconsider his notion of *duwende*. Thus religious beliefs and practices, like religious affiliations, can shift rapidly and often. The next section explores the religious atmosphere by looking at the ambiguity pervading spiritual matters—often regardless of religious affiliation and despite strong religious convictions.

SPIRITUAL AMBIGUITY

"Just as you can't tell the difference between an evil spirit and a good spirit, you can't tell the difference between the true religions and the false ones," observed a Bandong resident. In Bandong-Sinag, objects, images, rituals, words, and people are not usually inherently good or evil; rather, they can be used by either good or evil forces. Holy images—statues of saints or the Virgin Mary, for instance—are sometimes suspected of being possessed by evil spirits and bringing misfortune to their owners. Rosaries and *anting-anting* (good luck charms), usually associated with prayer and good fortune, can be possessed by evil spirits. So, too, can other personal items such as jewelry. In the same way, water and food are known to be not only instruments of divine healing and protection but also dangerous conduits of evil spirits.

Religious events can be ambiguous as well. Just talking of spiritual matters can attract evil spirits. One woman, for example, remarked that our conversation about religion and the Holy Spirit had attracted evil spirits into the house, causing her children to cry. During an El Shaddai healing session in a house, a butterfly circled the healing subject while she was being prayed over. The butterfly was the devil, some said, attracted when the Holy Spirit had been called. Once people are born again or "slayed," they are thought to be followed even more aggressively by harmful spirits wishing to derail them—to make them "backslide" in their new faith. Thus converting or being born again not only protects the adherent from harmful evil forces but may also attract evil entities.

Supernatural beings like *asuwang* and *duwende* can be ambiguous as well. One of my informants, a Catholic woman in her early forties, thought the Virgin Mary had visited her in a dream and healed her chronic stomach pain. The Virgin, however, had come in the form of an *asuwang*—an evil creature that flies at night and is thought to eat babies. The *asuwang* extended its characteristically long fingers to the woman's stomach and healed her. *Asuwang* are usually invisible but can assume different forms, both animal and human, to fool people. This woman's understanding of the changeable forms of both Mary and *asuwang* allowed her to interpret this dream as a healing miracle. *Duwende* too, as we have seen, may be regarded rather ambivalently by locals and can be viewed as either good or evil.

Even religious leaders and healers themselves may be morally and spiritually ambiguous—especially high-profile media figures like Mike Velarde and Eddie Villanueva. In the barrio, opinions of these figures vary widely: from generous prophet to selfish swindler, from a man used by God to a man used by the devil. Even among faithful El Shaddai affiliates there is debate over Velarde's character (which some see as irrelevant to his ability to inspire faith in God). Healers such as *albularyo, spiritista,* and others may also be spiritually ambiguous. Not only is their status debated, but even among those who esteem these healers, most cannot say whether the source of their healing power is good or evil. According to Vicente Rafael (1988:191), the Tagalog spirit world in the early Spanish period shared some of the ambiguity of the contemporary Tagalog spirit world in Bandong-Sinag:

> The *indio* spirit world was highly decentralized. Despite the elaborate typologies of beneficent and malevolent spirits and the popular lore regarding their characteristic disguises, their preferred victims, and modes of detection and defense against them, spirits had no reference to a comprehensive narrative of ultimate rewards and eternal punishments. Neither were they attributed to the workings of a single source that was simultaneously distant and omnipotent. As the repositories of all things strange that impinged on everyday life, spirits offered a multiplicity of possibilities—whether for loss or gain—in the world.

Unlike the changeable and ambiguous spirits of the early Spanish period and contemporary Bandong-Sinag, however, El Shaddai discourse on spirits makes absolute reference to good and evil entities and offers definitive judgments on the sources of power for other healers (who are usually judged to be evil). Brother Eddie and Brother Sonny, for example, the two El Shaddai healers based in Bandong-Sinag, devised a technique to test whether a person is being dominated by good or evil spirits. Eddie and Sonny bless drinking water in the name of Yahweh El Shaddai and then offer it to the unsuspecting subject. A person under the influence of good spirits (or the Holy Spirit) will drink the water readily and with pleasure. If the person does not drink the water or finds it unpleasant, Eddie and Sonny discern that he or she is being controlled by an evil spirit. They then can perform ritual healing to exorcise the spirits, "bind" the person with prayers to keep bad spirits away in the future, and make recommendations (often involving participation in the local El Shaddai group) for a life of health, peace, and stability with the power of Yahweh El Shaddai to overcome evil entities.

COMPREHENSIVE SPIRITUAL POWER

By performing these exorcising rituals and offering judgments on natural and supernatural events, the El Shaddai approach in this community not only validates people's experiences but also explains them by fitting them into a dichotomous system of good and evil. Unlike other local healers and religious leaders, El Shaddai healers give people constant assurance that the power of Yahweh El Shaddai will prevail over other supernatural, semi-supernatural, and natural forces, and that El Shaddai healers, who help to channel this power, can overpower evil entities most of the time.

When Lina, an El Shaddai member and fifty-eight-year-old housewife of a casual laborer, encountered a woman believed to be a *mankukulam* (witch), she was not afraid. Even though Lina believed this woman had cast a spell on her daughter-in-law Cellie, she disregarded her neighbors' warnings. El Shaddai healers who had blessed Lina's house confirmed that the woman upstairs was indeed a witch. When they burned incense ("the kind used in church") and sprinkled water (blessed by the healers themselves) in the name of Yahweh El Shaddai around the perimeter of the house, the woman upstairs closed her windows and doors and later "fled" the house. Lina told me: "In Jesus' name, Alleluia! Praise God!

After the burning of the incense, she went out." According to the El Shaddai healers and the *albularyo,* witches detest the smell of incense.

This woman, in Lina's opinion, had envied Cellie for her beautiful fingers: "My daughter-in-law, she was bewitched because she was beautiful. She had gone to Japan and returned. She has beautiful fingers, like candles, with jewelry. Every time she had a manicure, this woman . . . looked at her fingers and envied them. Then later my daughter-in-law's fingers swelled up, and she got wounds." Later, when the suspected witch cooked food for her neighbors on the occasion of her daughter's birthday, the neighbors refused to eat lest the food be a conduit for witchcraft. Lina, however, accepted it: "I took the food. I brought it here. I cooked it again. My neighbors said, 'Aren't you afraid?' I said, 'Why should I be? The Lord is with me. . . . The witch should be afraid of Yahweh El Shaddai.' I even said that in front of her: 'You should be afraid of the Lord.'"

To Lina and the others, El Shaddai beliefs did not invalidate claims of witchcraft; rather, they provided protection against them. This idea is evident in numerous other cases of spirit possession, cult control, and the like. In this case Lina had also consulted an *albularyo* who simply gave her advice on how to deal with the witch—whereas the El Shaddai healers actually performed the ritual. In dealing with an illness of her son, Lina had previously combined the services of *albularyo,* conventional medical doctors, *hilot,* Catholic priests, and El Shaddai healers. The only practitioners she did not believe in were the *spiritista*—because, she explained, they charge money for their services. The fact that they charge money, she said, invalidates their claims to have spiritual powers. Besides, she added, she had consulted them in the past and found them to be ineffective.

Because the devil can work through things, El Shaddai (both locally and in national contexts) stresses the blessing of all kinds of objects. Sonny, an El Shaddai healer who practices in Sinag, said that sometimes an object like a necklace will be used by the devil. The following is a paraphrase of Sonny's explanation reconstructed in fieldnotes: "During the pray-over, the necklace was bouncing on her chest. The devil was using the pendant as an instrument. In cases like this we have to rip off the necklace. That's why in the *gawain* you should hold up your objects to be blessed—hold up everything. Because once you bless it and say those words, it will not be touched by evil. Evil things will be repelled by it.

Blessing a person is similar—the person is sealed. And you should have an El Shaddai handkerchief with you at all times for protection. The devil can work through food and water, too. You should always bless what you eat."

El Shaddai healers protect against evil forces not only through their exorcising, healing, and purificatory rituals but through their teachings as well. In this they differ from other folk healers. Positive confession and faith teachings, characteristic of the "health and wealth" gospel, assert that one need only declare and believe something to be true for God to make it happen. Lina, in the witchcraft case, asserts out loud the overwhelming strength of Yahweh El Shaddai to her neighbors and to the suspected witch—giving her the confidence to eat the questionable food (although as a safeguard she recooks it). Lina's combination of healing strategies goes against the recommendations of local El Shaddai healers, however, who teach that all other folk healers are evil except for *hilot* (even though El Shaddai healers tolerate a diversity of affiliations with Protestant churches).

Like other folk healers, the El Shaddai healers sometimes incorporate Catholic imagery: holy water, Catholic prayers, the sign of the cross, purificatory incense. But unlike the others, they oppose the use of statues of saints and the Virgin Mary in healing rites or as intercessors to God in general. Nor do they use rosaries. When a rosary appears in local El Shaddai healing sessions, it is usually because it has been possessed by an evil spirit. Although El Shaddai members do not aggressively oppose statues and the rosary in the same way that born-again and other Protestant groups do, they downplay them and disapprove of what they see as idolatry in mainstream Catholic practice. In their eyes, praying to saints or even the Virgin Mary as intercessors is wrong.

Some El Shaddai members, following the teachings of Brother Mike, phrased their disapproval of statues in terms of the difference between worshiping dead saints versus worshiping the living God. For this reason, some members refuse to participate in All Souls' Day traditions involving cleaning and decorating loved ones' gravestones and celebrating on them with food and music. Nor do they keep a candle lit on the doorstep on All Souls' Day eve to light the way for spirits of loved ones, as I saw practiced by Sinag residents. Some members have even removed all religious images from their homes except those depicting Jesus or the infant

Santo Niño. One El Shaddai member, Danilo, stated that *albularyo* and other local healers are evil because they worship *"anito."* Surprised by his use of the term *"anito,"* which to me meant ancestral spirits, I asked him to clarify. He explained that *anito* and *rebolto* were the same thing. (He may have understood the word to mean "idol.") Vicente Rafael's description of early Tagalog beliefs in *anito* evokes an often noted fit between *anito,* ancestral spirits, and Catholic saints in Tagalog cosmology during the early Spanish period:

> As early Spanish accounts indicate, the "soul" of the dead was assumed to have joined the ranks of the *nono,* or *anito,* as they were also called. A period of mourning was marked by anticipation of the return of the spirit of the dead. In *tibao* feasts, a jar of water was placed at the entrance of the house so that the spirit could wash its feet. A special place at the table was also reserved for the spirit, and the best food was put there. The returning spirit, or *non,* was the privileged guest. As we saw earlier, spirits had the capacity to ward off danger and fulfill the desires of the living. . . . Mourning in this case seems to have involved a recognition of the dead as dead precisely because they could be petitioned for favors and protection. Thus the dead lingered on as part of the society of the living. . . . And their access to a realm unavailable to the living made them attractive sources of the means to ward off illness, hardship, and unexpected disasters. [1988:188–189]

The Spanish practice of using Catholic saints as intercessors fit into an existing cosmology of *anito.* In light of this notion, it makes sense for El Shaddai members to reject both *rebolto* and All Souls' Day rites: in their view, both instances represent worshiping "the dead" (or, as Danilo may have understood it, idolatry).

Many community members say that El Shaddai healers are more powerful and charismatic than church leaders in solving supernatural dilemmas. Such dilemmas include spirit possession and illness. Priests, with certain exceptions, are notoriously ineffective in exorcism and faith healing. El Shaddai healers are also seen as the most effective in releasing subjects from the spiritual grip of cults. El Shaddai healers approach people who belong to *kulto* as possessed by evil spirits. After exorcising these evil spirits— which sometimes takes two or three healing sessions—they then "bind" the person to ensure immunity to the cult's influence in the future.

LOCAL EXPRESSIONS

El Shaddai religiosity, as we have seen, is performed locally within the context of poverty, illness, and social problems. But it also contributes to a competitive religious scene and an active, fluid, and at times ambiguous supernatural world. Indeed part of El Shaddai's success lies in its ability to handle many different supernatural and natural situations. El Shaddai not only addresses local human conditions directly (defining them as spiritual problems) but also confers a transformative spiritual power that seems to triumph over other supernatural entities. The Catholic Church is perceived as incapable of addressing the problems faced by Bandong-Sinag residents in the same direct spiritual manner. Priests are considered unable to exorcise spirits and perform faith healing. El Shaddai differs from other religious options in its ability to offer people the spiritual power to overcome evil entities—both personal and supernatural—that cause family strife, illness, poverty, vices such as alcohol, and other spiritual and physical afflictions. And unlike other local solutions, El Shaddai offers definitive moral and social standards and unambiguous judgments of natural and supernatural events and entities.[9]

Despite the diversity of religious options in Bandong-Sinag—from traditional folk healers to both established and new Christian denominations —the Catholic Church is still a primary religious force in community life. Catholic holidays usually determine community events and celebrations, and church groups devoted to the Virgin Mary are numerous and popular. The Mama Mary figure can be mobilized for social causes and is often a site of debate over gender roles and relationships. El Shaddai Ministries, in contrast, criticizes what it sees as excessive popular veneration of the image and offers a more limited interpretation of Mary as an obedient and submissive role model for women. Many El Shaddai members believe this conservative notion of gender roles improves marital relations.

El Shaddai chapters are required to affiliate with Catholic parishes, and this relationship has produced mixed results not only in Bandong-Sinag but throughout the country. The San Marco chapter flourishes; the Holy Trinity chapter struggles with the parish for control over chapter prayer meetings. Local expressions of El Shaddai are enormously variable and depend on the chapter's relationship with the local Catholic parish and on the cultural and socioeconomic features of the community. Having become familiar with life in Bandong-Sinag and with the religious terrain of the area, in the following chapter we examine the dramatic form El Shaddai takes in this neighborhood by looking at the most active El Shaddai group there—the San Marco chapter.

7 Spiritual Warfare in Sinag and Bandong

> In here, I go house to house. Come with us so you can see what the problems of the people really are. You will see that most of the people's problems have to do with spiritual matters....
> —Brother Eddie, local El Shaddai healer, to the researcher

THE OFFENSIVE STANCE

Members of the core group of the Sinag El Shaddai chapter practice something akin to what is known in charismatic Christian contexts worldwide as "spiritual warfare" (Scotland 1995:123; Poewe 1994:7). Brother Eddie and Brother Sonny, the two healers associated with this group, utilize techniques and forms that combine charismatic spiritual warfare, local Roman Catholic religiosity, and the training and counsel they receive from elders at the El Shaddai office. This training inculcates the health and wealth gospel or "faith teaching" that is often evident in the counseling they do. Brother Eddie and Brother Sonny attended an international conference in Manila on spiritual warfare during the period of this fieldwork. Here are some excerpts from Brother Jaybee Ancheta's workshop on "Spiritual Warfare and the Church Militant" given at the First National Catholic Charismatic Congress at the Philippine International Convention Center, January 9–11, 1995:

> How can you fight the devil on your own? No way. And that is why Jesus made us realize that the objective of spiritual warfare is the dominion of one's power over another. This is our battle.
>
> Spiritual warfare is the battle that continues between the armies of God and the armies of the devil. It is not poetry or play, it is real. And

its splendor is the source of the free-willed human beings, like you and me. If it is merely a matter of power, then there is no doubt that God could conquer the prince of darkness in a moment . . . but it is not. Because the ebb and flow of the battle depends on the wills of humans to receive or reject divine good.

We are the church, therefore we are the people who are called forth to represent the purity of the holiness of God.

Today, many people who cater only to the gospel of prosperity, the practice of our faith, refuse to accept the reality of the Cross as a source of victory in our lives.

. . . No true soldier ever enjoyed waiting because it puts the battle timing in the hands of the enemy. To take the offensive stance provides certain elements of control. . . . [It is] the stance of one who knows he or she can actually do something to change the eternal outcome of the battle for human souls. When we have group prayer power, equipped with spiritual resources, we have been given all the fire power we shall ever need. We also have been given the guarantee of ultimate victory verified by Christ's resurrection from the dead. With this assurance, God is for us, on our side. We are ready to move forward to warfare. . . .

And so Paul [says] in his letter to the Ephesians (Eph. 6:10–18) . . . "Finally be strong in the Lord and in His mighty power. Put on the full armor of God so that you can take your stand against the devil's schemes. For our struggle is not against the flesh and blood but against the principalities and powers of this world and against spiritual forces of evil in the heavenly realms." [First National Catholic Charismatic Congress 1995:32–36][1]

According to this moral universe, the powerful evil entities in the world are in fact forces of the devil. Human beings are in a battle against these forces, and victory is assured if they accept God as the means to this victory. Life's problems and solutions are spiritual. By accepting this concept, they engage in a battle against their problems that they are sure to win.

Through El Shaddai's prosperity theology, members document positive events in their lives and give tithes as "seed faith" from which miracles will grow. This is an empowering stance. Members begin to see their own situation in a way that regards their hardships as temporary, personal, and not determining. The offensive stance of El Shaddai healers in

Sinag and Bandong is similarly empowering. These healers, as Ancheta said, not only preach the gospel of prosperity but also practice spiritual warfare in healing and counseling sessions: "To take the offensive stance provides certain elements of control. . . . [It is] the stance of one who knows he or she can actually do something to change the eternal outcome of the battle for human souls."

For people who have seen the 1986 People Power Revolution come and go without noticing any significant improvement in their life or relevant changes in the power structure of the country, this is an uplifting message. It recognizes the ultimate powerlessness of the individual—that is, the person who has not joined "God's army"—but grants ultimate power and victory to those who have. As we will see, it also represents a moral universe in which all people are equal, where wealth, position, beauty, education, material possessions, and conventional religious authority are irrelevant and may even become spiritual liabilities—but only for those who do not let the Holy Spirit rule their lives. These conventionally advantageous qualities (wealth, beauty, and so forth), including undue dependence on "traditional" (Catholic) religious practices, are seen to block the Holy Spirit and become avenues for the devil to enter one's life and create troubled personal relationships, broken families, sickness, alcoholism, drug addiction, and chronic financial problems. But if one is generous and "with the Holy Spirit," these qualities become godly and one's just rewards. From this perspective, the street vendor who is able to pay off his meager debts is just as empowered as the wealthy businessman who is healed of heart disease. Thus while the El Shaddai worldview in the barrio downplays social inequality and ultimately blames the victim for endemic poverty and distressing social and physical conditions, this blame on the individual brings about the possibility of a certain set of solutions that are also seemingly within the domain of individual agency. In other words: the individual is made to feel empowered and in control of his or her own life.

By aligning themselves with the most powerful entity in their world—the Holy Spirit—El Shaddai participants in a sense reclaim authority over their own moral universe. With El Shaddai they believe they do this, not only with spiritual backing, but also with support from the Catholic Church, from Brother Mike (who, people told me, "has friends in high places"), and from the multitudes of participants who lend the movement power and legitimacy.

THE SAN MARCO CHAPTER IN SINAG

The El Shaddai chapter in Sinag (San Marco parish) is defined by its weekly prayer meetings, which draw from sixty to one hundred people each week, and its healers—two local men who make house calls accompanied by a "choir" (also called the core group). In the context of these house calls (called counseling sessions) the choir is a fluid group of four to six local El Shaddai members who help with healing and exorcising rituals. The English term "healer" is used to distinguish them from *albularyo, yakal,* and *hilot.*

One of the El Shaddai healers, Brother Eddie, is also the coordinator of the chapter. As coordinator Brother Eddie is required to attend monthly training seminars organized by the El Shaddai main office. The coordinator is in charge of organizing the weekly *gawain* as well as handling the monetary offerings and prayer requests collected there. In both of these tasks, he is helped by other members of the chapter. It is also his duty to make sure the local Catholic Church and the central El Shaddai office receive the prescribed percentages of the offerings. If the allotted donations for the local chapter fail to cover the visiting preacher's travel expenses, the coordinator is (unofficially) expected to make up the difference out of his own pocket. Partly for this reason, the Sinag chapter had no volunteers for the coordinator position and Brother Eddie was assigned the job through a drawing of lots. He has proved to be an effective and dedicated leader.

Eddie's wife and two children are active members of the chapter, too, sometimes accompanying him on counseling sessions. This counseling is performed in the homes of members and nonmembers alike. The two healers, Eddie and Sonny, have gained a reputation for their skill in healing and exorcism and travel all over Manila and even in the provinces to do counseling. Although Brother Sonny discovered his healing power just before joining El Shaddai, Eddie did not discover his until much later. Both learned the ritual aspects of healing and counseling from El Shaddai's main office on Amorsolo Street. Eddie explains:

When we were at an El Shaddai rally, binding and praying, Sister Lora came and joined us in the binding, and it was there where she was possessed.[2] And Brother Sonny and I were just new there, and we didn't know what to do. We brought her to Amorsolo. We carried her. We didn't know what to do and Brother Sonny was still new with his healing power. When we went to Amorsolo, it was there where we saw how they do it—the prayers. And it is not as simple as that—the Lord really supports you.

After that, Eddie and Sonny would go on house calls together. Sonny would heal; Eddie would counsel. It was not until later that Eddie himself developed healing power and became what he calls an "evangelist." As Eddie tells it, he was called to heal a woman who could not walk. When he arrived, he did not know what to do, so he just trusted God. "Look, what message will I give to this person? What do I know? I prayed again, 'Lord, give me the right message for them, and may it be in their hearts. That you will talk and put holy oil on my lips and hide me at your back.' That was my prayer." Apparently it worked, for the woman who could not walk "stood up to greet her husband." Eddie explained:

> For the people who received the message of the Lord, it was as if from an evangelist! . . . I said, "Praise the Lord, what is happening?" . . . The Lord really used me.
>
> The category of a pastor is different from an evangelist. A pastor is . . . like he only recruits. He is only a way to bring them near the Lord. An evangelist, he will let you receive the power of the Lord. If the Lord says "Do this and say this," it is really what you will say and nothing else. If they will be hurt by the words of God, it is up to the Lord.

In Eddie's and Sonny's eyes, an El Shaddai preacher is different from a Catholic priest. A priest studies in order to know what to say; he also has a plan for his sermon, with Bible readings prescribed by the church. The El Shaddai preacher, by contrast, has no preparation. Even though El Shaddai decreed in 1996 that its preachers who travel to weekly *gawain* would also preach from weekly scheduled Bible readings, Eddie and Sonny insist that "it is direct from above." This is why one should never interrupt an El Shaddai preacher while he is preaching, they say, because "it is pouring out from the Holy Spirit."

Brother Eddie tells his subjects: "While I am giving a message, it is the Lord giving the message." Not unlike a shaman, the El Shaddai preacher, healer, or evangelist's appeal is based on his charisma and the community's approval; unlike a Catholic priest, the community's respect is not based on his office. This charisma is called "healing power" by El

Shaddai followers. As Weston La Barre has written: "The real difference between a shaman and a priest is who and where the god is, inside or out" (cited in Lindholm 1990:158). In this community, Brother Eddie operates much like a shaman. Both El Shaddai preachers and healers become conduits for the Holy Spirit—actually displaying the presence of the Holy Spirit through their own bodies and voices during the ritual.

Thus counseling sessions and *gawain* are the two main contexts for El Shaddai ritual in the Bandong-Sinag community. And in each context, the charisma and healing power of the healer or preacher are the most significant elements in his perceived success.

GAWAIN: HEALING POWER AND MIMICRY ON THE BASKETBALL COURT

The local El Shaddai prayer meetings are held every Friday night in the Bandong basketball court or in the yard of a nearby elementary school in Sinag. Often these *gawain* are highly emotional and cathartic events involving a lot of singing (led by the choir and band of seven or eight people), "sharing" (testifying) by members of the congregation, and dramatic sermonizing by a visiting preacher from the central office. Depending on the preacher's "healing power," praying in tongues may surface in the congregation during the preaching, especially when the band is playing a background of repetitive music. The preacher prays over members of the congregation through the laying-on-of-hands and sometimes may cast out evil spirits in people, perform healing, or "slay" people in the Holy Spirit. Slaying is a phenomenon well known in charismatic Christian circles worldwide. Sometimes it is called "resting in the spirit" (Poewe 1994). To be "slayed" is to be literally hit by the Holy Spirit with such force that you actually fall to the floor and partially lose consciousness for several minutes. In El Shaddai contexts, it is believed that an evil spirit leaves the body when the Holy Spirit enters.

* * *

The *gawain* had attracted a crowd of participants in the mesmerizing glow of the outdoor electric lights flooding the basketball court. The preacher from the central El Shaddai office was known to be an expert and powerful speaker. By the end of the prayer meeting, at least half the congregation of sixty to eighty people had been slayed. One slayed woman lay semiconscious in a puddle of rainwater on the concrete. Shaking and breathing irregularly, she was apparently unconcerned that letting the water touch her head might bring on illness, as many locals believe. Even very young children, who had next to no understanding of the ritual, had been slayed. Others continued to sway slowly and sing the soothing "Alleluia, Alleluia" song with hands raised up to the red night sky of the city. Some people were weeping.

During the preacher's sermon, he had asked the group: "Are you sick? Raise your hands if you are sick!" More than half of those gathered raised their hands. Later in the sermon, one woman started wailing loudly. This continued until the preacher approached her. Without interrupting his preaching, he laid his hands on her head and shouted, "Receive the Holy Spirit!" several times while mumbling other prayers. As she fell, slayed in the Holy Spirit, someone caught her and laid her on the ground. The preacher continued preaching, and the incident was woven into a crescendo that combined preaching, singing, and slaying.

During the singing and slaying/healing portion of the *gawain,* a frail older woman standing next to me began moaning. As the sounds continued to flow from her, she covered her mouth, trying to contain herself, as if embarrassed. The noises were largely ignored by those around her, who were either singing or uttering spontaneous prayers, some in tongues, facing the front where the choir stood. The old woman moaned for some time until one of the healers slayed her. But after she regained consciousness a minute later, she began writhing on the ground and wailing again. Her back arched as her whole body stiffened. Several people casually drew near her. Without breaking the trancelike flow of the singing and praying, they held their open palms over her body in an attempt to calm her in a gesture of blessing and pray-over. This effort was not immediately successful, but in time she became peaceful. As the meeting came to an end, she was the last one to stand up and join in the cheerful closing song.

The *gawain* was seen as very successful, and everyone seemed to leave happy. It was thought that because the preacher was so powerful, many people had been healed through slaying or had had evil spirits cast out. He had brought forth the power of the Holy Spirit—a power that spread to Brother Eddie and Brother Sonny, as well, for they too had been able to slay and heal many people.

It was announced during the *gawain* that the group was using a new drum set that had been donated by the vice-mayor of Manila (who was running for reelection). Although they were expecting the gift later in the year, it came early "due to prayers," they said. The *barangay* captain of Bandong appeared for several minutes and managed to say a few words into the microphone showing token support for the group.

* * *

Brother Eddie had told me not to take pictures during the preaching. When an El Shaddai preacher is preaching, he warned, the words are coming directly from God and the flash of the camera might disturb the flow of the Holy Spirit. When I asked Brother Mike Velarde about it in an interview, he said this was ridiculous: "How could the Holy Spirit be disturbed?"

At these *gawain,* often the preacher from the central office hands out blessed El Shaddai handkerchiefs, a common practice throughout the whole El Shaddai community. On each handkerchief is printed Psalm 91, "God Our Protector." El Shaddai members believe they are protected from all dangers when carrying the handkerchief with this verse, which says in part (usually in Tagalog):

> You need not fear any dangers at night or sudden attacks during the day or the plagues that strike in the dark or the evils that kill in daylight. A thousand may fall dead beside you, ten thousand all around you, but you will not be harmed. You will look and see how the wicked are punished.[3]

Psalm 91 is used outside the El Shaddai community as well. Indeed, it is "the quintessential statement of divine protection for Brazilian Pentecostals" (Chestnut 1997:96). One El Shaddai member in Sinag told me she had tried five or six different religions over the past decade or so—from Jehovah's Witnesses to Jesus Is Lord (a local born-again group) to Iglesia ni Cristo (an indigenous Protestant sect)—but finally settled on El Shaddai "because they have *this,*" she said, holding up her fist in which she clutched the El Shaddai handkerchief.

During the *gawain,* prayer requests are blessed and then forwarded to the central office, where, members believe, they are prayed over by Brother Mike. Many think these requests have a greater chance of being answered than those kept to oneself—not only because a lot of people pray over them (the Bible is cited to this effect) but also because Brother Mike is praying over them.

Although Brother Eddie told me that the priest from the San Marco parish says a Catholic mass at the *gawain* once a month, in my six months of observation I never saw this happen. There are, however, certain ceremonial elements of the *gawain* in Sinag that mimic the Catholic mass.[4] During one Sinag *gawain,* there was a sort of table that resembled an altar in a Catholic Church. Consisting of a table covered with white cloth, it was placed at the front of the meeting place (in this case the paved, enclosed schoolyard) in what would be the "stage" area. The preacher placed a glass of water (presumably to moisten his throat) on the table and laid a folded white handkerchief neatly across the top of the glass, mimicking the holy chalice of wine and water, with the cloth, on a priest's altar. On this table were two candles as well as a crucifix on a stand with a rosary draped over it—again references to the Catholic altar. Holding the Bible over his head with both hands, as a priest often does, the preacher entered. He then kissed the Bible ceremoniously (again mimicking a priest) before turning around to address the group. Before preaching, the man turned his back to the crowd, faced the bare cement wall of the schoolyard, and bowed his head in a short prayer. To my research assistant, this was amusing. When the priest does this he is facing both the holy tabernacle and the crucifix in a symbolic gesture; the El Shaddai preacher was facing a cement wall. It was done in such a way, however, that any practicing Catholic would have recognized the liturgical parallels.

The borrowed ritual elements seemed to give the novice preacher, an unschooled man in his early twenties, an aura of legitimacy. He also tried, several times, to address me in English as "the foreigner" during his Tagalog sermon, only botching it and eliciting much sympathetic laughter from members of the group, the majority of whom would not have done much better. Most Catholic priests, being educated and often coming from the upper echelons of society, can speak English, and sometimes Spanish, fluently. Their sermons may mix English with Tagalog, confounding the less-educated members of the congregation—the same people who gather for the El Shaddai *gawain.* In fact, the pastor of the local parish church in Sinag was an Italian. (I was told that the parish was founded by Italians and is thus always headed by Italians.) He spoke Italian and English, but no Tagalog.[5]

While the majority of El Shaddai preachers who travel to local chapters have Catholic backgrounds, some preachers I met had been trained at least partially by Baptists.[6] Most used American evangelical preachers as their models (in addition to Brother Mike)—in style, in voice modulation, and at least partially in content. Often they traded tapes and books of sermons available in local Christian bookstores. Some El Shaddai participants watched their preachers very carefully, however, to make sure they were not "Protestant infiltrators." Some preachers, in fact, were known to have come to El Shaddai from various Protestant sects. They were required, according to Brother Mike and Bishop Bacani, to convert to Catholicism during their training.[7] Preachers who had not converted could be spotted, according to my informants, if they failed to cross themselves or failed to take communion during mass. I heard rumors of such a case when I visited a provincial chapter, although no action was taken against the preacher. Among former El Shaddai members the rumor circulates that Brother Mike himself is not a Catholic and has never been seen taking communion. (He is usually backstage when the Catholic mass is said at rallies.)

Not every El Shaddai member in the Sinag area goes to the local *gawain.* Some alternate between the mass rallies at PICC and the local gathering. Many attend both prayer meetings, which means devoting both Friday and Saturday nights. The loudspeakers used during the Sinag *gawain,* especially in Bandong, broadcast the testimonies and preaching into the neighborhood, and often preachers will attempt to evangelize "those out there who can hear the Word of God but have not yet accepted it."

Gawain in Sinag are seen as successful when there is a high degree of involvement by the congregation. The preachers often draw in people by using real-life scenarios, avoiding intellectual topics, inviting responses, and repeating themes and sentence structures throughout the sermon. All of these features are evident in the following excerpt from the opening of a sermon at a Sinag *gawain.* The speaker is a preacher from the central office:

Are you having problems with your spouses? Raise your hands! [Many people raise their hands.] . . .

Those whose husbands are drunkards, raise your hands. [Five people raise their hands.] Do you believe that from now on you don't have a husband anymore? [Laughter.] Amen. You will not have a husband who is a drunkard. The Lord will change him, because the Lord will be the one to heal and set free those who are "slaves of gins."[8] Amen. Amen! [Applause.]

Who among you have arthritis? Raise your hands. [Two raise their hands.] You have arthritis? Do you believe that from now on your feet will not have arthritis? Amen! [*Amen!*] If you have faith in God, you will be healed. Amen! Alleluia, let us clap for the Lord! [Applause.] Clap louder! [Continued applause.] Alleluia. . . .

For me, my crosses now are my brothers-in-law. Maybe because they are all educated, they are difficult to invite [to El Shaddai]. . . .

There are also a lot of us who ask why, when she has started serving the Lord, why does she still have a lot of problems? Amen. Sometimes she is even ashamed in front of her fellow sisters that she is serving the Lord while her husband is still betting in the lotto! Amen. You know, that is our cross. Do you believe this? [*Yes!*] What does this mean? The Lord says that whoever wants to follow me should carry his own cross. When you carry your own cross, the only difference is that you are with Christ. Amen. Always pray, endure your hardships, always pray to the Lord that he will change your spouse's bad habits. Amen! [Applause.] Alleluia!

Why? Because you can't change a person if you don't have the power. . . . Trust in Yahweh in all things. . . .

You'll sacrifice every day. But look at the results of sacrifices. There are miracles and successes. There are rewards and blessings that await you. Amen! [Applause.]

During the testimonies, people express any recent triumphs in their lives—always interpreting positive outcomes as evidence of the active presence of Yahweh El Shaddai in their lives. These testimonies provoke a constant flow of responses from the audience in the form of "Amen, sister!" or "Praise God!" A *gawain* is considered successful if it involves joyful praise and singing. And if the singing and praising are heard by people not in immediate attendance (because they are nearby or the *gawain* has been amplified through loudspeakers), this is part of the spiritual battle for the whole community. The celebration is thought to offer a sense of overcoming the power of darkness for all who can hear. Prosperity theology is combined here with charismatic experience-oriented religiosity. And for those who have decided to follow El Shaddai, the *gawain* represents a continuous support group. When people accept healing or counseling from a local El Shaddai healer, he often tells them they have just made a promise to God to attend the *gawain* and follow the Lord.

COUNSELING: WRESTLING WITH THE DEVIL

Some Bandong and Sinag residents—even those not involved in the group in any way—think El Shaddai healers are more powerful than the *yakal* (local healer) in exorcising evil spirits. One reason for this is that El Shaddai healers work in groups whereas the *yakal* works alone. Nor do El Shaddai healers use the *yakal*'s divination techniques—for example, divining the source of an illness through an external source such as candle wax. But Brother Eddie, the local healer I observed for several months, does a sort of channeling during the counseling sessions that allows him to divine in other ways. At the start of the long ritual lasting up to five hours, he tells the group: "It is not Brother Eddie who is speaking but the Lord." This allows him to perform a sort of divination by claiming to see and understand things that are hidden even from the subjects themselves. He constantly emphasizes the difference between the fake and the real—between, for example, fake and real love, and fake and real problems (physical or social problems versus spiritual ones), and fake (ordinary) and real (El Shaddai) existence. "The truth will set you free," says Eddie, and it is his job, he says, to reveal the truth. As we shall see, however, the counseling session entails a redefinition of truth, love, problems, and so forth presented in the form of a revelation.

Eddie's Approach

Counseling sessions do not occur in every El Shaddai chapter. In fact, during my fieldwork I saw no other local chapter that replicated the counseling rituals I found in Sinag. Parts of the Sinag experience, however, are common elsewhere in the El Shaddai community and are typical of charismatic Christian experience worldwide. Eddie and Sonny learned some of their techniques in "spiritual warfare" seminars (not organized by El Shaddai) that often included evangelists from other countries such as the United States. Many of the elders at the El Shaddai headquarters are schooled in spiritual warfare as well. Essentially, then, Eddie eclectically combines ideas and techniques from El Shaddai, the Catholic Church, charismatic Christian experience, and local ritual to form his own ritual formula.

It should be mentioned here that Brother Mike Velarde himself does not practice spiritual warfare as such and seemed curious but slightly uneasy with the more dramatic charismatic elements such as slaying and speaking in tongues. Nonetheless—much to his continued surprise—his preaching and pray-overs sometimes provoke speaking in tongues in others and even knock down (slay) people.

Although not everyone believes in the efficacy of Eddie's healing and counseling team, many do. I had heard of him locally even before I knew there was a local El Shaddai chapter in the area. His reputation as a healer and exorciser extends beyond the El Shaddai community, and many of his clients are not El Shaddai members (at least initially). Eddie did develop his abilities through his involvement with El Shaddai, however. Eddie himself is a native of Manila, and he and his wife are longtime residents of the Sinag-Bandong community. In fact, members of his wife's family were some of the original landowners in this area when it became a *barangay*. At present Eddie and his family live in a cramped two-room apartment on the second floor of a house. Eddie is only a part-time healer/counselor. During the week he works as a clerk in the city's municipal offices. He has a tenth-grade education and speaks little English. He is in his mid-forties.

El Shaddai gains local legitimacy through counseling and healing sessions by causing strong emotional and physical responses in people through, for example, Eddie's own emotional intensity as he conducts the rituals. These sessions become proof of Brother Eddie's direct contact with the Holy Spirit (and evil spirits to be exorcised)—and, consequently, the El Shaddai ministry's privileged mediating position. By interpreting these responses as proof of the actual presence of the Holy Spirit or the devil, Eddie is able to tap into a preexisting Catholic and folk interpretive framework that corroborates his interpretations of ritual events and sees them as not only plausible but convincing. This in turn gives him credibility when he counsels people about problems and events in their lives.

After receiving the Holy Spirit through healing, slaying, counseling, and revelations, Eddie ties the person to a covenant involving promises to God, to Eddie, to the El Shaddai group, and to any bystanders at the ritual. In this way, the rite becomes a tool of recruitment to El Shaddai. Additionally, Eddie obligates them by making them aware that their problems are caused by evil spirits (which they themselves have allowed into their lives)—and now that he has expiated these spirits, the person must become even more vigilant in keeping them from returning. It is believed that evil spirits will hound the person even more intensely once the Holy Spirit is with them. Thus "binding" will be necessary to keep the evil spirits away, at least temporarily. "Binding the satanic" or "binding" a person against evil forces through prayer (and in Eddie's case holy water) is also a charismatic Christian technique (Scotland 1995:124).

Finally, although Eddie breaks down his subjects psychologically and emotionally (and perhaps physically through exhaustion) during the long ritual, he builds them up again (acting as a channel for Yahweh El Shaddai) by telling them that they are responsible for having let the devil into their lives in the first place. By connecting social, physical, and spiritual problems, Eddie redefines people's past and present and focuses attention on their inner state. By directing attention inward, he makes people feel personally responsible and empowered to solve their own problems.

Counseling at Gloria's

As the following description of a typical healing and counseling session shows, the main paradigm of Brother Eddie's counseling is personal transformation—that is, admitting to the "truth" and submitting yourself to the force of the Holy Spirit so that the evil spirits can be driven out of you. No matter what the problem, it can be solved through this process. There is no magic, for instance, that will make Gloria's husband return home. Rather, the personal transformation of Gloria, facilitated by exorcism, will be so compelling that the husband will want to come back.

During counseling sessions, both Eddie's legitimacy and his explanations for social and physical problems are affirmed through "slaying in the spirit." The Holy Spirit becomes an actual physical force that does battle with the devil in the subject's body and, sometimes, in the house. As Eddie told one of his subjects, a man suffering from an eye infection, "the words of God enter your flesh, go in the bones, and will go to the mind, then to the heart."

Through these rituals Eddie also reaffirms traditional gender and family roles. He points out that the subject's problems are often the result of failure to fulfill their duty as father, wife, or child—perhaps because of their job, money, drinking, or such. This role failure can block the Holy Spirit and allow evil spirits to control the person or vice versa: evil spirits may cause them to be a bad mother, wife, or husband. In any case,

Eddie says that the problems of the people in this community are mainly spiritual problems.

* * *

I am at Nelen's house having a conversation with her. It is around 9 A.M. Her small house is filled with candy toys she and her husband have assembled to take to the market—clear straws filled with tiny colored candy balls with a plastic toy stapled to the end of each, for example, or tiny bundles of candies and toys wrapped in transparent colored plastic. She and her husband conceived of this business idea almost a year ago and have since come up with these original designs themselves. They will sell the candies to stores for 10 pesos (around 40 cents) per dozen. This is their only livelihood. Their dwelling consists of two small rooms with dirt floors (they removed the linoleum because of constant flooding) right on the perimeter of the small basketball court.

The bundles surrounding us represent invested capital and hours of labor that may soon be turned into cash. Although I made the appointment well in advance, it is clear that had my research assistant and I not been there that morning, Nelen could have gotten an early start to the market and might have sold much of this candy by now. When we apologize for taking her time, she says: "No—this is God's work. God's work always comes first. I can feel that this interview is much more important than my other plans." That my research is somehow part of God's plan, that my report will be important for the world to hear, that my presence is mandated by God, that by talking to me they are bearing witness to their transformation with God—are all common themes during my interviews. It is not just an interview, it is "the Lord's work." As they tell of their spiritual transformations, they are performing one of their duties to God: "sharing," witnessing before others. Even more important, I can tell their stories of transformation to the world at large.

Nelen is recounting the story of her first counseling session with Brother Eddie. She tells me she has been with El Shaddai for ten months now. Prior to that, she had attended El Shaddai rallies but had "back-slided," or fallen away.[9] Ever since Eddie counseled her and her husband, their lives have been transformed for the better and they have been very active in the local chapter. She, for example, has stopped drinking and nagging her husband; her husband, too, has stopped drinking. Slaying, she tells me, is the evil spirit leaving you and the Holy Spirit entering you. This is why at first you feel hot, then you feel cool—because the devil is hot and the Holy Spirit cool. If you resist the spirit, you get a headache. But first you must confess your sins. This sets in motion the entire renewal process—it frees you, she says, so you can begin to change your ways. Eddie helps you understand how you need to change.

In the middle of Nelen's explanation, Brother Eddie, who lives only a few houses away, suddenly enters the house. Nelen is not surprised: it is as if she expects him to come. She is a member of Eddie's core healing group, so she often accompanies him on house calls. Brother Eddie declares that he has not yet eaten breakfast, but it is of no matter— he will be able to withstand his hunger because he is doing God's work. At first I think he is hinting that he wants Nelen to feed him, but she makes no gesture to do so. Later I find out that this declaration is common at Eddie's counseling sessions. God will give him strength, he says. His ability to perform without eating is evidence that he is really connected with God. Brother Mike at mass rallies does something similar—always emphasizing that he can endure the long hours of preaching at the *gawain* and not feel tired because the strength of God is in him. Afterward, however, he says his energy has been drained—it has gone out to the people gathered. He often compares this to the biblical story in which a woman, hoping to be healed, touches Jesus' cloak as he passes. Jesus doesn't see her but feels the energy being drawn from him.

Eddie asks Nelen for a cup of coffee. She boils water and mixes it with coffee powder. As she hands it to him, he continues to talk, not even pausing to thank her. He has been talking since the first moment he entered the house, as if from a memorized script. He has taken control of the scene; he is literally on a mission.

"You were bored, weren't you? When I entered, you were wishing the interview was almost over, weren't you?" I am shocked; Eddie is never this rude. I disagree. In truth I was disappointed about the interruption. Eddie doesn't listen to my protest and charges on. This is the opening act—the warmup for the ritual he is about to conduct. In fact, the ritual has already begun.

He tells my research assistant and I what a great coincidence it is that we are here at Nelen's this morning so that we can witness the true work of Yahweh El Shaddai. He invites us to observe the counseling he is about to do "so that we will know more about the root of the problems," he says, "why they are getting sick." He continues:

We will be guided by the Lord. . . . These people—the root is usually spiritual. They are weak. The problems are spread by the devil. . . . The Sinag prayer meeting—that's just a prayer meeting. After that we still have to go around and do counseling for problems. There is only one solution to these—that's El Shaddai. That is where you can see that people really should go back to the Lord.

The paradigm of "solving people's problems" is one supplied by Eddie. Eddie declares himself to be God's messenger. Before arriving at Gloria's house and throughout the ritual, he repeatedly tells us "the words of Brother Eddie are the words of the Lord. It is not Brother Eddie speaking. It is the Lord." He tells us:

> If the Lord is speaking, no matter who you are, your secrets in life will come out. If you want blessings, you have to accept the truth, and not the lies. . . . You bring all those problems to the counseling and I will give them to the Lord. If I'm delivering the words of the Lord, you should accept them no matter how painful, and that will set you free. Because if you don't accept them, you will never be free. It is the bad spirits working in us. The healing power given to me by the Lord— if I'm going to heal, the person should be open. Here we have no secrets because the words of the Lord are very striking [physically]. . . .
>
> When I entered the house, there were only the three of you talking so seriously. But what did you feel when the Lord entered the house?

With this, Eddie implies that he is already acting as the Lord. He even implies that the presence of the Lord can be felt when Eddie enters the house. My research assistant Liezle, a Catholic, is silently astounded by this last statement.

Eddie begins preparing my assistant and me for our first counseling. At this point Eddie is already planning to counsel us a bit alongside the intended subject, Gloria. He begins by stating "truths" about us that, although I try, are hard to refute. Liezle is dumbfounded and stays silent as he directs his unsolicited proclamations at her:

> When I entered a while ago, your smile was fake. But now the smile is coming from the bottom of your heart. Your name? She's cute, right? Behind all that beauty, the youth, the attraction, men should not push her aside, but men don't know all the problems behind that beauty. They're attracted to you for the wrong reasons. You have prob-

lems with your parents, your brothers and sisters. You have many plans in life, but . . . you can't achieve all this because something is blocking you. You want this, you want that.

Then he turns to me:

Sister Katie, you are intelligent, you'll have your children and your family, but there's something that's binding you. You can't move. You're not free. And that bondage is not known to other people. It will be removed if you come to know Yahweh El Shaddai. We should not rely on our strength, our intelligence, our money. Because if we rely on our money, we will make it our God. With money we can buy anything these days, even living people. . . . And if I'm intelligent, you can't command me, because I have a lot of knowledge. . . . But there's one thing we forget, and that's love for other people. People here on earth are all fake, but here in the counseling you will see joy and happiness, and there will be joy in your heart.

Although he knows very little about me at this point and nothing about Liezle—it is relatively early in my Bandong-Sinag research—he delegitimizes us and tells us what really matters: whether or not our hearts are with the Lord.[10] And Eddie is the one qualified to judge us at this moment, since he has already co-opted the role of the Lord's spokesman. In fact, he implies now—and later declares again and again—that everything is fake except that which comes from El Shaddai. Things are not what they seem, he constantly reminds us—we cannot trust our own thoughts and perceptions. Only Brother Eddie possesses the truth right now. Not only are we feeling slightly insulted and vulnerable, but our interpretations of ourselves have been contradicted. We are soon to find out that this is just a mild version of the process Eddie will apply to the woman who requested counseling. Like charismatics in the United States—who are more likely to say they've discovered the "real self" rather than a "new self" (Csordas 1997:50)—Eddie emphasizes that in this ritual, not only will authentic selves be revealed, but also "the *real* problems of the people." "In here," he says, "you will find out what's *really* going on," attributing falsity to other interpretations of local problems.

I am surprised to find out that the woman we are about to visit is Gloria. In fact, Liezle and I had interviewed her three months ago. At the time she was not an El Shaddai follower. She was thirty-five years old, having immigrated to Manila from Leyte after attending college at age twenty-three to work in an office. A nonpracticing Catholic, for a time she was forced to join the Catholic Cursillo movement in order to get promoted in her job. Since the president of the company was a Cursillo member, she said she had to "participate in the religious activities of our president" to move up in the firm. She did not resent this, however, because she felt some good had come of it—she learned something. But given her circumstances, she says, she has been unable to continue with what she learned. At the time of the interview, she was unemployed, having had to quit her job when she gave birth to her last child. Furthermore, her husband was living with another woman.

As we climb the stairs to Gloria's second-floor house nearby, Eddie stops for a moment to say another "sealing" prayer in anticipation of the evil spirits we will encounter there. We enter the hot, cramped room. We are six in the El Shaddai group—plus Gloria, her mother, her two children, and her house helper, a young girl who holds the older child. Ten people all told. There is little ventilation. Five of us sit on chairs, the rest on the floor. Gloria is in a housedress and slippers. She sits down on the floor, her back resting against the wall. Eddie asks her how she feels now. Gloria is upset. Her voice quivering, barely holding back tears, she begins to talk: "I feel so down. When I went there, I couldn't understand, because when I went there, they were watching *Mari Mar* [a popular TV soap opera from Mexico], so I watched too. And I said I should let my daughter sleep first. I don't know. My feeling is so heavy. . . . [Eddie interrupts her and then . . .] There was something I really wanted to know. There is an emptiness deep inside me. It's so hard to express and explain."

Eddie interrupts her several times, explaining to me that I will learn about faith here. Then he tries to show me that Gloria's mother has been healed of deafness through El Shaddai (during Eddie's previous visit with Gloria and her mother). I am confused about Gloria's story, her problem, and the relevance of her mother's deafness because Eddie does not permit her to tell her story until several hours later. Eventually I piece together the events that preceded this counseling.

At the time of our first interview, Gloria had been living in this apartment—a two-room section of a house in Bandong—for only six months, having moved from another part of Manila. This house was owned by her husband's parents. Gloria's biggest problem, she had told us, was that her husband was a womanizer. He had rented an apartment elsewhere and was living there with his "Number Two"—his mistress. Moving Gloria and their two children in with his parents, he himself took up residence with the mistress in what Gloria described as a big apartment elsewhere in the city, a nice apartment originally intended for Gloria and the children.

Gloria said she prayed a lot. She did not participate in El Shaddai, however, because she didn't believe in "raising your hands and letting people know that you are suffering or relieved. Because if you really have problems, you can solve them by yourself." She was grateful that as a result of her prayers, her husband had been supporting them financially ever since she quit her job. When asked her opinion of the typical El Shaddai view that women should submit to men, she disagreed. Males and females are equal, she said, and equally capable.

According to Gloria, her husband's mistress did whatever she could to hang onto Gloria's husband, including going to an *albularyo* (traditional healer/diviner) and using love potions. Gloria said she didn't believe in things like love potions. When she consulted a priest (in her company's church) about her marital problems while she was still employed, he had told her, somewhat contradictorily, not to believe in them because they are the work of the devil.[11] She would have to "fight it and prevent the work of the devil," the priest told her.

Gloria had clearly grown more depressed and frustrated with her situation since our first interview and had called on Brother Eddie for help. That was two days ago. Brother Eddie told her to go directly to Jerry, her husband, and bring him back, but apparently that didn't work. Gloria describes her inability to confront Jerry when she arrived at the apartment where he and his mistress were watching *Mari Mar* on TV. Today she is even more desperate and called on Eddie early this morning.

Eddie focuses attention on Gloria's mother first in order to demonstrate to me that he had healed her of deafness. But despite the healing she received yesterday, the mother does not respond to Eddie's questions because she cannot hear him. Furthermore, she doesn't understand Tagalog, only Waray. Eddie first blesses his own hands and "seals" himself so that the evil sprits that are driven from the woman do not enter him. Then he begins healing her. Rubbing blessed oil on her eyes and around her ears, he prays over her to cast out the evil spirit that is binding her. After making the sign of the cross with her, he holds her head in his hands and shouts:

> In the name of Jesus, I cast out you evil spirits that bind this woman! Bad spirit of deafness, I remove you and cast you to the furthest mountain! I command the veins inside her head to loosen! In the name of Jesus, be healed! Glory be to God! Glory be to Jesus! Whatever this person's sins are, forgive these sins. Bad spirit of sickness, never return to my sister!

His words continue for a long three or four minutes punctuated by what seem to be unintelligible "Latin" words.[12] Then he begins diagnosing the problem. She is deaf not only because she was "overdosed with medicine," as Gloria has told us. Eddie declares:

> You know, Gloria, your mother is deaf not only because of the medicine. When the devil said "medicine, medicine," you gave her medicine. The truth is, she's the one suffering from the sickness that you should be suffering from. What are those sicknesses? Broken heart in the family—Valentines. Another is pride.

Eddie attributes the deafness to Gloria—first because Gloria followed the devil's instructions and gave her mother too much medicine (actually it is not clear who was responsible for the overdose) and second because her mother is not receiving enough love from Gloria. Eddie continues:

> She has, until now, kept all the old hurts of the family with her—carried them inside her. She's hurt, but you don't know it, as a result of what you're doing. You lack love. . . . You say you love your mother, but you don't truly love her! . . . Maybe you're going to admit everything now, aren't you? Admit everything now so you'll be free, and so with your mother! . . . You buy her medicines but you never ask about her problems. . . . You just put her aside in a corner, just like a rag, like old clothes. . . . When the garbage truck comes, you just throw it out. Your mother is just waiting for the time when you're just going to throw her away. . . . When you were young, she didn't even let the mosquitoes bite you. But now that she's old, you just shove her aside! . . . You should go back to the Lord, all of you siblings, and stop your quarreling! You are all full of excuses! Every one of you! But [address-

ing the mother] none of your children truly cared for you! Is this true or not? Amen! . . . [The mother doesn't respond.]

You're just concerned with your money. . . . The truth hurts, but the truth will set you free. The love they show their mother is fake. They just give you food and money, prepare something on your birthday, but it's all fake! The truth is that on your birthday, you were crying because it's all fake! . . . Though they feed you fancy foods, this makes you suffer because everything is fake! You can't even swallow it! That's why you're getting weak! . . .

From your youth until now, Mother, you didn't even know El Shaddai. She just goes to church, enters, goes out, enters, goes out. But it's not from the heart. Mother, you will be set free here, and your healing will be continuous. . . . The doctor . . . only gives medicine for her ears but not something for the heart. Soon we will face Yahweh El Shaddai, but not physically. It's the heart that will face him. Mother, . . . what good have you done to others? [The question is translated to her. She answers *"pakikisama"* (getting along with others).] But that's fake too! When you're giving others food, you're praying that they'll give something back, right? . . . Even Sister Gloria, she gives to the church, too, but she wants it donated to something that "is seen." . . . It's not really from the heart. . . . You're asking for something in return, right? That's also what you did to your children. . . . You should wait for what El Shaddai gives you. It's El Shaddai who's going to return everything, not your children.

The idea that "it's El Shaddai who's going to return everything" reflects Eddie's training in prosperity theology: what you give to God will be returned to you, often a hundredfold. This idea fits well with local suspicions of healers who charge for their services. Eddie often says that if you consult a healer who is not of God (that is, non-El Shaddai), he may heal you but you will get sick again—even sicker than the first time. The reasoning is that the devil is an unfair exchange partner who asks for payment that is much greater than what the healed person has received. Yahweh El Shaddai, by contrast, is not only fair but returns *more* than what the healed person has "paid for."

Eddie goes on to preach about selfishness, giving to the church or El Shaddai, and giving from the heart. If Gloria was not selfish regarding "material things, love, position, and intelligence," her life would be at peace and her mother would not be suffering. Eddie accuses Gloria of being stingy with her knowledge at work and not sharing it with coworkers. Thus there is a precondition for receiving blessings from Yahweh El Shaddai: you must give without expecting a return. Ironically, the "return" requires a "pure gift."

Eddie forces Gloria to admit to gambling (playing the card game *tong-it* for money). And because she did not attend the local *gawain* last night, he accuses her of trying to hide from him and El Shaddai. Today, he says, the Lord will reveal all the lies she is trying to hide. He accuses her of watching *Mari Mar* instead of attending the *gawain*. He continues:

> You, sister, if El Shaddai called you now, "Come now, my child," would you go with him? [Gloria says, "I would go with him."] You would go with him? [He laughs.] You see, the resistance is there! You see, what people say is different from what they do! You see, everything is fake!

The effect of this attack is devastating not only to Gloria but to those of us who are listening. Eddie continues to cut down Gloria in this fashion for more than two hours. Eddie also continues to refer to his words as the Lord's words and his presence as the Lord's presence. He declares that while the room was hot when we entered because the devil was here, it is now cool, reflecting the presence of the Lord. (To Liezle and me, the room felt hot throughout the five-hour ritual.) When Gloria's child begins screaming while Gloria weeps, Eddie says that an evil spirit is taking advantage of the child. Typical of many charismatics, Eddie exorcises through repentance.

Once Gloria is broken down emotionally, Eddie addresses her marital problems. The problem is with Gloria, he says, not with Jerry. Gloria has failed in her role as a wife. Because she feels cheated and betrayed, she is not giving her husband enough love. She should be attentive to his every need, going so far as to even chew his food for him. Even if she does not receive love in return, she should not doubt him. When Gloria protests by saying she does do these things for her husband, Eddie says: "You show him something good, but it's *plastik* [fake]." He doesn't come home, says Eddie, "because it's hell here." With the mistress it's heaven, because she is fulfilling the role of the wife completely. She serves him food and "performs it as a wife." Eddie continues:

If your husband is changing his clothes, she is doing it for him. Your husband arrives and has not yet eaten, and she is already sitting on his lap, which you were not able to do! That's why the devil has destroyed your mind. Your anger and hurt feelings are piling up in your heart. That is why you see your husband as a devil. That is why your life is hell. You called the devil, the devil came to you, and the devil is with you. But now, this is the way, this time, this day, reform, sister! Can you approach your husband and ask for forgiveness?

This preaching is punctuated by spontaneous religious songs by Eddie and his choir, and by more discussion of selfishness, forgiveness, and fakeness. He scolds Gloria for not attending the *gawain* the night before:

> We will say, "Lord, today is Saturday. Next Friday I will go to the Sinag *gawain*." . . . Thursday the Lord was here, and there was a *gawain* on Friday. You were changed on Thursday and when Friday came, you erased the Lord. Is that how weak we are now? Is that how we praise? Will the devil enslave us forever? The teaching of the Lord, the teaching in the *gawain*, is to pray early in the morning to clear your path. What is your path? You are watching *Mari Mar Acapulco*, which is all about revenge! There is no love in those things. You were watching it, weren't you? Especially with Sister [referring to the main character, Mari Mar]—when it comes to Sergio, she is angry at him. You say, "That is like my husband."

She must humble herself, forget her college degree, her "class," her money, her pride, and visit Jerry and his mistress—again. She will thank the mistress for taking care of him and declare that now it is time for her to take back what the mistress "borrowed" from her. Eddie advises:

> You hold the key, and you will be the one who will open your spirit. You are the one who will knock, open the door, enter, and eat together. . . . This is your life. The servant of the Lord cannot be with you because of the thickness of that wall. Open your spirit. Jericho is an example, but this is your life, sister. Now you are able to praise, to sing, and to clap. You can do it now. You can destroy the wall so long as you humble yourself. Go to your husband. . . . Repent. . . . It is your fault. . . . You are the reason your husband left here and will not come back. . . . But Yahweh El Shaddai will return him to you. He will help you, sister. . . . Wear perfume, and hug him so tight that he won't be

able to hug "Number Two." . . . The Lord will do the hugging for you. . . .

Sister, there is no cure for your sickness if you will not return to God.

Gloria is weeping once more. Again she is soothed by a song from the choir. One by one, Eddie begins "slaying" nearly everyone in the room except for his choir members, who catch the subjects as they fall. Each slaying is a five to ten minute ordeal. This is the emotional catharsis and climax of the ritual. Eddie prays over each person as they stand in front of him. As he holds his hands around the person's head (without touching it), he commands the evil spirits to leave the person, just as he did while trying to cure Gloria's mother of deafness. He stands slightly to the side so that the bad spirit, as it leaves the person's body, does not enter him. Through his hands he "throws" the Holy Spirit into the person. Eventually, after a few minutes, the person begins to lose consciousness, falls backward into the hands of the choir, and is laid gently on the floor. Eddie and the choir then surround the subject and continue praying out loud for the person.

Such moments as these during healing and counseling rituals are very emotionally charged. Some subjects regain consciousness with tears streaming down their faces; some cry out loud. Others describe feeling cold and clammy, shaking, and sensing a certain hotness in their chest. One woman (during another session), after falling, did not lose consciousness but lay screaming and writhing on the floor. According to Eddie, this was the bad spirit leaving her. Subjects are made to know they have been literally hit with the Holy Spirit.

After the slaying, Eddie asks Gloria for containers of water to be brought out. He blesses the water "in the name of Yahweh El Shaddai" and asks everyone to drink. Eddie asks those present how the water tastes, and someone answers "sweet," as usually happens. Eddie interprets this as a sign that the water is holy and has God in it. Eddie then purifies the entire house by dousing everything in it with water, uttering blessings as he does so. He focuses particularly on the *apirador* (cabinet) that was used by an Indian relative—an in-law of Gloria's husband—who practiced fortune-telling. Both the fortune-telling and the non-Christian implications of Indian ethnicity arouse some suspicion.

In Search of Resolution

With this ritual, as we have seen, El Shaddai can enter people's lives on a very personal and powerful level. Eddie acts as both a spokesman for God and a representative of El Shaddai. As such, he is able to create a convincing sense of spiritual presence and transformation through confession, catharsis, slaying, and exorcism. He first makes the person defenseless by breaking them down and insulting them. He is able to do this legitimately by claiming that it is not Eddie but God who is delivering these painful words. He later builds up the person by giving them a feeling of empowerment. By reasserting their social roles—and attending the *gawain*—they can effect changes in their own lives. This is declared to be "true" while everything in the previous life is "fake." This allows the person to mark a point at which a transformation has occurred—a sense of renunciation of one's previous life that is common in Pentecostal and charismatic Christian experience. Through this dichotomy he redefines the person's problems and personal history, which can now be understood only through the prism of this Christian language. Connecting social, physical, and spiritual problems, the counseling hinges on personal transformation. The focus shifts away from externalities and rejects larger social or structural problems and solutions. Finally, Eddie compels the person to begin attending the El Shaddai *gawain.*

I was able to follow Gloria's case only up to a certain point. Gloria did as she was instructed and visited Jerry and his mistress again. The following week, Jerry returned to Gloria and reportedly even received some counseling from Eddie. The couple was seen at the *gawain* together for two weeks in a row, but they were only marginally participating. Shortly thereafter Jerry returned to his mistress. Eddie and Vangie (a member of the initial counseling group) explained that of course he cannot leave the mistress suddenly—it needs to be done gradually. Vangie added:

At least he heard the words of God and he realized his sins—whether he accepts it or not, we are not responsible for it anymore. . . . We do not force him. Because a person, if he hears the words of God and really accepts the words of Christ in his heart, . . . they accept and surrender their sin, they will immediately accept the Holy Spirit. But if the way they respond is *pilosopo* [skeptical], we don't accept those. Because the Holy Spirit will have difficulty in entering the body and will not enter.

With this they seemed to close the case. Blame for the unsatisfactory resolution was focused on the individuals involved—supported by the initial framing of the problem as one of faith and authenticity. Now the focus has shifted to Jerry, who has blocked the Holy Spirit from entering his body with his skepticism (and was likely not slayed as a result). In the words of Jaybee Ancheta: "The ebb and flow of the battle depends on the wills of humans to receive or reject divine good" (Ancheta 1995). The ultimate nonresolution of the case does not disprove Eddie's world-view, of course. In fact, it can be used to support it. To the participants, moreover, the ritual may well have demonstrated proof of El Shaddai's privileged mediating position by evoking strong physical and emotional responses whose meanings are defined in the context of El Shaddai and charismatic spiritual warfare.

EDDIE'S WORLD

Counseling sessions and *gawain* seem to encourage participants to recover a sense of power over their lives—a recovery that can be long-term or short-lived. In spiritual warfare, Eddie exorcises evil spirits through charismatic Christian techniques of counseling and repentance. The actual manifestation of the Holy Spirit through other charismatic elements such as slaying, testimonies, and speaking in tongues is seen as proof of the presence of God and the legitimacy of El Shaddai beliefs and rituals. Like other varieties of charismatic religious practice, El Shaddai here offers itself as the only authentic avenue to God—and the charismatic experience confirms this. In the context of counseling and exorcising, El Shaddai healers lay great stress on traditional family and gender roles. By incorporating Catholic elements into the prayers and rituals, these religious experiences gain legitimacy in the eyes of participants. And by focusing on the person's internal state, El Shaddai effectively advances an ideology that does not challenge larger social, economic, and political structures.

Through counseling, slaying, and *gawain,* people reinterpret their own lives in El Shaddai terms. Counseling and slaying serve as an induction into this world. Once one has been slayed, one is automatically "born again," according to El Shaddai elders. The *gawain* then reinforces the person's new status and new viewpoint on life. This change is marked by speaking of all previous emotions, intentions, and actions as "fake," while everything since the person's first encounter with Yahweh El Shaddai is seen as "true" or "real." In sum, this process translates into a transformative spiritual power that creates a new life of health and prosperity standing apart from the old life of poverty and suffering.

Epilogue

The many specific *hows* and *whys* that motivated Father Bert to attend an El Shaddai rally in the opening pages of this book have driven my curiosity, too, in this investigation. In Brother Mike's view, El Shaddai is simply removing the man-made impediments to the Holy Spirit's bounty:

> I have a revelation now that has not yet been pronounced. . . . The reason I haven't pronounced it yet is that it will upset religious institutions. . . . And it is this: "Set my people free so they can worship." People can't worship now because of religious bondage, because religion builds walls that try to block out the spirit. Religion is binding people, holding them back from experiencing the Holy Spirit.[1]

My investigation, by contrast, has revealed two types of transformation. The first is a transformation of self. In remaking themselves through El Shaddai, members open up a creative if controversial space of change within Philippine Catholicism. Thus the second transformation is in the way Roman Catholicism is practiced in the Philippines—particularly by the 10 million people who call themselves "children of El Shaddai." Brother Mike was quick to point out in an interview that he does not intend to lead his people away from the Catholic Church but, rather, to bring the church closer to the people. Both of these transformations reveal the yearnings of a sector of society for whom the time-worn ideologies and rites of the church and the left have lost some of their relevance.

El Shaddai transforms the way its members practice Catholicism by changing the site of sacredness and the mode of mediation of spiritual power through its use of mass media and outdoor rallies. El Shaddai members see the airwaves of radio and television and the open air of mass rallies as conducive to the free movement of the Holy Spirit. In contrast to Catholic churches this air seems to ease mediation with others within the El Shaddai ritual sphere and with the local elites and power brokers of Philippine society. An El Shaddai member's communicative possibilities extend to the nation and beyond—to a global arena. By bringing ritual space into the home and the self, radio healing empowers ordinary people to heal and to mediate with God in other ways.

Resisting an imposed urban order that expresses a history of marginalization, El Shaddai's engagements with public spaces contribute to a new sense of power and critical mass for its members. El Shaddai has colonized various public spaces throughout its own brief history and indeed has reclaimed the spaces of the Philippine International Convention Center along Manila's seafront. This contested space remains haunted literally by the casualties of Imelda Marcos' ruthless projects on this land and haunted symbolically by the attitudes toward the urban poor of successive Philippine presidencies.

But El Shaddai's prosperity theology and the ways in which it is put into practice also transform the self. El Shaddai's orientation toward individual rather than social transformation rejects determining notions of poverty and seeks to retell life histories and futures in narratives of transformative miracles. Poverty becomes a catalyst for blessings, healing, and other positive changes. Seed-faith offerings, tithes, prayer requests, and the resulting testimonies of miracles recontextualize and rewrite suffering and success.

Despite shifting religious and denominational boundaries, Catholicism is a source of legitimacy for the movement and an important aspect of identity for its members. While prosperity theology and its associated rituals represent a significant divergence from the way in which Catholicism has traditionally been practiced in the Philippines, El Shaddai has negotiated a controversial but legitimate Catholic identity. Moreover, the El Shaddai movement has positioned itself uniquely to effect change in popular Catholicism because it has combined a critical stance on traditional Catholic practices with a tempered loyalty to Catholic affiliation, hierarchy, and doctrine. This combination has produced new cultural forms as the movement finds creative ways to bridge these divergent sentiments of independence from and dependence on the church. El Shaddai has avoided direct competition with the Catholic Church while creating a distinctive sacred and quasi-physical space from which critique is possible.

The marriage between shamanic traditions of spiritual mediation, on the one hand, and native conceptualizations of charisma and sacred power, on the other, has produced a revitalized spiritual arena in which authentic "healing power" has shifted to El Shaddai contexts. Combining elements of Roman Catholicism, prosperity theology, charismatic Christianity, and local shamanic traditions—all bound together by the person of Brother Mike along with the preachers and leaders—El Shaddai brings its members into direct contact with the spiritual realm through "healing power" and new sacred space. El Shaddai ritual elements associated with mass mediation, healing and counseling sessions, local prayer rallies, and customized applications of prosperity theology within Catholic and Philippine cultural contexts have all produced a sense of spiritual potency and authenticity that sets the movement apart from other available options in the Philippine religious landscape.

* * *

In the un-air-conditioned office at the back of Holy Trinity church, just days after dissolving the popular El Shaddai chapter in his parish, Monsignor Tomas gave me his copy of the Acts and Decrees of the Second Plenary Council of the Philippines of 1991 to photocopy. In it the Bishops Conference defines the concept of "Church of the Poor":

> To the shanty dwellers of Favela dos Alagados, Pope John Paul II forcefully asserted: "Do not say that it is God's will that you remain in a condition of poverty, disease, unhealthy housing, that is contrary in many ways to your dignity as human persons. Do not say 'It is God who wills it.'"
>
> In the Scriptures, the poor are blessed. "Blessed are you who are poor, for the kingdom of God is yours." It is not their poverty that is "blessed." Nor are they blessed because they are necessarily better Christians than their prosperous brothers and sisters. But they are blessed because their poverty has been historically the privileged place of the gracious intervention of God's saving grace. Just as the sin of Adam ("O happy fault!"—Easter Proclamation) occasioned God to decide that his Son become savior, so the poverty of people brought in God's intervention. . . .
>
> [Church of the Poor] means a Church that embraces and practices the evangelical spirit of poverty, which combines detachment from possessions with a profound trust in the Lord as the sole source of sal-

vation. While the Lord does not want anyone to be materially poor, he wants all his followers to be "poor in spirit." [Catholic Bishops Conference of the Philippines 1992:47–48]

This compelling passage reveals a Filipino Roman Catholic Church attempting to connect to a segment of the population that has been marginalized in the nation's efforts toward modernization—a segment beset by the continuing economic and social strains of poverty.

But this passage also reveals the deeply divergent understandings of Christian life, poverty, and engagements with modernity that constitute the significant fault lines between the Philippine church and El Shaddai. While the Church of the Poor movement speaks of a spirit of poverty that rejects material attachments, El Shaddai's prosperity theology directly engages and affirms desires for the material signs of modernity. And while the very label "Church of the Poor" seems further to entrench class positions—it is hard to imagine anyone proclaiming proudly that they are part of the "poor" movement—El Shaddai provides a potent spiritual and personal language for rejecting deterministic class labels. Even liberation theology's revolutionary worldview is still based on class analysis and identification. El Shaddai, instead, achieves a powerful reframing of cultural models implied in such language and thinking. Brother Mike's preaching, as well as such practices as positive confession and prayer requests, propel a radical recasting of identity and life events. Far from being a church of the poor, or the "poor in spirit," El Shaddai becomes a church of the self-identified rich. When El Shaddai members chant *"I am rich! I am strong! Something good is going to happen to me!"* they expect miracles. And because they are "rich in spirit," they indeed *see* miracles happen.

NOTES

CH. 1: SEEKING EL SHADDAI

1. In El Shaddai contexts Velarde formally goes by the name Brother Mariano "Mike" Z. Velarde. Informally he is known as Mike Velarde or "Brother Mike."

2. In April 2002, Mel Robles, now Brother Mike's spokesman and liaison to the government, reported that the group's membership has remained relatively stable since 1997.

3. The seven ministries of the El Shaddai Foundation are the music ministry, the education ministry, the outreach (operations) ministry, the international chapters ministry, the administrative general services ministry, the finance ministry, and the media ministry.

4. Bishop Bacani is auxiliary of Manila and spiritual director of the Catholic Charismatic Movement.

5. In contrast to these studies, which focus on popular Catholicism, others (such as Youngblood 1990) have focused instead on the role of the institutional church in political and social change.

6. I am referring especially to Asad's critiques of anthropologist Clifford Geertz's well-known and seminal definition of religion (Geertz 1973), which emphasizes meanings and ignores power and social discipline. Asad urges anthropologists and other scholars to investigate religion with attention to power and the specific social and historical conditions that are necessary for particular religious forms to arise.

CH. 2: GOLDEN RULES, MIRACLE INVESTMENTS, AND
THE SEED-FAITH PRINCIPLE

1. Personal interview, Nov. 28, 1996. This priest asked not to be identified by name.

2. In 1993, an estimated 84 percent of the population was Roman Catholic (Demaine 1996).

3. I have unverified reports that Velarde, when beginning the movement, told friends that his new "business"—religion—would be a big moneymaker if it followed the trends and appealed to the majority: the Catholics. I also have firsthand accounts from movement insiders who report that Velarde described his new movement at the time as "good business" for "making money and capital."

4. Mike Velarde, live broadcast of a rally from PICC in Manila on DWXI, Apr. 4, 1996.

5. Mike Velarde, live broadcast of a rally from Rizal Baseball Stadium in Manila on DWXI, Feb. 13, 1996; translated from Tagalog by Yda Arce Liongson.

6. Interview with Mike Velarde, Sept. 28, 1996, El Shaddai office, Makati City.

7. The idea of miracles for offerings is used by other religious groups in Manila, as well, such as "Jesus Christ the Name Above Every Name" and "Jesus Is Lord."

8. Mike Velarde, live broadcast of a rally from PICC in Manila on DWXI, Holy Thursday, Apr. 4, 1996; translated from Tagalog by Miren Sanchez.

9. Ibid.

10. Mike Velarde, live broadcast of a rally from Rizal Baseball Stadium in Manila on DWXI, Feb. 13, 1996; translated from Tagalog by Yda Arce Liongson.

11. That Velarde draws heavily on the teachings of Hagin was confirmed by Cesar Roxas, formerly known as the cofounder of El Shaddai, in a personal interview.

12. Mike Velarde, live broadcast of a rally from PICC in Manila on DWXI, Holy Thursday, Apr. 4, 1996; translated from Tagalog by Miren Sanchez.

13. Ibid.

14. Personal interview with Archbishop Jaime Cardinal Sin, Nov. 14, 1996, at the archbishop's residence, Manila, in English.

15. This priest requested anonymity.

16. Grameen Banking is a strategy for poverty alleviation that was started in Bangladesh and has recently been applied in Manila. The program gives poor people (mostly women) microloans to start small businesses. In the Philippines, Grameen Banking is being used by around thirty church-related and secular nongovernmental organizations (Mask 1995).

17. I have personally witnessed this recordkeeping in the El Shaddai office.

18. The English "pray-over" is a pseudo-Tagalog word, as is "prayer request." For example, *"nagprayerrequest ako"* means "I made or submitted a prayer request."

19. Sister Norma, for example, a Filipina worker in the Netherlands, testified as follows in El Shaddai's newsletter: "When I was still in the Philippines, I used to receive a monthly salary of only 1,800 pesos. Yet I did not neglect to give my tithes for the work of the Lord at DWXI–PPFI, together with my prayer request for a salary increase. Praise the Lord, He has given me a job in this country, and now my monthly tithe alone amounts to 2,440 pesos! I have a good-natured boss, and my job is simply wonderful!" (Velarde 1992:2).

20. Sources at the central El Shaddai office, however, say it may also be one of the elders who prays over the requests.

21. Several informants have described this to me; it was also reported by Jiminez-David (1999).

22. Mike Velarde, live broadcast of a rally from PICC in Manila on DWXI, Holy Thursday, Apr. 4, 1996; translated by Miren Sanchez.

23. Tithes collected at national rallies or at El Shaddai headquarters yield higher net collections for El Shaddai DWXI–PPFI since 100 percent of these offerings stays within the foundation whereas local chapters forward only 50 percent of their offerings to the foundation.

24. These numbers do not include emergency visits to the medical tent at El Shaddai rallies.

25. Records obtained from the El Shaddai medical and dental offices. In 1995 the medical and dental clinics had 5,652 and 1,584 patient visits, respectively.

26. Due to traffic congestion and distances, traveling from one section of Metro Manila to another may involve a prohibitive investment of time, effort, and money.

27. Recent legal cases against Velarde have raised awareness of the distinctiveness of each entity. (See the following section, "Money Troubles," for details.)

28. The NPA is the armed wing of the Communist Party of the Philippines.

29. His story is taken from my field notes of Mar. 29, 1996.

30. The eight-page pamphlet is titled "The El Shaddai Golden Rule Company, Inc. (For Incorporation), *Super Bodega at Super Murang Lupa't Bahay* 'Vision Projects,' *Pahayag* [Statement/Agreement] Survey and Application Form." It is written almost completely in Tagalog. Other sources, however, such as *El Shaddai Bagong Liwanag Magazine* (Jan.–Mar. 1996), state that participants in the program must hold El Shaddai ID numbers in order to join.

31. The five provinces are Batangas, Laguna, Bulacan, Rizal, and Cavite.

32. This information comes from copies of official legal documents from the Regional Trial Court of the National Capital Municipal Region, Makati, Metro Manila, Sept.–Oct. 1988, obtained from a source who wishes to remain anonymous. The incident was widely reported in Filipino newspapers.

33. *People's Journal Tonight,* a tabloid in Manila, first broke this story; it was later picked up by other tabloids and English-language newspapers.

34. Velarde split with the church over the changes to the Philippine Constitution proposed by President Estrada. Velarde backed the unsuccessful campaign that would have allowed presidents to serve two terms instead of just one.

CH. 3: MASS MEDIA AND RELIGIOUS EXPERIENCE

1. Interview recorded in Makati City, Sept. 28, 1996. The interview was conducted in English and is transcribed here with minor grammatical changes.

2. Velarde says he had already been involved in the charismatic movement for a couple of years at this time.

3. The booklet, "El Shaddai," was written by Rev. Kenneth E. Hagin (see Chapter 1) and describes "El Shaddai" as Abraham's name for God, a meaning Brother Mike has taken up as well. The booklet's teachings expound on Psalm 91, which later became one of the El Shaddai ministry's theme prayers and is reproduced on El Shaddai handkerchiefs. Of the song "El Shaddai," Velarde said: "I think it came from the States—one of those evangelist movements."

4. It was unclear during interviews with Velarde and El Shaddai officers how long this development took. Velarde said the movement was starting to become popular by 1984. In 1996, El Shaddai Ministries celebrated its twelfth year anniversary. El Shaddai officers could not indicate, however, which event in 1984 designated that year as the official beginning of the movement.

5. Based on an unpublished survey of radio listening levels in Metro Manila, Nov. 19–27, 1995, conducted by Applied Marketing Research, Inc., commissioned by the Radio Research Council, Inc., Philippines, obtained from El Shaddai Ministries.

6. The El Shaddai Foundation broadcasts its programs in California and in Hong Kong.

7. El Shaddai DWXI–PPFI's TV programming in 1995 existed in the following cities: Metro Manila; Sorsogon City, Sorsogon (two stations); Tuguegarao, Cagayan; Cebu City, Cebu; Puerto Princesa, Palawan; Baao, Camarines Sur; and Naga City. See El Shaddai Foundation (1995).

8. There is at least one other ministry in Manila with a similar emphasis on mass media and open-air rallies: the slightly less popular Jesus Is Lord led by Eddie Villanueva. Because this group is Protestant, however, its dynamics of religious identity and practice are in many ways different from El Shaddai's. The vast majority of El Shaddai participants consider themselves Catholics. They define themselves and describe their own religious practices and beliefs overwhelmingly with reference to "ordinary Catholics" or to their own preconversion state of being "just Catholic" or just nominally Catholic. Only when specifically asked did my El Shaddai informants compare themselves to Protestants—despite the many similarities in religious ideology between El Shaddai and certain Protestant groups.

9. In provincial areas the configuration is different: local prayer groups and radio broadcasts are the primary ways in which the El Shaddai community is

formed. Attending mass rallies in Manila then becomes a possibility for pilgrimage. Smaller mass rallies (between five thousand and thirty thousand people) are sometimes hosted by Velarde in provincial areas for large El Shaddai chapters on their founding anniversaries. The majority of El Shaddai members, however, reside in the Manila area.

10. The PICC compound is a large piece of land on which stands the Philippine International Convention Center.

11. Translated here from Tagalog.

12. Interview recorded in Makati City, Nov. 4, 1996, in English.

13. Although Brother Mike and El Shaddai members insist that Velarde is not needed in communicating with God, El Shaddai practice indicates that he is highly sought after as a mediator. Velarde's actions seem to encourage this mediation as well.

14. Personal interview with Velarde. See also Velarde (1995): the back cover of this booklet contains a short piece in which Brother Mike describes how he misinterpreted a "mysterious voice" that told him in 1982 to "build me a center." He thought God was asking him to build a church or basilica. Three or four years later, however, the spirit of the Lord revealed to him the real meaning of that call: "It is you whom I need to be built as a holy temple and serve as a living sacrifice in order to renew the Church." It was not an actual church but Velarde himself that would be the temple. The piece also contains a picture of Velarde holding the plans for his church, with the pope looking on, with the caption: "Taken at St. Peter, Basilica Square, Vatican City."

15. Personal interview with Velarde, Makati City, Nov. 4, 1996, in English.

16. The words "Let the weak say 'I am strong.' Let the poor say 'I am rich'" are lyrics from an English-language Christian song that is sung by participants at nearly every El Shaddai event.

17. Whether or not El Shaddai is legitimately Catholic is widely debated among non–El Shaddai Filipino Catholics and, as mentioned, some PRCC clergy.

18. Since 1995, when Velarde stipulated that all local chapters must be affiliated with Catholic parishes, many of the small local El Shaddai prayer meetings have been held in Catholic parish churches. A proportion of the tithes collected at these chapter meetings goes to the local parish. The majority of El Shaddai events, however, still occur outside Catholic Church structures. The PRCC officially claims to supervise El Shaddai practice, and Catholic bishops participate in the training of El Shaddai preachers.

CH. 4: URBAN SPACES OF COMMUNITY AND CONGREGATION

1. The City of Manila is divided into six districts. Each district is divided into "areas," which are further divided into *barangay*. Some *barangay* are divided into *sitio*, the smallest unit of administrative organization. A *barangay*

is also a community of people. For discussion of the *barangay* as a social unit in precolonial and colonial times see Scott (1994).

2. Makati City was formerly called Makati as part of the City of Manila. In 1995 it formally became a city of its own as part of Metro Manila.

3. My informants could page me from a public phone, but I could not contact them by phone. Our neighbors, who owned the building where we stayed, would also give us phone messages. During the last few months of my fieldwork I obtained a cell phone, but it proved to be completely useless for communicating with informants in Bandong-Sinag because my cell phone number was unreachable via public phones.

4. Henceforth "Manila" or "Metro Manila" refers to the greater Metro Manila area; "City of Manila" refers to just the city area, which is contained within the greater Metro Manila area. This is not to say, however, that the City of Manila constitutes "the center" of Metro Manila. Metro Manila has no real center as such.

5. Manila was experiencing (and still is) tremendous traffic problems throughout the city; hence a sixty-minute trip was considered to be near average.

6. See "Barangay Annual Report" (1995:2). Information that could be used to identify the *barangay* has been omitted.

7. Office of the Mayor, Makati City. This number has been disputed by local residents, who accuse *barangay* officials of lowering the population estimate in order to influence election outcomes.

8. Since 1 hectare = 2.5 acres, the area of Bandong is 3.75 acres and the area of Sinag is 22.5 acres. If a standard American block is one-tenth of a mile squared, then a square block is roughly 6 acres.

9. I define a household as a group of people who eat together and sleep in a shared space. Membership in households is often fluid and partial. Thus household also refers to the common dwelling space.

10. On average, fourteen or fifteen people inhabit each house in Bandong. But considering that single-family houses are included in this average, the number of people in the majority of houses in this *barangay* is actually higher. These estimates are from the "Barangay Annual Report" (1995:2). My own nonrandom survey of thirty-four households confirmed that a large portion of Bandong residents live in houses containing as many as twenty-five people.

11. In relative terms, a pair of roller blades could cost the equivalent of another family's entire living stipend for one or two months.

12. I use the term "blocks" as the locals do: areas of land on which houses are built. They are bordered by narrow lanes or wider paved paths but are not necessarily square or rectangular.

13. During my fieldwork period, the basketball court was used for these prayer meetings only occasionally; most often the group met in the elemen-

tary school's paved yard. I have been informed, however, that sometime in 1997 these prayer meetings were permanently moved to the basketball court.

14. Thomas Pinches has written extensively about this intimacy and inter-household cooperation, not only as a preferred way of living, but also as residents' collective response to exclusion from legal housing property and the danger of expulsion and demolition. (See, for example, Pinches 1994 among others.)

15. When meetings are officially *barangay* oriented, such as *barangay* council meetings or the *barangay* fiesta, a place is found within the technical *barangay* boundary. In the case of Bandong, for instance, the Bandong fiesta stage was not set up in the basketball court because the court is technically located in Sinag. Instead the stage was set up at the junction of two wide walkways in Bandong.

16. These data are based on a nonrandom survey I conducted of thirty-four households in Bandong in 1996.

17. The fiesta involves the *caracha,* a dance that is traditionally featured at the hometown fiesta in Leyte (originally from Spain), as well as *tuba,* a traditional homemade palm liquor brought from Leyte each year for the fiesta. The Holy Cross that was brought to Manila from the hometown in 1952 (some sources say the late 1940s) reportedly has been decorated and displayed at this fiesta every year since then. The cross, approximately 3 feet tall, is displayed on a table during the dance portion of the fiesta. During the week preceding the dance, members of the religious civic organization use the cross for novenas (a series of daily prayers usually lasting nine days). According to my informants, the Holy Cross, as well as the *caracha* and the *tuba,* symbolize their connections to their hometown. The *caracha* dance involves an exchange of money and thus helps to raise money for the next year's fiesta.

18. These figures are based on a nonrandom survey I conducted of thirty-four households in Bandong in 1996.

19. Legal tenants must, according to law, demonstrate that they have lived on that land for a certain number of years (around twenty years according to residents, though I was unable to confirm this) and demonstrate that they have developed the land.

20. This land was purchased by national government from a private owner under a national law that gives long-term tenants who have developed land the opportunity to purchase it from the government at a predetermined price. In 1995 and 1996, these rights were challenged in Bandong when the *barangay* captain illegally mediated the sale of some of these lots to an outside party. Because the National Housing Authority had not yet actually purchased the lots, the business deal was conducted illegally. Residents organized under the leadership of one local woman and successfully resisted the illegal purchase with the support of the local Catholic parish priest.

21. Ben Razon, pers. comm. Razon is a Filipino photojournalist and long-time resident of Manila.

22. The Folk Arts Theater was built for the 1974 Miss Universe beauty pageant; the PICC was built for the 1976 International Fund and World Bank Conference (Pinches 1994:14).

23. The story has been widely reported by Filipino journalists; see also Manapat (1991:51) cited in Pinches (1994:14).

24. To my knowledge, El Shaddai members have not been part of these seance groups (pers. comm.; see also de Guzman 1996).

25. The sale of parts of the reclamation area south of PICC by the government under former President Ramos and J. de Venecia was the subject of an inquiry by a Philippine Senate blue ribbon committee; its conclusions were indefinite.

26. For an extended discussion see Pinches (1994).

27. This sense of awe created by numbers is not unexpected in the context of Southeast Asian and Philippine ethnography. Shelly Errington (1990) has noted that in island Southeast Asia, spiritual potency and power have often been demonstrated not by material things but by the size of audience one is able to attract. See also Manalansan (2003).

28. Ben Razon, pers. comm.

29. Ibid.

CH. 5: STORIES OF TRANSFORMATION AND DESIRE

1. Interview, Mar. 29, 1996, El Shaddai headquarters, Makati City.

2. I was permitted to conduct this survey by El Shaddai DWXI–PPFI and was urged to accept their assistance in structuring the questionnaire and administering it. This assistance was extremely helpful in that we were able to survey a much larger number of people in a short period of time. Another effect, however, was that some open-ended questions were inserted at the expense of questions designed to elicit detailed socioeconomic data.

3. Emil P. Jurado (1996) uses this nickname, which, he writes, comes from a story in *Asiaweek*.

4. *"Masa"* and *"mga mahirap"* are sometimes used interchangeably since "the poor" are seen as composing such a large segment of the population. They have different meanings, however. *Masa* describes a slightly broader socioeconomic spectrum—anyone from a homeless person to a casual laborer to a midlevel office worker—people also called *tao lang* (ordinary person). *Masa* is a term that can also connote, derogatorily, a "mindless mass."

5. Taglish is a mixture of English and Tagalog.

6. Doronila did not go further in his explanation.

7. This priest wished to remain anonymous.

8. Ten thousand pesos is much more than an average working-class Fil-

ipino family with children lives on in one month. In fact, the El Shaddai Social Services Department's standard for indigency was 5,000 pesos per month at the time. My informal poll of Tagalogs in Manila indicated that most of them had never heard of the custom of handing out money on one's birthday.

9. Velarde brought these two priests to Manila for the El Shaddai twelfth-anniversary celebration so they could testify during the rally about the El Shaddai chapters in their parishes at home.

10. Stunned and in fact confused by this cash gift, I let it sit on the table in front of me throughout the meal as some of the other guests did. A few pocketed the gift with a warm thank you. It is customary in the Philippines to open gifts in private, not in the presence of the giver. It is also offensive to reject a gift. Velarde left the lunch first, without eating, saying he had an appointment. After he left, I expected some discussion of the gifts to arise, but none did. I ended up putting the money back into this research, using it to hire a video cameraman and a photographer to record some El Shaddai and *barangay* events that would otherwise have been unaffordable given the research budget. To this day I wonder whether I should have returned the gift to Velarde or perhaps given it to El Shaddai members, who would have likely interpreted it as confirmation that their tithes had yielded miracle returns.

11. The letter, like most of this episode, was in English.

12. Personal interview, Mar. 29, 1996.

13. Velarde in his address at the seventh EDSA anniversary celebration, Ortigas Center, Philippines (Velarde [1993c?]: 11).

14. The EDSA Revolution was the culmination of many oppositional efforts in the Philippines, not the least of which were populace-based and church-based, although it was a military coup that tipped the scales in the final days of the Marcos regime. Some do not consider EDSA to be a true revolution, however. Although it replaced a military dictator with a legitimately elected head of state who restored a democratic form of government, many people think there was no radical change in the lives of ordinary Filipino people in terms of economic stability, peace, and justice (Labayen 1995).

15. One tape labeled "February 1986" (no specific day) was available in the El Shaddai collection at their office in Makati City. Velarde's preaching on this day made no mention of current political events; it simply addressed themes typical of Velarde's preaching already mentioned here.

16. This priest requested anonymity (original in English).

17. One exception was when an El Shaddai preacher told me that Velarde had toned down his practice of encouraging followers to seek employment abroad as domestic and other workers. This change was precipitated by a series of stories in the Filipino press about the abuse of Filipino domestic workers abroad.

18. For an extensive study of liberation theology in the Philippines see Nadeau (2002).

19. The phrase "Church of the Poor" was used first by Pope John Paul II.

20. The BCC movement was an "early forerunner of the BEC movement" (Nadeau 2002:xv).

21. Cited in Coumans (n.d. (a): 13); from the diocesan survey, 1981, coordinated by Sr. Marie Therese C. Bulatao, O.S.B., conducted for the diocese of Boac and financially assisted by MISSIO. See also Herrera (1992).

22. I use the word "miracles" to describe events or good fortune that are thought by their beneficiary to have occurred due to the intervention of God or the Holy Spirit.

23. The refrain begins with the line "And now, let the weak say 'I am strong,' let the poor say 'I am rich.'"

24. Mike Velarde speaking to a rally congregation, Feb. 1986.

25. See Stromberg (1993) for a detailed analysis of the Christian conversion narrative in American contexts.

26. At the time of this fieldwork, the exchange rate was approximately 25 Philippine pesos per U.S. dollar. Thus 200 million pesos equaled approximately U.S. $8 million at 1996 exchange rates.

27. There is some discrepancy between these dates, cited by Mike Velarde, and those I have seen reported elsewhere (also from Mike Velarde).

28. The conversation was in Tagalog and later translated by Miren Sanchez. All quotes of El Shaddai members in this chapter were originally in Tagalog.

29. Interviews with Manila Archbishop Cardinal Jaime Sin and Bishop Ted Bacani, spiritual adviser of Catholic charismatic lay movements in the Philippines. I personally heard this view expressed in various other Catholic settings, including sermons at mass. See also Chapter 2.

CH. 6: LOCAL RELIGIOUS LIFE

1. While all El Shaddai experience is local—that is, specific to particular places and times—"local" is used here in opposition to "national" insofar as mass rallies, media broadcasts, and the El Shaddai national headquarters, to greater or lesser degrees, affect all El Shaddai participants and serve a national, widespread, and anonymous audience whereas local El Shaddai chapters pertain mainly to people in particular residential communities.

2. Monsignor Tomas' attempts to establish BECs had been only marginally successful when I had contact with the parish in 1996. For an in-depth discussion of why the BEC model may be less successful in urban settings than in the countryside in the Philippines see Nadeau (2002:61–71).

3. In many Filipino wedding ceremonies, a "marriage rope" is customarily draped over the shoulders of the bride and groom during the ritual to signify how the marriage will bind the two together.

4. The term "Aglipayan" is applied to members or clergy of the Philippine Independent Church, an indigenous church that broke away from the Catholic Church in the early twentieth century. Although it once comprised nearly 25 percent of the population, it has since diminished in influence (Schumacher 1979).

5. "Slaying," also called "falling down" or "resting in the spirit," is a practice primarily associated with charismatic Christians. It occurs in some El Shaddai rituals, especially at local *gawain*. During a slaying, a person experiences a sudden and intense contact with the Holy Spirit that causes the person to literally fall down and lie semiconscious for several minutes.

6. Velarde's disapproval of intercessors and mediators such as the saints and the Virgin Mary may reflect Protestant influences in his theology, but it also secures his position as the sole mediator to God for El Shaddai members. Although Velarde encourages direct communication with God, the term "Christ-centered" does not accurately represent his theology.

7. Velarde, Mother's Day and Celebration for Our Lady of Fatima, Luneta, Manila, May 12, 1996.

8. The English word "nagging" is used.

9. R. Andrew Chestnut's (1997) observations of Pentecostalism in the urban barrios of Brazil offer a striking parallel to the situation in Bandong-Sinag.

CH. 7: SPIRITUAL WARFARE IN SINAG AND BANDONG

1. The talk was printed in the Resource Book of the same congress. Representatives from El Shaddai attended this conference, too, in which Mike Velarde gave a talk titled "The Amazing Grace of Generosity in the Church of the Poor and Its Miracle Working Power."

2. "Binding" is a sort of blessing that protects a person from evil spirits.

3. Psalm 91:5–8; *Good News Bible: The Bible in Today's English Version* (New York: American Bible Society).

4. Prayer meetings vary from chapter to chapter, as parts of the ceremony depend on the preferences of the visiting preacher. I have visited several chapters, however, where ritual elements from Catholic mass were reproduced in the *gawain* while the distinctly charismatic Christian mood—less solemn, more emotional, with many songs and healing and slaying—was preserved.

5. To be fair, this pastor had only been in the parish for a year or so when I arrived and was just beginning to learn some Tagalog words. Monsignor Tomas of Holy Family parish, however, as a native Tagalog, spoke fluent Tagalog.

6. It was not clear which Baptist denomination participated in this training or to what extent Baptists were involved.

7. Bishop Bacani is in charge of the Philippine Roman Catholic Church's charismatic groups and is "spiritual adviser" to Brother Mike Velarde and to El Shaddai DWXI–PPFI.

8. This is a play on the expression "slaves of sins."

9. The English word "backslide" is used and conjugated as a Tagalog verb.

10. Eddie and I had already met several times at the Sinag *gawain*. He knew that I was an American scholar doing funded research on El Shaddai and that I had conducted interviews locally.

11. Large companies in Manila may have a chapel within the building and may even have a priest who customarily administers to the employees.

12. Found elsewhere in the Philippines in ritual healing contexts (Wiegele 1993), the use of "Latin" words in healing is controversial in Bandong and Sinag. Some Protestants and even El Shaddai members in Bandong and Sinag consider "Latin" words and incantations to be "of the devil."

EPILOGUE

1. Mike Velarde, personal interview, Nov. 4, 1996.

BIBLIOGRAPHY

Abelman, Robert, and Steward M. Hoover, eds.

  1990 *Religious television: Controversies and conclusions.* Norwood, N.J.: Ablex.

Ackerman, Susan E., and Raymond L. M. Lee

  1988 *Heaven in transition: Non-Muslim religious innovation and ethnic identity in Malaysia.* Honolulu: University of Hawai'i Press.

Agoncillo, Teodoro A., and Milagros C. Guerrero

  1987 *History of the Filipino people.* 7th ed. Quezon City: Garcia.

Aguilar, Filomeno V.

  1998 *Clash of spirits: The history of power and sugar planter hegemony on a Visayan island.* Honolulu: University of Hawai'i Press.

Ancheta, Jaybee

  1995 "Spiritual warfare and the church militant." In First National Catholic Charismatic Congress, *One body one spirit.* Manila: Philippine International Convention Center.

Ang, Ien

  1996 *Living room wars: Rethinking media audiences for a post-modern world.* London: Routledge.

Annis, Sheldon

  1987 *God and production in a Guatemalan town.* Austin: University of Texas Press.

Anonymous

  1991 "Fundamentalism: Twist of faith." *IBON: Facts & Figures* (Manila), May 15.

  1994 "El Shaddai: Promise of miracles draws Catholics." *Manila Chronicle,* Mar. 7.

  1995 "A willing vessel." *National Renewal* (Manila), December.

  1996 "The prophet of profit: El Shaddai's Mike Velarde brings religion down to earth." *Asiaweek,* Sept. 20.

Applied Marketing Research Inc.

  1995 Unpublished survey of radio listening levels in Metro Manila, Philippines, commissioned by Radio Research Council, Nov. 19–25.

Aragon, Lorraine V.

  1992 "Divine justice: Cosmology, ritual, and Protestant missionization in Central Sulawesi, Indonesia." Ph.D. dissertation, University of Illinois at Urbana–Champaign.

Armstrong, Karen

   1993   *A history of God: The 4000-year quest of Judaism, Christianity, and Islam*. New York: Knopf.

Asad, Talal

   1983   "Anthropological conceptions of religion: Reflections on Geertz." *Man* 18:237–259.

   1993   *Genealogies of religion: Discipline and reasons of power in Christianity and Islam*. Baltimore: Johns Hopkins University Press.

Asian Development Bank

   1996   *Country Economic Review: Philippines*. Manila: Asian Development Bank.

Babb, Lawrence A.

   1995   "Introduction." In Lawrence A. Babb and Susan S. Wadley, eds., *Media and the transformation of religion in South Asia*. Philadelphia: University of Pennsylvania Press.

"Barangay Annual Report for 1995, Barangay [deleted] Zone [deleted], City of Manila"

   1995   Report submitted by Punong Barangay (Barangay Chair).

Barron, Bruce

   1987   *The health and wealth gospel: What's going on today in a movement that has shaped the faith of millions?* Downers Grove, Ill.: InterVarsity Press.

Barry, Coeli M.

   1996   "Transformations of politics and religious culture inside the Philippine Catholic Church (1965–1990)." Ph.D. dissertation, Cornell University.

Bauman, Gerd

   1992   "Ritual implicates 'others': Rereading Durkheim in a plural society." In D. de Coppet, ed., *Understanding rituals*. London: Routledge.

Bell, Catherine

   1994   *Ritual theory, ritual practice*. New York: Oxford University Press.

Beltran, Benigno

   1987   *The Christology of the inarticulate: An inquiry into the Filipino understanding of Jesus the Christ*. Manila: Divine Word.

Bendroth, Margaret Lamberts

   1993   *Fundamentalism and gender: 1875 to the present*. New Haven: Yale University Press.

Beyer, Peter

   1994   *Religion and globalization*. London: Sage.

Blanc-Szanton, Cristina

   1990   "Collision of cultures: Historical reformulations of gender in the Lowland Visayas, Philippines." In J. Atkinson and S. Errington, eds., *Power and difference: Gender in island Southeast Asia*. Stanford: Stanford University Press.

Bowen, John R.
1993 *Muslims through discourse: Religion and ritual in Gayo society.* Princeton: Princeton University Press.
1995 "The forms culture takes: A state-of-the-field essay on the anthropology of Southeast Asia." *Journal of Asian Studies* 54:1047–1078.

Bruce, Steve
1990 *Pray TV: Televangelism in America*. London: Routledge.

Brusco, Elizabeth
1986 "The household basis of evangelical religion and the reformation of machismo in Colombia." Ph.D. dissertation, City University of New York.
1993 "The reformation of machismo: Asceticism and masculinity among Colombian evangelicals." In V. Garrard-Burnett and D. Stoll, eds., *Rethinking Prostestantism in Latin America*. Philadelphia: Temple University Press.

Buhay, Sr. Hilda, O.S.B.
1992 "Who is Mary?" In M. J. Mananzan, O.S.B., ed., *Woman and religion* (rev. ed.). Manila: Institute of Women's Studies, St. Scholastica's College.

Burdick, John.
1993 *Looking for God in Brazil*. Berkeley: University of California Press.

Caldarola, Victor J.
1994 "Embracing the media simulacrum." *Visual Anthropology Review* 10 (1): 66–69.

Cannell, Fanella
1999 *Power and intimacy in the Christian Philippines*. Cambridge: Cambridge University Press.

Caoili, Manuel A.
1988 *The origins of Metropolitan Manila: A political and social analysis.* Quezon City: New Day.

Catholic Bishops Conference of the Philippines
1992 *Acts and decrees of the Second Plenary Council of the Philippines, 20 January–17 February 1991*. Manila: Secretariat, Second Plenary Council of the Philippines.

Chambers, Ross
1984 *Story and situation: Narrative seduction and the power of fiction.* Minneapolis: University of Minnesota Press.

Chestnut, R. Andrew
1997 *Born again in Brazil: The Pentecostal boom and the pathogens of poverty.* New Brunswick: Rutgers University Press.

"City map of Manila and suburbs"
  1979   Manila: National Bookstore and Heinrich Engeler.
Clammer, John
  1984   "Secularization and religious change in contemporary Asia."
         Southeast Asian Journal of Social Science 12 (1): 49–58.
Claussen, Heather L.
  2001   *Unconventional sisterhood: Feminist Catholic nuns in the Philippines.*
         Ann Arbor: University of Michigan Press.
Coleman, Simon
  2000   *The globalisation of charismatic Christianity: Spreading the gospel of
         prosperity.* Cambridge: Cambridge University Press.
Comaroff, Jean, and John Comaroff
  1991   *Of revelation and revolution: Christianity, colonialism, and
         consciousness in South Africa.* Vol. 1. Chicago: University of
         Chicago Press.
Coronel, Sheila S.
  1989   "The exploding phenomenon of evangelicalism." *Sunday Times
         Magazine* (Manila), Mar. 26.
  1993   "Apocalypse now: The explosion of evangelical sects." In
         S. Coronel, ed., *Coups, cults, and cannibals: Chronicles of a troubled
         decade (1982–1992).* Manila: Anvil.
  n.d   "Right-wing religious movements in the Philippines." Manila:
         Philippine Center for Investigative Journalism.
Coumans, Catherine E.
  1993   "Building basic Christian communities: Religion, symbolism, and
         ideology in a national movement to change local level power
         relations in the Philippines." Ph.D. dissertation, McMaster
         University, Canada.
Coumans, Catharine (Rineke)
  n.d.(a) "'Re-Christianization' in Marinduque." Unpublished manuscript.
  n.d.(b) "Constructing BCC–CO ideology in the Philippines 1972–1990:
         Intellectual, cultural, and political *bricolage.*" Unpublished
         manuscript.
Cox, H.
  1995   *Fire from heaven: The rise of Pentecostal spirituality and the
         reshaping of religion in the twenty-first century.* Reading, Mass.:
         Addison-Wesley.
Cruz, Jericho
  1996   "El Shaddai's Velarde." *Bagwis* (Hong Kong), Nov.
Csordas, Thomas
  1997   *Language, charisma, and creativity.* Berkeley: University of
         California Press.

Cueto, Donna S.
　1996　"783,000 families displaced by Apec." *Philippine Daily Inquirer*,
　　　　Dec. 3.
Cunningham, Clark
　1989　"Celebrating a Toba Batak national hero: An Indonesian rite
　　　　of identity." In S. Russell and C. Cunningham, eds., *Changing
　　　　lives, changing rites.* Ann Arbor: Center for South and Southeast
　　　　Asia.
de Coppet, Daniel, ed.
　1992　*Understanding rituals.* London: Routledge.
de Guzman, Susan A.
　1996　"Cultural Center will exhume Film Center bodies." *Philippine
　　　　Daily Inquirer*, Nov. 1.
Demaine, Harvey
　1996　"The Philippines: Physical and social geography." In *The Far East
　　　　and Australasia 1997.* London: Europa.
Doherty, John F., S.J.
　1985　*The Philippine urban poor.* Honolulu: Philippine Studies Program
　　　　Center for Asian and Pacific Studies, University of Hawai'i.
Doronila, Amando
　1999　"Can the president win against the oil companies?" *Philippine
　　　　Daily Inquirer,* Nov. 5.
Doyo, Ma. Ceres P.
　1993　"Why El Shaddai?" *Sunday Inquirer Magazine* (Manila), Aug. 22.
　1996　"The man who has more than enough." *Philippine Daily Inquirer,*
　　　　July 14.
Eagleton, Terry
　1991　*Ideology.* London: Verso.
El Shaddai Foundation
　1995　"Profile of El Shaddai DWXI–Prayer Partners Foundation
　　　　International, Inc." Unpublished information packet for the Pope
　　　　during his visit to the Philippines.
Errington, Shelly
　1990　"Recasting sex, gender, and power: A theoretical and regional
　　　　overview." In Jane Monnig Atkinson and Shelly Errington, eds.,
　　　　Power and difference: Gender in island Southeast Asia. Stanford:
　　　　Stanford University Press.
Fabros, Wilfredo
　1988　*The church and its social involvement in the Philippines, 1930–1972.*
　　　　Quezon City: Ateneo de Manila University Press.
First National Catholic Charismatic Congress
　1995　*One body one spirit: A call to united action.* Resource book of the First

National Catholic Charismatic Congress. Manila: Philippine International Convention Center.

FitzGerald, Frances

1990 "Reflections: Jim and Tammy." *New Yorker,* Apr. 23.

Frankl, Razelle

1987 *Televangelism: The marketing of popular religion.* Carbondale: Southern Illinois University Press.

Garrard-Burnett, Virginia, and David Stoll, eds.

1993 *Rethinking Protestantism in Latin America.* Philadelphia: Temple University Press.

Geertz, Clifford

1973 *The interpretation of cultures.* New York: Basic Books.

George, Carol V. R.

1993 *God's salesman: Norman Vincent Peale and the power of positive thinking.* New York: Oxford University Press.

Ginsburg, Faye

1994 "Some thoughts on culture/media." *Visual Anthropology Review* 10 (1): 136–140

Giordano, S. J.

1988 *Awakening to mission: The Philippine Catholic Church 1965–1981.* Quezon City: New Day.

Gonzales, Stella O.

1999 "Bishops start move to rein in Bro. Mike." *Philippine Daily Inquirer* (Manila), Sept. 14.

Hacket, Rosalind I. J., ed.

1987 *New religious movements in Nigeria.* Lewiston, Maine: Mellen.

Hagin, Kenneth E.

1980 *El Shaddai: The God who is more than enough, the God who satisfies with long life.* Tulsa: Faith Library.

Harding, Susan. 1991. "Representing fundamentalism: The problem of the repugnant cultural other." *Social Research* 58:2.

1994 "Imagining the last days: The politics of apocalyptic language." In M. Marty and R. Appleby, eds., *Accounting for fundamentalisms,* vol. 4. Chicago: University of Chicago Press.

Hart, Donn V.

1977 *Compadrinazgo: Ritual kinship in the Philippines.* DeKalb: Northern Illinois University Press.

Hefner, Robert W.

1993 *Conversion to Christianity: Historical and anthropological perspectives on a great transformation.* Berkeley: University of California Press.

Herrera, Teresita A.

1992 "Liberation theology and its praxis in the Philippine context: A

people-empowering response." Ph.D. dissertation, University of
Hawai'i.

Hollenweger, Walter J.
1997 *Pentecostalism: Origins and developments worldwide.* Peabody, Mass.:
Hendrickson.

Hollinger, D.
1991 "Enjoying God forever: An historical/sociological profile of
the health and wealth gospel in the USA." In P. Gee and
J. Fulton, eds., *Religion and power, decline and growth:
Sociological analysis of religion in Britain, Poland, and the
Americas.* London: British Sociological Association, Sociology
of Religious Study Group.

Horsefield, Peter
1984 *Religious television: The American experience.* New York: Longman.

Horton, Donald, and R. Richard Wohl
1976 "Mass communication and para-social interaction: Observations
on intimacy at a distance." In J. E. Combs and M. W. Mansfield,
eds., *Drama in life: The uses of communication in society.* New York:
Hastings House.

Hulsman, Alexander
1992 "Christian politics in the Philippines." In J. P. Nederveen
Pieterse, ed., *Christianity and hegemony: Religion and politics on the
frontiers of social change.* New York: Berg.

Ileto, Reynaldo
1979 *Pasyon and revolution: Popular movements in the Philippines,
1840–1910.* Quezon City: Ateneo de Manila University Press.

Jiminez-David, Rina
1999 "Caught between boulders." *Philippine Daily Inquirer,* Aug. 29.

Johnston, Hank, and Bert Klandermans, eds.
1995 *Social movements and culture.* Vol. 4 of *Social movements, protest, and
contention.* Minneapolis: University of Minnesota Press.

Johnston, Patrick
1993 *Operation world.* Carlisle, UK: OM Publishing.

Jurado, Emil P.
1996 "Metro Manila is not the Philippines." *Manila Standard,* Feb. 23.

Keyes, Charles F., Laurel Kendall, and Helen Hardacre, eds.
1994 *Asian visions of authority: Religion and the modern states of East and
Southeast Asia.* Honolulu: University of Hawai'i Press.

Kipp, Rita Smith
1991 "A practice approach to conversion as a change of identity." Paper
prepared for the annual meetings of the Association for Asian
Studies, Apr. 11–14, New Orleans.

Kramer, Eric W.

1997 "The faith which possesses: Rituals and representations of money in the Universal Church of the Kingdom of God." Unpublished manuscript, Institute for the Advanced Study of Religion.

Labayen, Julio X., O.C.D.

1995 *Revolution and the church of the poor*. Manila: Socio-Pastoral Institute and Claretian Publications.

Lancaster, Roger N.

1988 *Thanks to God and the revolution: Popular religion and class consciousness in the new Nicaragua*. New York: Columbia University Press.

Lee, Raymond L. M., and Susan E. Ackerman

1980 "Conflict and solidarity in a Pentecostal group in urban Malaysia." *Sociological Review* 28 (4): 809–827.

Lehmann, David

1996 *Struggle for the spirit: Religious transformation and popular religion in Brazil and Latin America*. Cambridge, Mass: Polity Press.

Lieban, Richard

1965 "Shamanism and social control in a Philippine city." *Journal of Folklore Institute* 2:43–54.

1967 *Cebuano sorcery: Malign magic in the Philippines*. Berkeley: University of California Press.

1977 "Symbols, signs, and success: Healers and power in a Philippine city." In R. D. Fogelson and R. N. Adams, eds., *The anthropology of power*. New York: Academic Press.

Lindholm, Charles

1990 *Charisma*. Cambridge: Blackwell.

Lindstrom, Lamont

1999 "Cargo cult 2000." Paper presented at the University of Illinois at Urbana–Champaign, Oct.

Lopez, Bernardo V.

1993 "El Shaddai: A counter-reformation?" *Manila Chronicle*, Aug. 30.

Manalansan, Martin F.

2003 *Global divas: Filipino gay men in the diaspora*. Durham: Duke University Press.

Manapat, R.

1991 *Some are smarter than others: The history of Marcos crony capitalism*. New York: Aletheia.

Marcus, George E., ed.

1996 *Connected: Engagements with media*. Chicago: University of Chicago Press.

Marfil, Martin
  1996   "Ramos attends El Shaddai rites." *Philippine Daily Inquirer*
          (Manila), Aug. 19.
Marti, Fr. Thomas
  1987   "Fundamentalist sects and the political right." SPI Series 3,
          Special Issue. Quezon City: Socio-Pastoral Institute.
Martin, David
  1990   *Tongues on fire: The explosion of Protestantism in Latin America.*
          Oxford: Blackwell.
Marty, Martin E., and R. Scott Appleby, eds.
  1993   *Fundamentalisms and society: Reclaiming the sciences, the family, and
          education,* vol. 2. Chicago: The University of Chicago Press.
  1994   *Accounting for fundamentalisms: The dynamic character of movements,*
          vol. 4. Chicago: University of Chicago Press.
Mask, Russell P.
  1995   "Grameen banking in Metro Manila, Philippines: Religion and
          other facts in borrower and program performance." Ph.D.
          dissertation, University of Wisconsin–Madison.
McCoy, Alfred, and Ed. C. de Jesus, eds.
  1982   *Philippine social history: Global trade and local transformations.*
          Honolulu: University of Hawai'i Press.
Mercado, Leonardo N., ed.
  1977   *Filipino religious psychology.* Tacloban City: Divine Word
          University.
Mercene, Recto
  1994   "FVR courts El Shaddai: A moderate voice on population." *Today*
          (Manila), Aug. 22.
"Metro Manila Citiguide: The Encyclopedic Map of Metro Manila"
  1995   Manila: Citiguide.
Miller, Daniel R., ed.
  1994   *Coming of age: Protestantism in contemporary Latin America.* New
          York: University Press of America.
Mitchel, Timothy
  1991   *Colonizing Egypt.* Berkeley: University of California Press.
Mitchell, W. J. T., ed.
  1980   *On narrative.* Chicago: University of Chicago Press.
Morley, David, and Devin Robins
  1995   *Spaces of identity: Global media, electronic landscapes, and cultural
          boundaries.* London: Routledge.
Muzaffar, Chandra
  1987   *Islamic resurgence in Malaysia.* Petaling Jaya: Penerbit Fajar Bakti
          Sdn. Bhd.

Nadeau, Kathy

1993 "Christianity and the transformation of Philippine lowland life: A critique of Rafael." *Philippine Quarterly of Culture and Society* 21:25–38.

2002 *Liberation theology in the Philippines: Faith in a revolution.* Westport, Conn.: Praeger.

National Statistics Office

1990 *Census of population and housing. Report no. 3: Socio-economic and demographic characteristics.* Manila: National Statistics Office.

1994 *Philippine Yearbook.* Manila: National Statistics Office.

1997 *Census of population. Report no. 2: Socio-economic and demographic characteristics.* Manila: National Statistics Office.

Nemenzo, Francisco

1984 "The millenarian-populist aspects of Filipino Marxism." In F. Nemenzo, *Marxism in the Philippines: Marx Centennial Lectures.* Quezon City: Third World Studies Center, University of the Philippines.

Ness, Sally Ann

1992 *Body movement and culture: Kinesthetic and visual symbolism in a Philippine community.* Philadelphia: University of Pennsylvania Press.

Office of the Mayor, Makati City

1996 Miscellaneous unpublished printed materials.

Peck, Janice

1993 *The gods of televangelism: The crisis of meaning and the appeal of religious television.* Cresskill, N.J.: Hampton Press.

Pertierra, Raul

1988 *Religion, politics and rationality in a Philippine community.* Honolulu: University of Hawai'i Press.

"Philippine City Plans"

1945 2nd ed. Prepared under the direction of the chief of engineers by the Army Map Service (AM). Washington, D.C.: U.S. Army.

Pinches, Michael

1994 "Modernisation and the quest for modernity: architectural form, squatter settlements, and the new society in Manila." In Marc Askew and William S. Logan, eds., *Cultural identity and urban change in Southeast Asia: Interpretive essays.* Victoria: Deakin University Press.

Poewe, Karla, ed.

1994 *Charismatic Christianity as global culture.* Columbia: University of South Carolina Press.

Rafael, Vicente L.

1988 *Contracting colonialism: Translation and Christian conversion in Tagalog society under early Spanish rule.* Ithaca: Cornell University Press.

Rafael, Vicente L., ed.
  1995 *Discrepant histories: Translocal essays on Filipino cultures.*
        Philadelphia: Temple University Press.
Roberts, Richard H., ed.
  1995 *Religion and the transformations of capitalism: Comparative approaches.*
        London: Routledge.
Roelofs, Gerard
  1994 "Charismatic Christian thought: Experience, metonymy,
        and routinization." In Karla Poewe, ed., *Charismatic
        Christianity as global culture.* Columbia: University of South
        Carolina Press.
Rosaldo, Michelle Z.
  1980 *Knowledge and passion: Ilongot notions of self and social life.*
        Cambridge: Cambridge University Press.
Russell, Susan D., and Clark E. Cunningham, eds.
  1989 *Changing lives, changing rites: Ritual and social dynamics in Philippine
        and Indonesian uplands.* Ann Arbor: Center for South and Southeast
        Asia.
Sales, Dia
  1996 "Mike of the multitudes (the real man behind El Shaddai)." *Plus!*
        (Manila), Apr.
Samarin, William J.
  1972 *Tongues of men and angels: The religious language of Pentecostalism.*
        New York: Macmillan.
Samonte, Sheila A.
  1996 "As they say, religion is good business." *Business World* (online
        ed.), Apr. 3.
Saunders, George R., ed.
  1988 *Culture and Christianity: The dialectics of transformation.* Westport,
        Conn.: Greenwood Press.
Schirmer, Daniel B., and Stephen R. Shalom, eds.
  1987 *The Philippines reader: A history of colonialism, neocolonialism,
        dictatorship, and resistance.* Boston: South End Press.
Schmetzer, Uli
  1997 "Letter from Manila: A reality hard to swallow." *Chicago Tribune,*
        Dec. 15.
Schneider, Jane, and Shirley Lindenbaum, eds.
  1987 "Frontiers of Christian evangelism." *American Ethnologist* (special
        issue) 14:1.
Schultze, Quentin J.
  1991 *Televangelism and American culture: The business of popular religion.*
        Grand Rapids: Baker Book House.

Schumacher, John, S.J.
  1979 *Readings in Philippine church history.* Quezon City: Loyola School of
        Theology.
Scotland, Nigel
  1995 *Charismatics and the next millennium.* London: Hodder & Stoughton.
Scott, William Henry
  1994 *Barangay: Sixteenth-century Philippine culture and society.* Manila:
        Ateneo de Manila University Press.
Spittler, Russell P.
  1994 "Are Pentecostals and charismatics fundamentalists? A review of
        American uses of these categories." In K. Poewe, ed., *Charismatic
        Christianity as global culture.* Columbia: University of South
        Carolina Press.
Spitulnick, Debra
  1993 "Anthropology and mass media." *Annual Review of Anthropology*
        22:293–315.
Stoll, David
  1993 "Introduction." In V. Garrard-Burnett and D. Stoll, eds.,
        Rethinking Protestantism in Latin America. Philadelphia: Temple
        University Press.
Stout, Daniel A., and Judith M. Buddenbaum
  1996 *Religion and mass media: Audiences and adaptations.* London: Sage.
Straub, Gerard
  1986 *Salvation for sale: An insider's view of Pat Robertson's ministry.*
        Buffalo: Prometheus Books.
Stromberg, Peter G.
  1993 *Language and self-transformation: A study of the Christian conversion
        narrative.* Cambridge: Cambridge University Press.
Sturtevant, David R.
  1976 *Popular uprisings in the Philippines, 1840–1940.* Ithaca: Cornell
        University Press.
Tadiar, Neferti Xina
  1995 "Manila's new metropolitan form." In V. Rafael, ed., *Discrepant
        histories: Translocal essays on Filipino cultures.* Philadelphia: Temple
        University Press.
Torres, Carlos Alberto
  1992 *The church, society, and hegemony: A critical sociology of religion in
        Latin America.* Westport, Conn: Praeger.
Tsing, Ann Lowenhaupt
  1993 *In the realm of the diamond queen.* Princeton: Princeton University
        Press.

Turner, Victor
   1969   *The ritual process: Structure and anti-structure*. Cornell: Cornell
         University Press.
   1974   *Dramas, fields, and metaphors: Symbolic action in human society*. Ithaca:
         Cornell University Press.
United Nations Children's Fund (UNICEF)
   1987   "Situation of children and women in the Philippines." Manila:
         Government of the Republic of the Philippines.
Valenzuela, Fr. Bayani G.
   1988   "The Philippine Catholic Church and fundamentalist Christian
         groups: A baseline study." Research proposal presented by
         Archdiocesan Ministry of Ecumenical and Inter-Faith Affairs to
         His Eminence Jaime Cardinal Sin, Nov. 15, Manila.
van der Veer, Peter, ed.
   1996   *Conversion to modernities: The globalization of Christianity*. London:
         Routledge.
van Zoonen, Liesbet
   1994   *Feminist media studies*. London: Sage.
Varias, Lorenzo
   1953   "Map of Manila and Environs." Manila: Plans and Maps Section,
         Bureau of Public Works.
Velarde, Brother Mariano "Mike" Z.
   [1991?]   *El Shaddai the Almighty God* (Makati), vol. 1.
   1992a   *El Shaddai's miracle of seed-faith*. Makati: El Shaddai
         DWXI–PPFI.
   1992b   *How to win your battles all the time*. Makati: El Shaddai Miracle
         Publications.
   [1992c?]   *El Shaddai the Almighty God* (Makati) 2:1.
   [1992d?]   "Something good is going to happen to me today!" *El Shaddai
         God Almighty* (Makati) 2:2.
   1993a   *El Shaddai's miracle assurance policy against sickness, famine, and
         bankruptcy*. Makati: El Shaddai DWXI–PPFI.
   1993b   *An invitation to store riches in heaven and enjoy El Shaddai's prosperity
         plan on earth now*. Makati: El Shaddai DWXI–PPFI.
   [1993c?]   *El Shaddai God Almighty* (Makati) 3:2.
   [1993d?]   "El Shaddai's master plan for real success and prosperity for
         you and me." *El Shaddai God Almighty* (Makati) 3:3.
   1994   "The miracles of believing and doing likewise." *El Shaddai God
         Almighty* (Makati) 4:1.
   1995   *General pastoral guidelines and manual for service volunteer workers*.
         Rev. ed. Makati: El Shaddai DWXI–PPFI.

Villadiego, Rita
   1996 "'Miracle investment.' Coseteng sues El Shaddai, Velarde."
      Philippine Daily Inquirer (Manila), July 11.
Weber, Max
   1946 *From Max Weber: Essays in sociology.* Translated by H. H. Gerth and
      C. Wright Mills. New York: Oxford University Press.
   1968 *On charisma and institution building.* Selected papers edited and
      with an introduction by S. N. Eisenstadt. Chicago: University of
      Chicago Press.
Wiegele, Katharine L.
   1993 "Men who chant and women who pray: Luck and ritual in a
      Philippine fishing village. M.A. thesis, Northern Illinois
      University.
Wilks, Richard
   1994 "Colonial time and TV: Television and temporality in Belize."
      Visual Anthropology Review 10 (1): 94–102.
Wooster, Henry
   1994 "Faith in the ramparts: The Philippine Catholic Church and the
      1986 revolution." In D. Johnston and C. Sampson, eds., *Religion,
      the missing dimension of statecraft.* New York: Oxford University
      Press.
Wuthnow, Robert
   1994 *Producing the sacred: An essay on public religion.* Urbana: University
      of Illinois Press.
Youngblood, Robert L.
   1990 *Marcos against the church: Economic development and political repression
      in the Philippines.* Ithaca: Cornell University Press.

INDEX

ABOUT THE AUTHOR

Katharine L. Wiegele is an adjunct assistant professor of anthropology at Northern Illinois University in DeKalb, Illinois. She received a Ph.D. in sociocultural anthropology from the University of Illinois at Urbana-Champaign in 2002. Wiegele's interest in the Philippines began in 1988 when she served there as a Peace Corps Volunteer. Since then she has spent nearly four years living in Pangasinan, Batangas, Laguna, and Metropolitan Manila.

Production Notes for Wiegele / *Investing in Miracles*

Cover designed by Leslie Fitch in Meta and Filosofia Unicase
Interior design by UH Press Production Department in Garamond 3,
after series design by Rich Hendel

Composition by Lucille C. Aono

Printing and binding by The Maple-Vail Book Manufacturing Group

Printed on 60# Text White Opaque, 426 ppi